KAY HOOPER
SHANNON DRAKE
LISA KLEYPAS
DIANE WICKER DAVIS

Celebrate the joys of the season with love—
four tender, passionate and enchanting
holiday tales from a quartet of your favorite
romance authors. Now the magic of
Christmas is combined with the soul-
stirring ecstasy of rapturous romance in an
unforgettable collection of stories certain to
touch your heart at Yuletide...and all
through the year.

*And for more
of the magic of romance
at Christmastime*

Avon Books Presents:

*For More Christmas Love
from Your Favorite Romantic Authors
Don't Miss*

AVON BOOKS PRESENTS: CHRISTMAS ROMANCE

Avon Books Presents:

Christmas Love Stories

KAY HOOPER   SHANNON DRAKE
LISA KLEYPAS   DIANE WICKER DAVIS

AVON BOOKS ◆ NEW YORK

AVON BOOKS PRESENTS: CHRISTMAS LOVE STORIES is an original publication of Avon Books. This work, as well as each individual story, has never before appeared in print. This work is a collection of fiction. Any similarity to actual persons or events is purely coincidental.

AVON BOOKS
A division of
The Hearst Corporation
1350 Avenue of the Americas
New York, New York 10019

Holiday Spirit copyright © 1991 by Kay Hooper
Gifts of Love copyright © 1991 by Heather Graham Pozzessere
Surrender copyright © 1991 by Lisa Kleypas
A Creole Christmas copyright © 1991 by Diane Wicker Davis

Published by arrangement with the authors
Library of Congress Catalog Card Number: 91-92056
ISBN: 0-380-76572-1

First Avon Books Printing: November 1991

AVON TRADEMARK REG. U.S. PAT. OFF. AND IN OTHER COUNTRIES, MARCA REGISTRADA, HECHO EN U.S.A.

Printed in the U.S.A.

RA 10 9 8 7 6 5 4 3 2 1

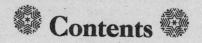 Contents

Holiday Spirit

Kay Hooper

True love is like ghosts,
which everybody talks about
and few have seen.

—François, Duc de La Rochefoucauld
(1613–1680)

 1

IN THE HUGE, DRAFTY, AND CHILLY DRAWING ROOM was an intense and profound silence; the sort of silence, Antonia reflected bitterly, that her grandmother had perfected over fifty years of methodical practice. Like the icy blue eyes gazing out of the aged but still handsome face, the silence indicated extreme offense.

"I beg your pardon, Grandmother," Antonia said stiffly, her own blue eyes still as fierce as when she had spoken the offending words, but her face schooled into a mask of regret and apology. "Wingate Castle is your home, not mine; I had no right to question your choice of guests."

"Question?" The Countess of Ware's voice was measured. "I should rather have termed it an attack, Antonia."

Even more stiffly, Antonia said, "I was taken off guard, and spoke without thinking, Grandmother. Again, I beg your pardon."

Thawing ever so slightly, Lady Ware inclined her head regally. "I observe Sophia has at least seen to it your manners are not wholly wanting."

3

Antonia flushed, sensing a faint sarcasm. "If I lack anything with regard to social graces, it isn't Mama's fault, Grandmother, and I won't have you abusing her."

This direct statement, though it could properly be termed rude, brought a spark of approval to Lady Ware's eyes. In a milder tone, she said, "Very well, Antonia, there's no need to mount a second attack against me on behalf of your mother. I have always thought Sophia a silly goose, but neither you nor anyone else can claim I do not appreciate her true worth; she has a kind heart and a generous disposition, and well I know it."

Regarding her granddaughter sternly, Lady Ware continued, "However, that is neither here nor there. I should like to know, Antonia, why you object so violently to Lyonshall's presence here. It has, after all, been nearly two years since your engagement ended, and I daresay you have encountered one another countless times in London since that shameful episode."

Antonia gritted her teeth. In the eyes of her grandmother—and, indeed, in the eyes of society—Antonia's jilting of the Duke of Lyonshall had most certainly been a shameful, and inexplicable, action. Even her mother had no idea what had gone wrong; Lady Sophia had suffered most dreadfully from the ensuing gossip, and had nearly swooned when, some months later, she had been forced to greet the duke in public.

As for herself, Antonia had encountered him at a number of the *ton* parties; she had even danced with him at Almack's at the beginning of the present Season. It was, after all, vital to maintain an appearance of cool politeness. Nothing so offended the sensibilities as a private disagreement paraded before the gawking eyes of the public; Antonia might have committed a social solecism, but she was not lost to all sense of propriety.

"I have encountered the duke," she replied in measured tones, "and I expect to encounter him again since we are often invited to the same parties. But you must see, Grandmother, that for him to be invited to my family's home for the Christmas holidays will give rise to just the sort of gossip I have been at some pains to silence. Furthermore, I don't understand why you would put me in such a position. Nor do I understand why you have chosen to house both the duke and myself in the South wing—alone.''

Lady Ware offered her a frosty smile. ''Since it has been recently renovated after being closed off for fifty years, the South wing is the most comfortable section of the castle, Antonia, with apartments far grander than any of the rest—even my own rooms. Are you complaining of your accommodations?''

For the first time, Antonia had the uneasy suspicion that her grandmother—famed as much for her sly machinations as for her blighting social graces—had an ulterior motive when she had arranged this little house party. But it was absurd! What could she possibly hope to accomplish?

Ignoring the question put to her, Antonia said, ''Grandmother, I trust you understand that the mere idea of—of in any way reconciling with Lyonshall is profoundly distasteful to me. If you have *that* idea in your head—''

Lady Ware let out a sound which, in anyone less dignified, would have been termed a snort. ''Don't be absurd, Antonia. Do you suppose I would for one moment believe that Lyonshall could bring himself to offer for you a second time after your disgraceful conduct? No man of pride and breeding could even consider such a thing.''

Antonia had flushed vividly, then gone rather pale at the crushing remarks, and her lips were pressed tightly together as she met that eagle-eyed stare. ''Very well, then. This is your home, and it is for you to decide where your guests shall sleep. However, Grandmother, at the risk of offending you yet again, I must request that my coach be brought around; I am returning to London immediately.''

Lady Ware's expression was one of faint surprise. ''You cannot have looked out a window in the past hour, child. It began to sleet and snow some time since; you would hardly set out for London in such weather. In fact, I can only hope Lyonshall has not been constrained to put up at some inferior inn on his journey here.''

Angry and—if the truth were told—intensely uncomfortable at the thought of spending several days in the company of her former betrothed, Antonia could only hope he *had* been compelled by inclement weather to delay—indefinitely—his arrival at the castle. But she doubted that was so. Lyonshall not only owned the finest horseflesh in England, he was also famous for his disregard of any obstacle in his path; if he intended to reach the castle, he would do so.

Balked in her determination to avoid the situation, Antonia could only curtsy and stalk from the room, head high.

Lady Ware, left alone in the huge room and comfortable in her chair before a blazing fire, chuckled softly. She had managed to divert her granddaughter's thoughts from the—really quite improper—allocation of rooms, and that had been her primary intent. Sophia would no doubt protest the arrangement, in her fluttery way, but Lady Ware had every confidence of being able to handle *her*.

And since the ''house party'' consisted of only the duke, Antonia and her mother, and the countess herself, there would be no one to carry tales of what went on here back to London.

Lady Ware congratulated herself. Providing Lyonshall reached the castle, her plan should come off rather well, she thought. The weather would serve to explain why her house party was no larger; since the castle, located in the northern Welsh mountains, had seen icy weather each Christmas for decades, Lady Ware had been able to factor that into her careful scheme. She had been doubtful only of her ability to get Lyonshall here; his own country seat was his customary retreat for the holidays, and he was notoriously disinclined to respond favorably to a summons from one who, though lesser in rank, commanded considerable social power.

At her best when slyness was called for, Lady Ware had been maneuvering for months to find a way of getting the duke here. After studying the situation—and the man—she had finally hit upon an outrageous solution.

Smiling to herself as she sat in her chair, the countess reflected that a lesson in the tragedy of mistakes would do both the duke and Antonia good. In fact, if she knew Antonia—and she did, far more completely than that young lady could guess—the lesson would have a profound effect.

The stage was set. Now if only the actors who had sustained their roles for so many years would lend their support on this very important anniversary, the play could begin.

Since her father had been a younger son of the Earl of Ware, Antonia had not grown up in Wingate Castle, and she had never put much stock in the tales of its being haunted. Still, as she strode briskly along the second-floor hallway of the South wing, she admitted silently that if there was a more likely habitation for spirits of the departed, she had never seen it.

The original castle dated before the Norman conquest, though it had naturally been renovated and even rebuilt numerous times over the centuries. Along the way, its appearance and purpose had changed from fort to residence, though the Wingate family had lived and died here from the beginning.

If ghosts walked for the reasons common to folklore—tragic, untimely deaths, for instance—numerous Wingates could be said to meet the accepted criteria. The family history held more than its share of strife, illness, and violence, as well as the usual lesser troubles all families are heir to. There were records of at least half a dozen murders, two suicides, and a score of brutal accidents—all taking place either within the castle walls or on the estate grounds.

Antonia was only vaguely familiar with most of her family's long and colorful history, and had always considered Wingate Castle a moldy old relic. But one couldn't help being aware of centuries of existence, she thought, when one was surrounded by thick stone walls, velvet hangings, and long corridors lined with immense doorways.

The restoration of the South wing had returned this part of the castle to the glory of a century before, but Lady Ware had refused to modernize in any way except for the installation of steam heat. The corridor presently echoing with the sounds of Antonia's footsteps was merely chilly rather than freezing, and her bedchamber, while not exactly snug, was at least tolerably comfortable.

Antonia passed a bedchamber two doors from her own and across the hall, and noted that two of the maids were still working to ready it for the expected arrival of the duke. It had been that sight earlier, and an explanation by the maids regarding the identity of the expected guest, which had driven her to confront her grandmother. The remainder now brought a frown to her face, and the expression earned her a stern rebuke from her maid as she entered her own chambers.

"What if your face should freeze like that, milady? It's likely enough in here!"

Antonia laughed. Plimpton had been her maid since she had left the schoolroom, and despite the older woman's frequent blunt reprimands, Antonia never took offense; she often thought that even her own mother did not know her as well as Plimpton did.

"Oh, it isn't that cold in here," she said, watching as Plimpton continued to unpack her trunks. "And you can hang the silk gowns in the back of the wardrobe, for I certainly won't wear them; it *is* too cold for low-cut evening gowns."

Plimpton glanced at her mistress, shrewd eyes direct. "Lady Ware requires her guests to dress in the evenings."

Antonia lifted her chin. "I have the two velvet gowns, and the merino—"

"High-necked and dowdy, milady, and well you know it! Even Lady Ware isn't such a stickler as all that. It's the duke you want to hide yourself from, not the countess *or* the cold!"

Antonia went to her dressing table and busied herself with the already exquisite arrangement of her fiery hair, stubbornly avoiding her maid's eyes in the mirror. "You're talking nonsense, and you know it. I've met Lyonshall countless times in company, and fully expect to continue doing so in future."

Plimpton was silent for a few moments as she went on unpacking Antonia's trunks, but it soon became obvious that she had no intention of allowing the subject to drop. With casual innocence, she said, "There must be a full dozen bedchambers on this floor, and only two of them occupied. And this wing so far from the rest of the household. Odd, how Lady Ware put you and the duke so far from the others. Alone."

Antonia was conscious of another pang of uncertainty,

but pushed it resolutely aside. As her grandmother had so accurately stated, only a fool would entertain even the faintest hope that Lyonshall could be brought up to scratch a second time when the lady in question had jilted him so shamefully—and Dorothea Wingate was no fool.

Antonia responded with composure, "Lyonshall will have his valet, and I will have you; therefore, we are not alone—"

"My room, milady, is in the East wing. Another room is prepared in that wing for His Grace's valet."

Antonia was shaken by the information, but tried not to show it. She also refrained from saying instantly that she would have a cot brought into the dressing room so that her maid could sleep there. She refused to appear foolishly nervous or overly concerned with her reputation. There would have been talk in London at such an improper arrangement—but this was not London. And no one in the city was likely to hear news of what went on in this isolated part of Wales.

Her voice, therefore, was a masterpiece of unconcern. "As for choosing to house the two of us in this wing, Grandmother merely wished to show off the renovations, that's all."

"Then why is Her Ladyship's chamber situated in the North wing?"

When Plimpton used the title, "Her Ladyship" always referred to Antonia's mother, Lady Sophia Wingate.

"Because Grandmother wanted someone near her own rooms," Antonia replied.

Plimpton sniffed. "I daresay. *And* I daresay Lady Ware never gave a thought to how cold your morning coffee and bathwater will be after it's been hauled up three flights of stairs and along two corridors to reach you. You are not accustomed to such vexatious service and neither, I daresay, is the duke."

It did sound a bit daunting, Antonia thought. "We

shall have to make the best of it," she said finally. "It's only for a few days, after all."

"A few days, is it? I was speaking to Mr. Tuffet just after we arrived, milady, and he's served here in the castle for nigh on to forty years; he says when winter sets on as it has today, travel is unthinkable for weeks."

The very possibility of being shut up in the castle—no matter how large it was—with the duke for weeks on end sent a shudder of nervous dread through Antonia. It was at least bearable to encounter him socially at brief intervals, when she was able to maintain her coolly pleasant mask without strain; she doubted her ability to sustain the pretense over a period of days, much less weeks. She doubted it very much.

Sooner or later, she would give herself away. Sooner or later, Richard Allerton, the Duke of Lyonshall, would realize that the woman who had jilted him was still foolishly in love with him.

Dorothea Wingate, Countess of Ware, kept Wingate Castle fully staffed, despite the fact that she was the sole occupant throughout most of the year. Other residents of such out-of-the-way and inconvenient estates as hers wondered how on earth she managed to keep servants, especially since hers tended to be a quiet life, with few visitors and fewer social events. But the truth was that Lady Ware paid her people very well. The butler, four footmen, six housemaids, three kitchen maids, and cook—as well as numerous gardeners and stable men—were amply compensated for the drawbacks of service at the castle.

The countess seldom visited London; her most recent trip had been two years previously, when Antonia's engagement had been announced. She had returned to Wingate several months later when the engagement ended, and after Antonia had refused to discuss the situation with anyone. The scandal had obviously distressed her, for Antonia knew that her grandmother had had her heart set on the match.

Her eldest son, the present Earl of Ware, was a dedicated bachelor who spent his time in London and on another of his estates outside the city, and was not much concerned with the continuance of his family line; in all likelihood, the title would perish with him. The family had dwindled over the years, and since the countess's younger son, Antonia's father, died leaving no male offspring, only Antonia remained to carry on the family line—if not the name itself. And since the castle was not entailed, it would most probably be left to Antonia.

She wondered if that was part of her grandmother's reason for this house party. Antonia had made no secret of her aversion to the castle; it was entirely too large, too damp, too chilly, and too far from London. She did not want it. Despite her Uncle Royce's determined bachelorhood, she continued to cherish the hope that he would fall head over heels in love and start his nursery before gout or an apoplexy carried him off.

Still, it seemed possible that Lady Ware was attempting to arouse in her granddaughter's breast some flicker of feeling for the ancestral home—as well as a reminder of what she owed to her family—and had chosen this holiday visit as a first step toward that goal.

Antonia considered the situation as she dressed for dinner that evening, wrestling her distantly polite social mask into place with all her will. There was nothing she could do except keep her wits and her calm. Ignoring Plimpton's meaningful glances and mumbled remarks, she chose a heavy velvet gown in olive green. Neither the high-necked style nor the drab color was particularly flattering, which satisfied Antonia inordinately.

Lady Ware was a stickler for promptness, and dinner at the castle was served at the unfashionable hour of six;

it was just after five o'clock when Antonia left her room for the long walk to the drawing room on the ground floor. She had hoped that by going down early, she could avoid a chance encounter with Lyonshall. But fate was against her.

He stepped from his room when she was still several feet away, allowing her little time to collect herself. Normally, in social situations, she saw him first across a crowded room and was granted ample opportunity for the shoring up of her defenses; now, although she had tried to prepare herself, his sudden appearance caught her off guard.

It was clearly not so with him. He bowed with the exquisite grace for which he was famed and offered his arm. His deep voice was the caressing drawl she hadn't heard from him in nearly two years.

"Toni. You're looking lovely, as always."

To say that Antonia was taken aback would have been a considerable understatement. Expecting the distant courtesy he had shown her since their engagement had ended, she had no idea how to react to his voice, the compliment, or the unsettling warmth in his gray eyes. She had a small feeling that her mouth was open, but accepted his arm automatically.

As they began walking down the long, silent corridor, she tried to collect herself, and was unable to keep from stealing glances up at him. Gifted with an old and honorable title as well as a considerable fortune, Richard Allerton had also been blessed with a tall, powerful frame set off admirably by his usual sportsman's style of dress, and a handsome face that had broken any number of thudding female hearts.

He had been called a nonesuch, his skill with horses and his athletic prowess unequaled—and uncommon in one of his rank. He was not held to be a rake, since he neither toyed with the affections of innocent young ladies nor scandalized society by openly indulging in indiscretions. He was not above being pleased in company, and could be counted on by any hostess to dance with the plainest damsel or spend half an hour charmingly entertaining even the rudest or most outspoken of matrons.

He was a paragon.

So, at any rate, Antonia had believed when she had tumbled into love with him during their first dance together. He had no need of her fortune, and had seemed interested in her views and opinions, encouraging her to share her thoughts rather than accept the usual platitudes so common among persons of their social order.

It had been a magical, dizzying experience for Antonia, being loved by him. He had treated her as a person in her own right, a woman whose mind mattered to him. Antonia had long been appalled by the "civilized" arrangements that passed for marriage; she had desired a partner, an equal with whom to share her life—and she had believed, with all her heart and soul, that Richard was that man. Until she found out otherwise.

Now, walking beside her former betrothed, her thoughts tangled and confused, she fought to raise her defenses again in the face of his changed attitude.

"This is quite a place," he said, looking around. His voice still held that drawling, caressing note, though the words were casual. "Lady Ware has done an excellent job with the renovations."

Conscious of the strength of his arm under her hand, Antonia blurted, "I hardly expected to see you here, Your Grace."

"You know very well what my name is, Toni—don't use my title," he said calmly.

Antonia caught the gleam in his gray eyes and looked hastily away. "That wouldn't be proper," she said stiffly.

"Would it not?" His free hand covered hers, the long

fingers curling under her own in a strangely intimate touch. "You have called me Richard many times. You have even whispered it, as I recall. Remember that early spring ride at Lyonshall? We were caught unexpectedly in a storm, and had to take shelter in an old stable while the groom rode back for a carriage. You whispered my name then, didn't you, Toni?"

She wanted to display a dignified offense at the reminder of a scene any gentleman would have wiped from his memory, but she found herself unable to utter a word. He was stroking the sensitive hollow of her palm in a secret caress, and an achingly familiar warmth was stealing through her body.

"How delighted I was that day," he mused, a husky note entering his deep voice. "I had believed you were everything I wanted in a woman, with your excellent mind and strong spirit; that day I discovered the wonderful passion in you. You responded to me so sweetly, with none of the missish alarm or dismay our society mistakenly insists must be the response of a lady of quality to passion. I held a loving, giving woman in my arms, and thanked God I had found her."

"Stop," she managed finally, her cheeks burning as she made a useless attempt to pull her hand from his grasp. "To remind me of such a—a shameful episode—"

"If I thought you really believed that, I'd box your ears," he said, and his eyes then were a little fierce. "There is nothing shameful about the desire two people feel for one another. We were to be married—"

"But we were *not* married, not then and not afterward," Antonia said unsteadily, grateful to see the first flight of stairs just ahead, but painfully aware that it was still some distance to the ground floor of the castle where the presence of other people would certainly curb her companion's shocking conversation. She didn't know how much more of this she could bear.

"I am aware of that," he said evenly. "What I don't know is why we were not married afterward. You never gave me a reason, Toni. You talked a great deal of nonsense, saying that you had realized we wouldn't suit—"

"It was true!"

"Balderdash. We were together nearly every day for months, and found one another splendid company. Parties, the theater, riding, driving in the park, spending quiet evenings in your home and mine—we suited admirably, Toni."

She remained silent, staring straight ahead.

"I intend to discover your reason for jilting me. I know there *was* a reason; you are far from being so flighty as to do such a thing on a whim."

"It has been nearly two years," she said at last, refusing to look at him. "Past. Do me the—the courtesy of allowing the entire incident to remain undisturbed."

"Incident? Is that how you recall our engagement, as a meaningless *incident* in your past? Is that how you remember our lovemaking?"

It required an enormous effort, but Antonia managed to make her voice cold. "Is that not how any mistake should be termed?"

Lyonshall did not take offense at what was, in essence, an insult, but he did frown. "So cold. So implacable. What did I do to earn that, Toni? I have wracked my brains, yet I cannot recall a single moment when we were not in harmony—except for that last morning. We had been to the theater the night before, along with a party of friends, and you seemed in excellent spirits. Then, when I came to see you the following morning as usual, you informed me that our engagement was at an end, and that you would be . . . obliged if I would send a notice to the *Gazette*. You refused to explain, beyond the obvious fiction that we didn't suit.''

They were descending toward the entrance hall now, and Antonia caught a glimpse of one of the footmen, splendid and stalwart in his livery, stationed near the foot of the stairs. She had never been so relieved to see another person in her life, and a tinge of that emotion was in her voice when she replied to Lyonshall.

''You acceded to my wishes and sent the notice—why must you question me now? There is no reason to do so. It is past, Richard. Past, and best forgotten by everyone.''

He lowered his voice, apparently because of the footman, but the quieter tone did not at all lessen the relentlessness of his words. ''If only my pride had been bruised, I would agree with you; such shallow hurts are best put aside and forgotten. But the blow you dealt me went far deeper than pride, my sweet, and in all the months since, I have not forgotten it. This time, there will be an end to things between us. One way or another.''

The endearment surprised her; it was one he had used only in passion—and it triggered a scalding rush of memories that tore at her hard-won composure. But that shock was small compared to what she felt at the clear threat of his words. Dear heaven, had he waited two years to punish her for jilting him? Or had Lady Ware's invitation presented him with an opportunity he intended to take advantage of, merely to enliven a boring holiday?

She had never believed him to be a cruel man, at least not intentionally so, and found it difficult to believe now. Had she indeed hurt him so badly? And what did he intend now? *An end to things . . .*

It was only years of practice that enabled Antonia to school her features into an expression of calm as she walked beside Lyonshall into the huge drawing room. He released her hand in order to greet her mother and grandmother, but that was no more than a brief respite since he fetched her a glass of sherry and stood near her chair as he talked with his usual charm to the two older ladies.

Any other time, Antonia would have been hard put not to laugh. Her mother, a still-pretty woman with large, startled blue eyes and fading red hair, was clearly baffled and unnerved by Lyonshall's presence, and hardly knew what to say to him. Lady Sophia had been delighted by the engagement, both for the worldly reason of her daughter's assured position in society and because she knew Antonia had loved her betrothed. But she was, by nature, a timid woman, and a situation such as this one was bound to be a strain on her nerves.

Lady Ware, on the other hand, was utterly calm and obviously pleased with herself. She was not one to charm, but she was more courteous to Lyonshall than Antonia had ever known her to be to anyone else. She seemed to have an excellent understanding with him.

"I believe we may make your holiday here a memorable one, Duke," she said at one point, her tone one of certainty rather than hope, and her use of his title a bland indication that she considered them equals despite the difference in their ranks. "Here at the castle, we observe most of the usual Christmas traditions, as well as some which are uniquely our own. Time enough to discuss those tomorrow, of course, when you have completely settled in—but I do trust you mean to be a participant rather than merely an observer?"

He inclined his head politely. "I try always to be a participant, ma'am. What is the point of a holiday if one cannot enjoy oneself, after all? I am looking forward to a very special memory of Christmas at Wingate Castle."

Antonia sipped her sherry, feeling peculiarly detached. Christmas? That *was* the reason they were all here. It was difficult to think about the usual trappings of Christmas when her mind was so filled with him. This was supposed to be an interlude of peace and good cheer, of high spirits and joy and contentment.

But all Antonia could think of were the memories Lyonshall had dragged from the locked rooms of her mind. Secret memories. To some, they might even be shameful memories.

As they seated themselves in the dining room, she looked at her mother and grandmother, wondering. What would they think if they knew about that rainy spring day? They would undoubtedly condemn her for what she had done. It was shocking enough that she had given herself to a man—even her betrothed—without the sanctity of marriage, but then to end her engagement within a week, seemingly without reason . . .

Lyonshall could have ruined her completely had he chosen, with only a few words spoken to the right people. Antonia knew he had remained silent. For his own sake, perhaps; the tale would not have ruined him, but it would have marred his excellent reputation as a gentleman. Oddly enough, it had never occurred to her then that he might do so. It occurred to her now only because of his implied threat to "end things" between them.

But surely he wouldn't . . .

"You're very quiet, my sweet."

She looked up hastily from her plate, cheeks burning; he had not troubled to lower his voice, and everyone from Tuffet and the footman serving them to her mother and grandmother had heard the endearment.

Lady Sophia all but dropped her fork, but Lady Ware, undisturbed, met her granddaughter's eyes with a faint, bland smile.

Grimly holding on to her composure, Antonia said, "I have nothing to say, Your Grace."

He was seated on her grandmother's right, with Antonia on his right, and her mother across the table. Antonia's chair was near the duke's, so near in fact that he was easily able to reach the hand lying over her napkin in her lap. Once again, his long fingers curled around hers in a familiar, secret touch.

"That, surely, is a rare event," he said with a smile so private it was like a touch.

Antonia couldn't reclaim her hand without an undignified—and obvious—struggle, so she was forced to remain still. But her cheeks burned even hotter when Tuffet came around to serve them. Naturally, the butler did not betray by so much as the flicker of an eyelid that he saw the clasped hands, but there was no doubt he did see.

"I have learned to rein my tongue," Antonia said with a meaning of her own. "I no longer blurt every thought aloud."

"But your thoughts are part of your charm," Lyonshall said smoothly. "I always found your plain speaking quite refreshing on the whole. Pray say whatever you wish; no one here, surely, would censure you."

Antonia gritted her teeth. Very slowly, she said, "If I were to say what I wished to say, Your Grace, I am very much afraid that both my mother and grandmother would find me sadly lacking in manners."

"I am persuaded you are wrong."

Antonia did not know what to think, and her earlier brief detachment had flown. How dared he do this to her! What did he mean by it? She could feel the warmth and weight of his hand even through her clothing, feel one of his fingers stroking her palm in a slow caress, and a tingling heat spread slowly outward from the very core of her body in a helpless response.

She wanted to be angry. She wanted that so desperately. But what she felt most was a longing too powerful to deny and almost beyond her ability to fight.

Lady Sophia, looking anxiously at her daughter's flushed cheeks and glittering eyes, and unsettled by the oddly intimate conversation going on between Antonia and the duke, rushed hastily into speech. "I do trust, Your Grace, that this wretched weather won't keep you tied by the heels here and cause you to miss very many of—of your usual pleasures! You were promised to Lady Ambersleigh's cotillion in a fortnight, were you not?"

It was such a transparent hope that the duke's unnerving presence would not be unnecessarily prolonged, it was actually rather comical. Antonia caught herself glancing at Lyonshall, and felt a spurt of reluctant amusement when she met the laughter shining in his eyes. His voice, however, was perfectly grave.

"I was, ma'am, but I sent my regrets." His gaze flickered to Lady Ware's impassive face. "Having been warned I was likely to find myself snowbound here."

Her amusement vanishing, Antonia looked at her grandmother as well. "I was not warned," she said.

"You did not ask, Antonia. Lyonshall, being a man of good sense, did ask." Placing her napkin beside her plate, the countess regarded her noble guest with a questioning lift of her brows. "Shall we ladies withdraw and leave you to enjoy your port in lonely splendor?"

He inclined his head politely. "I would prefer to forgo that custom, ma'am, with your permission."

If Antonia had cherished hopes that Lyonshall would release her when they rose from the table, those hopes were swiftly dashed. He tucked her hand in the crook of his arm and held it there as they returned to the drawing room.

He was, in short, behaving as though he and Antonia were still engaged! She did not understand what was in his mind . . .

"Play for us, Antonia," her grandmother commanded with a nod toward the pianoforte. "I am sure Lyonshall would be delighted to turn the music for you."

Antonia considered rebelling, but at least he would be forced to release her since both her hands would be required for the task. She seated herself on the bench, and was further disturbed by the swift pang of loss she felt when he let go of her hand. Automatically, she began playing the piece already set before her, realizing too late that it was a soft, gentle love song.

Lyonshall leaned against the pianoforte, ready to turn the pages. His voice was low. "I have missed your playing, Toni."

She kept her eyes resolutely on the music, grateful only that her mother and grandmother could not overhear whatever shocking things he said while she was playing. "I am merely adequate, Your Grace, and you well know it," she said repressively.

He turned the first page for her. "If you use my title one more time, my sweet, I shall take my revenge in a manner calculated to shock your mother very much."

Antonia hit a wrong note, and felt her cheeks flaming yet again. Her practiced mask was in splinters, and her voice was much more natural—and, to her fury, helpless—when she said, "What are you trying to do to me, Richard?"

"Have you not guessed, love? I am doing my poor best to court you. Again. In fact, I have a special license, and fully intend to marry you before the new year."

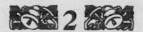 2

IT WAS TRULY REMARKABLE, ANTONIA THOUGHT MUCH later that evening as she paced her bedchamber, how the social manners drummed into one from childhood had the power to hide even the most intense emotions. The moment Lyonshall had stated his astonishing intentions, her mask had almost magically rebuilt itself, and she had actually been able to behave as though nothing out of the ordinary had happened.

She knew she had remained calm, that she had continued to play the pianoforte; she could even recall responding to several of his more casual remarks. But the wild emotions churning beneath her mask had enabled her to ignore—almost to the point of literally not hearing—the shockingly intimate things he had murmured to her under cover of the music.

Perhaps his intentions, if he had meant what he said about wishing to marry her, should have made his behavior more bearable, but for Antonia that was not so. The bitter hurt that had caused her to end their engagement was still strong in her despite the months that had passed, but even though her mind fiercely refused the very idea of marrying him, both the painful longing of her heart and the powerful desire he had rekindled whispered seductively.

It had been nearly two years. Perhaps *she* was no

longer a part of his life now. Perhaps he had decided—
this time—that he could be content with a wife, and feel
no need for a mistress as well. Or perhaps Mrs. Dalton
had grown too demanding for his taste, and he had not
yet found a replacement for her. And perhaps Antonia
could forgive, even forget, the terrible hurt . . .

Perhaps. Perhaps. *Perhaps*.

Antonia flung herself into a comfortable chair by the
fire, absently drawing her dressing gown tighter. The
afternoon storm had continued into the night, adding its
threatening chill to the cold stone walls and floors. Outside, the wind moaned fretfully, and sleet pelted the
windows in a whispery cadence. The mournful sounds
were a perfect accompaniment to her miserable mood.
Her thoughts chased their own tails, and her feelings
remained in a painful tangle.

Her mother, she knew, would never understand; that
was why Antonia had never confided her reason for
breaking the engagement. Her own father had kept a
mistress; according to gossip, most gentlemen did. Their
wives were expected to pretend that such creatures simply
did not exist. But Antonia knew herself too well to believe she could be happy in such an arrangement.

Even worse, he had *lied* to her. Early in their engagement, with the frankness he had claimed to admire, she
had told him that she believed both partners in a marriage
should remain faithful. He had agreed with her, saying
with equal bluntness that although he had enjoyed several
agreeable connections in the past—he was, after all,
thirty-three at that time—she was the only woman in his
life, and he fully intended that that would remain true.

That he had been so clearly willing to begin their
marriage with a lie had hurt even more than the thought
of another woman. It had shattered her trust in him.

Even now, she didn't know why she had not told him
the truth. Perhaps because she could not bear the thought

that he would lie again. And although he had said in the drawing room that he meant to know the truth about their breakup, she didn't want to tell him. She was afraid he would have some ready answer, and that she would allow herself to believe it even if it was a lie.

It was nearly midnight, and though the room was reasonably comfortable with the fire blazing, she shivered a bit. She felt so alone. The thought had barely crossed her mind when she became aware of a slight stirring of the air, as if someone had passed near her, and all her senses came suddenly alive and tense. She turned her head slowly, and gasped aloud.

He stood by one of the windows looking out, frowning slightly as if the storm disturbed him. He was wearing a dressing gown, its colors muted. He was dark, with a hawklike profile, and for an instant Antonia thought it was Lyonshall. Indeed, she very nearly cried out a sharp demand to be told what he was doing in her bedchamber.

Her bewildered anger vanished quickly, however, to be replaced by a pang of chill fear when she realized that she could clearly see the tapestry hanging just beyond him—*through his body*.

Unable to believe her own eyes, Antonia swallowed hard and managed to hold her voice steady enough to ask, "Who are you?"

He did not answer. In fact, he appeared to take no notice of her at all, as if—to him—she was not even in the room. Turning away from the window, he drew a watch from the pocket of his dressing gown and studied it, still frowning. Returning the watch to his pocket, he moved a few steps nearer to Antonia and seemed to pick up something as if from a table long since vanished. A book appeared in his hands, no more solid than he was, yet she could almost hear the whisper of pages as he leafed through them.

Antonia was still afraid, yet she was fascinated as well.

She felt almost numb, her mind working with a strange clarity. Huddled in her chair, she stared at him, seeing that he did indeed resemble Lyonshall. His height and build were much the same, as was the dark hair and hawklike handsomeness. But this—man's—hair was worn long, tied at the nape of his neck with a black ribbon, and she vaguely recognized the style as that of a century past. His face was thinner, his eyes deeper-set than the duke's, and she thought he was—had been—a bit younger.

She was not dreaming; Antonia knew that. She could feel the heat of the fire and hear its crackling energy, hear the wail of the storm outside, and sense her own heart pounding rapidly. She forced herself to move, rising slowly from her chair. Again, he did not react to her presence.

"Who are you?" she repeated in a louder voice. She started when he moved suddenly, but it immediately became clear that he had no awareness of her presence. She had the eerie feeling that this was no longer her room, that it had become his. It even looked subtly different to her, as if she was the one caught between times and she could *almost* see the room as it had been in his time. Almost. But it was more of an emotional sense than an actual one, she thought; she was fixed in her own time, allowed only a kind of doorway to see into his.

For a fraction of a moment, a superstitious terror sent ice through Antonia's veins. She could not draw him into the world of the living—but what if he could pull her into the world of the dead? The fear was brief, but strong enough to leave her feeling shaken. Her rational mind reasserted itself, and she reminded herself that he had taken no notice of her; obviously, he was no danger to her.

Nevertheless, she started a bit when he dropped the book—it vanished the instant it left his hands—and consulted his watch a second time. A smile curved his lips as the watch was returned to his pocket. Then he strode toward the door.

Antonia had no intention of following him, but she found herself doing just that, as though compelled. She felt almost like a puppet, pulled along as if she had no will of her own, and that sensation, added to the appearance of the man, made the impact of these unnatural events even stronger. Fascinated, numbly frightened, inexorably drawn, she followed him.

She had a bad moment when he passed through the closed door as if it had been open, but she forced herself to turn the handle, open it for her own passage, and step out into the hall. He had paused just outside the door, and for a moment she was unaware of anything but him. Then he went on. It was easy for Antonia to see the man in the hallway; sconces placed high on the wall between each door lined the entire corridor, and they were kept burning all night.

The man was met several feet away in the hallway by a slender, very young woman, dressed in a flowing dressing gown, with a lovely, delicate face and a crop of riotous red curls worn loosely. Her huge, glowing eyes lifted to his as they met, her lips parted, and she was in his arms as if it was the one place in all the world where she belonged.

Antonia felt a vague shock when she saw the young woman, but she was uncertain as to the cause. Surely, two ghosts were no more shocking than one? No, it was something else. A sense of familiarity, perhaps, though she had no idea why that should be so, for she could not remember ever seeing a likeness of this young woman and she did not know her identity. Before she could ponder the matter further, she realized that she was not alone in observing the lovers.

Lyonshall stood in the open doorway of his room,

staring just as she did. She could see him hazily through the lovers. It was a strange and eerie sight, evoking a feeling of even greater unreality within Antonia, yet she was more affected by the passionate embrace than by the ghostliness of two people long dead and buried.

Their passion for one another was so powerful Antonia could literally feel it. They kissed with the aching pleasure of two people deeply in love, their faces transformed by tenderness and desire. Their lips moved in speech that only they heard, though it was obvious they spoke words of love and need. Her arms were tight around his neck, and his held her pressed to his body. She tilted her head back as he kissed her throat, her expression filled with such sensual delight that Antonia wanted to turn her eyes from so intimate a moment.

But she could not. Just as she had felt compelled to follow the man from her room, so now she was compelled to stand there and watch. She felt caught, trapped in a spell of sensuality that tugged at all her senses. Her heart beat faster, and she felt hot, her body feverish and tense. It seemed to go on forever, but it was actually no more than a few minutes later when the couple turned with one mind and moved toward the duke's bedchamber.

Antonia felt rather dazed, but a shaken laugh escaped her when Lyonshall automatically stepped aside for them. They passed into his room. He looked after them for a moment, then reached for the handle and pulled the door closed. He strolled down the hall to Antonia.

With utter composure, he said, "I believe they would rather be alone."

"How can you be so calm?" she asked, her gaze moving between him and the closed door down the hall. Her voice was shaking, and she felt appallingly unsteady. "I knew the castle was supposed to be haunted, but it was not something in which I believed. I—I was never more shocked in my life."

He slid his hands into the pockets of his dressing gown and smiled faintly. "Lyonshall is not so old as Wingate, but it can claim a number of centuries. And a few ghosts. In the portrait gallery, it is quite usual to see a cloaked gentleman moving about on stormy nights such as this one. I have seen him myself. In fact, he tipped his hat to me with perfect courtesy one night." He paused, then added, "I wonder why spirits choose to walk most often when the weather is uneasy. And why the hour of midnight seems to be their time."

Antonia had no answer for him, and in any case he did not wait for one.

"Well, as it appears my room will be occupied for some time to come, and since it is somewhat drafty in this hallway, I suggest we wait in your room."

Too startled to voice an instant refusal, Antonia found her arm taken in a firm grasp as she was guided back into her bedchamber. She pulled away from him, her voice even more shaky when she said, "We most certainly cannot wait here! I am astonished you would suggest anything so improper."

"Don't be missish, Toni; it hardly becomes you." He strolled over to the fireplace and stood gazing at the flames. "I have left the door open, as you see. In any case, but for our ghostly friends we are quite alone in this wing, so you need fear no scandal. By the way— do you happen to know who the lady was?"

"No."

"Undoubtedly an ancestor of yours; you are the living image of her."

That startled Antonia so much that she forgot to be affronted by his presence in her room. "I?"

Lyonshall looked at her. "Didn't you notice? The same red hair and blue eyes, of course, but there is a much stronger resemblance than mere coloring. You share the same delicacy of feature, the same large eyes and flying brows. She was less stubborn, I imagine; your jaw is sharper. And though the shape of your mouths is very alike, you have more humor than she could lay claim to, I believe.''

He smiled slightly, his gaze intent on her. "As for . . . other attributes, I would say that you are far superior to your ancestor. She seemed quite frail, almost sickly. You, however, possess a magnificent body, beautifully voluptuous without an ounce of excess flesh. A body made for the passion we both know you are capable of.''

Antonia felt an almost feverish heat stealing through her body once again, and silently cursed his seductive wiles. She had to regain control of this situation, be-fore . . . before something irrevocable was said. Or done. "Please leave at once," she said stiffly.

"And where am I to go?" He raised one brow.

"There must be thirty rooms in this wing!"

"None of which have been prepared for a guest. Cold fireplaces and unaired sheets? And the furniture likely in holland covers? To say nothing of the difficulty my valet would have locating me in the morning. Would you really be so cruel as to consign me to such discomfort only to satisfy the boring notions of propriety, Toni?''

She struggled to remain calm. "There is no reason for you not to return to your room. The—the ghosts probably vanished the moment they entered; I am sure you will find them gone if—''

"No. They were moving toward the bed as I shut the door.'' His voice had deepened to a husky note.

Remembering the passionate kisses they had observed, Antonia flushed. The scene had profoundly unsettled her. She couldn't seem to shake the queer sensual spell that had enveloped her as she had watched them, especially since Lyonshall seemed bent on reminding her.

She could not help but think of those two lovers bliss-fully together in the duke's bed, or in a ghostly bed of their own century, she surmised, and that mental image brought others with it. A quiet stable, filled with the sweet scent of new hay. His mouth on hers, arousing emotions and sensations she had never known before. The burning, throbbing longing of her body for his. The incredible, shocking pleasure of lying in his arms and discovering her own passion . . .

Antonia stood with her arms crossed beneath her breasts, and tried to push the disturbing memories from her mind. That proved impossible. She was vividly conscious of how alone they were, of the nearness of her bed and the scant covering of her nightclothes. Gradually, the eeriness of the ghostly encounter was completely overwhelmed in her mind by its sensuality, and by the flesh and blood stirrings in her body as all her senses responded to the man who stood only a few steps away.

"Sit down, Toni. We may be here a while."

"I would rather stand." She was afraid to move, certain that if she did, it would be to throw herself into his arms. Dear heaven, he had barely touched her when they had entered the room, and casually, yet her entire body longed for his touch so intensely that resisting the pull toward him was like fighting an uncontrollable force of nature. Not even her most bitter and hurt memories of what he had done could stop the building desire.

He shook his head. "So stubborn. Do you expect me to try and ravish you, is that it?"

She lifted her chin and glared at him, reaching for dignity, offended hauteur—anything to combat the clash of longing and bitterness inside her. "I *expect* you to remember you are a gentleman. Though, given your behavior today, I must admit my hopes are not high."

"Indeed? Wise of you. For I don't mean to pretend with you, my sweet. I won't play the gentleman, happily content with a light flirtation and a few chaste kisses. There is blood in my veins—and yours—not water. I refuse to behave as though my desire for you is easily tamed. It is not. I refuse to forget that you have already given yourself to me, even if you choose to ignore that fact.''

''Stop.''

''Why? Because a gentleman wouldn't remind you? Because society insists that if such a shocking thing were to happen, all memory of it must be wiped away? That isn't so easy, is it, Toni? To forget. Is that why you accepted none of the offers of marriage made to you this last year, because you could not forget? Or was it because your bridegroom would know he was not the first in your bed?''

''Why must you taunt me with that?'' she whispered, wishing she could hate him. Anything would be better than this awful, aching need for his touch.

His hard face softened. ''Not a taunt, sweet. How could I scorn such a beautiful memory? I know you felt as I did that day, that our loving was intended. You could not have given yourself to me so freely if you had believed anything else.''

Antonia couldn't move or speak as he came slowly toward her. She could only wait, heart thudding, body trembling. She felt suspended, poised on the brink of something she wanted desperately even while a large part of her mind struggled not to give in.

''No, Richard,'' she said in a smothered voice as he reached her, suddenly very much afraid that if he touched her now she would be lost.

''Yes,'' he said huskily, his hands lifting slowly to frame her face. ''Whatever caused you to hate me didn't change this. We both know it. You want me, Toni, as much as I want you. And if desire is all I can claim from you, I will claim that. Marriages have begun with less.''

Even if she had been granted a moment to prepare herself, no barrier she might have raised could have stood against him. He took her mouth with all the passionate intensity she remembered so vividly, and her entire body responded. Her arms lifted to his neck as his went around her. She felt the hard warmth of him against her, and the strength drained from her legs in a rush.

She had forgotten how it felt . . . No, she had forgotten nothing. The heat spreading through her body, the building tension of need, the hunger that brought her out of herself until she was returning his kisses with a passion only he was able to ignite in her—all of it was achingly familiar. Just as it had been in the stable, her response to him drove everything else from her mind, until only the two of them existed in a world of sensuality.

She was barely aware of being lifted and carried a few short steps, then she felt the softness of the bed under her back. She gasped when his lips left hers, her eyes opening dazedly to stare up at his taut face. He was sitting beside her, bending over her, his hands smoothing loosened strands of her long hair away from her face. He lowered his head and kissed her so fiercely that it was like a brand of possession, and she heard the small muffled sound of pleasure that escaped her.

It was as though she had been deprived for a long time of something her body and spirit craved, and her hunger rose higher and higher, beyond her ability to control it. Just as it had been before, she didn't think of a price to be paid or the potential for pain—only the irresistible necessity of belonging to him.

His lips trailed down over her throat, then lower as his fingers untied the ribbon of her nightgown. He pressed a hot kiss in the valley between her breasts, and the vibrations of his words were an added caress.

"Tell me you want me, Toni."

It was not the demand that sent a cold rush of sanity through Antonia; it was his voice. There was something in it she had never heard before, a driven, implacable note. And when he raised his head to stare down at her, his eyes were the flat gray of a stormy sky. Angry. He was angry.

She wondered suddenly, painfully, if he really did intend to marry her. She didn't think so. She thought he wanted her physical surrender, wanted to prove to them both that she could not refuse him in this, at least.

If he wanted revenge because she had jilted him, he could hardly have chosen a better means. Because if she gave herself to him now, knowing they had no future together, in her own mind—and undoubtedly his—she would be little better than a whore.

Her throat was aching, but her voice was steady when she said, ''No.'' Her arms around his neck fell to her sides, and she closed her eyes. ''No.''

He went utterly still, then she felt the bed shift as he moved away. A few moments later, the door closed quietly, and she knew she was alone.

Antonia opened her eyes and sat up slowly. Her lips were throbbing from his kisses, and her entire body felt feverish and tense. Until that moment, she had not realized just how much she still loved him. Enough so that she wanted to call out to him, or go after him. Enough so that if he had kissed her one more time, she would have been unable to say no again.

She loved him so much that she would have made herself a whore without an instant's hesitation, if only he had said he loved her.

But he had not.

That, more than anything else, caused Antonia to believe he wanted nothing from her except the satisfaction of knowing she could not resist his seduction.

The room was very quiet, growing chilly as the fire died. Antonia felt alone, and this time not even a ghost came to prove her wrong.

* * *

The following day was strange and unsettling. Antonia had not slept well; between the ghostly visitation and Lyonshall's near-seduction, she had been left in a state hardly conducive to sleep, and it had been close to dawn before she had finally managed to close her eyes. When Plimpton had awakened her only a few hours later, the lack of rest and her emotional turmoil made her feel raw and tense. She said nothing about the ghosts to her maid, and certainly nothing about the duke's midnight presence in her bedchamber, but drank her tepid morning coffee in silence.

When she went downstairs, it was with a certain trepidation, but she found only her mother in the breakfast room. Lady Sophia was not a particularly observant woman, but where her only child was concerned affection lent her acuity.

"Darling, are you feeling well?" she asked immediately, her large eyes filled with concern. "You seem tired and—and quite pale."

Antonia had already made up her mind not to mention the ghosts to her mother; Lady Sophia was of a nervous disposition, and would certainly be unable to sleep a wink if she were told that spirits roamed the castle at night.

Helping herself to toast and more coffee from the heavily laden sideboard, Antonia replied calmly. "The storm kept me awake, Mama; I am only a little tired—nothing to signify."

Lady Sophia waited until her daughter was seated at the table, then glanced around to make certain they were alone. Lowering her voice, she said in her fluttery way, "Darling, I trust you locked your door last night. I was never more shocked! I had intended to speak to your grandmother about the situation, but . . . but she looks at one in *such* a way, I felt myself quite unable to make the attempt."

It required a moment before Antonia realized her

mother was referring to the arrangement of bedchambers. "I am sure you need have no fears, Mama," she said, pushing aside the memory of hot kisses. "Remember, if you please, that the duke and I agreed we wouldn't suit."

Eyeing her, Lady Sophia said, "Well, so you said at the time, but—Forgive me, Toni, but it appeared to me last night that Lyonshall was behaving with far more— more *warmth* than was at all seemly. The way he spoke to you and looked at you . . ." Blushing slightly, she added, "My dear, though you judge yourself quite grown-up, there are some things you simply cannot know about men. Even the best of them may find themselves at the mercy of their *baser* instincts and—and for you to be all alone with the duke in that big, empty wing—and you so pretty as you are—it just seems to me—"

Rescuing her parent from the morass of her tangled sentence, Antonia said a bit dryly, "Are you referring to passion, Mama?"

"Antonia!"

She felt a pang of sad wisdom. She should have been innocent of passion, as her mother so clearly believed she was. For an unmarried young lady of twenty-one to have the knowledge Antonia possessed was shocking and should be a source of heartache. But the shame of having given herself to a man before marriage was not so dreadful to her because she had given herself in love. No matter what had happened afterward, and despite her words to Lyonshall about the "mistake," Antonia did not regret what she had done.

Quietly, she said, "Mama, the duke is most certainly a gentleman, and would do nothing to force me against my will." He had not, after all; when she had refused him, he had left her alone without another word.

Lady Sophia hesitated, biting her lip. "Darling, I have often thought you were not . . . not as indifferent to him

as you have insisted. Indeed, you seem very aware of
him when he is in the room. If your feelings for him are
confused, it could cloud your judgment. And his behavior
last night . . ."

"He is amusing himself with a light flirtation, nothing
more," Antonia said. "As for me, I am quite certain of
my feelings for the duke, and quite able to exercise sound
judgment. I assure you, Mama, I have no intention of
further disgracing my good name by doing anything I
ought not." The words should have burned her tongue,
she thought wryly—or at least pricked her conscience,
considering what she had already done.

The conversation might have continued, but the countess entered the room then. Lady Sophia looked so self-
conscious that Antonia was mildly surprised her grandmother did not instantly demand to know what they had
been discussing, but it became obvious she had another
matter on her mind.

"Antonia, since the weather makes outdoor amuse-
ments impossible, I believe you young people will find
some enjoyment in arranging the Christmas decorations.
A tree was cut some days ago, and Tuffet is having it
brought into the drawing room now, along with mistletoe
and holly boughs. The maids have spent the past week
or so stringing berries and making other decorations, so
you need only put them in place."

Antonia would have objected, but before she could
the duke entered the room. "An excellent scheme,
ma'am. I am glad you have adopted the recent custom
of bringing a tree inside; it is especially pleasant in
weather such as this."

The matter settled to her satisfaction, Lady Ware nodded. "Since Christmas Eve is day after tomorrow, you
should have plenty of time to get the decorations in
place."

So Antonia found herself once more thrown into the

duke's company. Her grandmother carried her mother
off immediately after breakfast, obviously intending to
occupy her in another part of the castle, and even the
servants made themselves scarce as soon as the couple
went into the drawing room to find the tree and promised
decorations.

Lyonshall behaved as though nothing had happened
the night before. He was very casual, not nearly so intense as he had been during the previous evening.

Antonia could not help but feel grateful for that; she
could no longer don her social mask in his company. If
he had attempted to make love to her, or even to flirt,
she knew she would have betrayed herself. Instead, because he was relaxed and carelessly charming, she was
able to be calm herself.

The festive nature of the holiday had its own effect,
as well. The sharp scent of holly and of the big spruce
tree mingled with the spicy fragrance of potpourri from
the bowls the maids had set out in nearly every room,
and even as vast as the castle was, the enticing aroma
of plum pudding and other dishes being prepared for
Christmas dinner drifted up from the kitchen.

The yule log was prepared, candles put into place, and
holly boughs arranged to please the eye. The maids had
strung berries of different colors for the tree, and Antonia
was surprised to find among the other decorations small,
exquisitely sewn sachets in various shapes, obviously the
work of her grandmother.

"I didn't realize she cared so about the holiday,"
Antonia murmured as she fingered one lovely, potpourri-
filled sachet in the shape of a star. "She must have sewn
these sachets every year for a long time. Look how many
there are."

"Beautiful work," the duke observed. "It's going to
be a fine tree."

Antonia agreed with him. In fact, she had to admit

the castle would look and feel quite different once it had donned its holiday dress. Already, the huge drawing room seemed warmer, brighter, the colorful decorations adding light and cheerfulness.

She was beginning to see why her family had loved the castle. There was something stately in the sheer size of the place, and a feeling of permanence in the solid stone walls and floors. This place, she realized, had surrounded the Wingate family for centuries. It had sheltered and protected them, hidden their secrets, housed their happiness, their anger, and their tears.

Ever since the ghostly lovers had appeared the night before, Antonia had been aware of a growing feeling that the castle itself was a living thing. That over the centuries, it had absorbed so much of the Wingate family emotions that it, too, had become part of the family. She almost told Lyonshall of this feeling, but kept it to herself in the end. It sounded very fanciful, she decided.

She and Lyonshall worked together in harmony, and for a time Antonia nearly forgot everything except the pleasure of being in the company of a man who talked to her as an equal. But even as they hung decorations on the tree and argued amiably about their placement, she could not help being wary of his changed attitude. More than once, she caught him watching her, and the brooding look she saw so fleetingly caused tension to steal over her.

To her surprise, he continued to behave casually for the remainder of the day, and she blamed her imagination for the dark expression she had seen. He neither said nor did anything to upset or confuse her. He was pleasant and charming at dinner, even drawing a laugh from Lady Sophia, and when the evening was over he escorted Antonia to her door and left her there with a composed and polite good night.

Antonia told herself it was all for the best. He had

obviously accepted her refusal—or had, at least, realized
he was more of a gentleman than he had believed himself
to be, and had given up the idea of seduction. But the
apparent end of his brief courtship did nothing to ease
her chaotic emotions.

Once again, she could not sleep, and though her mind
automatically marked the approach of midnight with both
anticipation and anxiety, she was nevertheless surprised
to turn from the fireplace and see that her ghostly visitor
had returned. Her fear of the previous night was absent,
but the eeriness of what she saw as she watched him
moving about the room had a decided effect on her. She
felt almost like an intruder, watching him without his
awareness, yet she couldn't force herself to look away.

Just as the night before, he moved around the room
restlessly for a time before he eventually headed for the
door. She followed without making a conscious decision
to do so. In the open doorway of her room, she watched
a repetition of the previous night's scene enacted in the
hall, and the same sensual awareness stole over her.

The dark man and his fiery-haired lady shared a love
that had lived beyond their time, surviving the death of
mortal flesh to haunt this hall of stone and silence. No
one, Antonia thought, could look upon such unquenchable emotions and not feel the power of them. It made
her throat ache, made her peculiarly aware of her own
body as her heart beat and the blood coursed through her
veins. And it made her feel a profound sense of loss,
because she had believed just such a love as theirs had
once been within her own grasp. That grief grew even
stronger when she saw Lyonshall through the entwined
lovers. It was as if fate was mocking her.

She remained unmoving in the doorway as the ghostly
pair went into his room. As on the previous night, he
closed the door and came to her, but before he could

speak she caught a glimmer of movement beyond him in the hallway.

"Look," she murmured.

A third ghostly form had appeared at the end of the hall near the stairs. She came toward them, a pretty woman past the first blush of youth but not yet near middle age, her dress made up of dark colors and fashioned in the style of a century before. She gave a clearer idea of the time than the other two had, since she was fully dressed. She wore a high, stiff cap of frilled linen with a short veil on her neatly arranged dark hair; an outer garment, trailing in back, with semi-long sleeves and linen cuffs, was worn open in front over a laced bodice and flounced skirt.

She was attractive in a colorless way, but seemed far more lifeless than the other two. Like the lovers, she took no notice of the two living spectators. She was moving along the hallway, but stopped when she reached the duke's bedchamber door.

Like a person attracted by some sound, she stood with her head turned a little toward the door and her attention fixed on that room. She was very still for a long moment, the expression on her face curiously intent, even mask-like. Then her lips twisted in an ugly grimace, and she continued on her way.

Antonia felt chilled as she watched the woman. It was a feeling quite unlike what she had experienced upon first seeing a ghost in her room. This was something far more acute, and deeply troubling. She had a strange and powerful urge to rush to the lovers and warn them to take care, because someone in the castle intended them harm. She *knew* that somehow, felt it with every fiber of her being. The lovers were in danger.

Her rational mind reminded her that these people had been dead for a hundred years, but she couldn't seem to throw off the oppressive feeling of dread or her anxious desire to prevent a tragedy.

Standing beside Lyonshall, she watched the woman continue down the hallway and vanish into one of the rooms. Slowly, Antonia turned and went into her own room, her emotions so disturbed she didn't realize immediately that Lyonshall had followed her.

"Toni?"

Antonia went to the fireplace, still feeling chilled, and stretched her hands out toward the flames. "That other one," she murmured. "She means them harm."

"Yes, I saw."

"I feel so helpless. It's like watching the first seconds of a carriage accident in the streets and feeling powerless to stop what you know is coming."

He stood several steps away, watching her, and his voice remained low. "Whatever will happen—already *has*, Toni. A hundred years ago."

"So my mind tells me. But what I feel . . . is difficult to overcome. They seemed so happy together, with their whole lives before them, yet I have an awful certainty they didn't live much beyond what we have already seen." Antonia shook her head a little, trying to push away the dread. "I wonder who they were."

"You don't know?"

"No, I—I know very little of my family's history in this place. That is a dreadful thing to say, isn't it?"

"Natural, if you haven't lived here. Most of us do tend to live in the present."

"I suppose."

"Have you asked Lady Ware about the ghosts?" he asked. "She would very likely know the history of the castle, and of the family."

"No," she replied. When he continued to gaze at her with one brow raised, she shrugged. "Grandmother is such a brusque and matter-of-fact person, I have no doubt she would tell me I imagined the whole."

He was silent for a moment, and odd look of hesitation in his eyes. "Somehow I feel sure she wouldn't tell you that. I believe she knows about the ghosts. My valet tells me only the South wing of the castle is held to be haunted. Perhaps Lady Ware put the two of us here for that reason."

"Because of the ghosts?" Antonia frowned. "Why would she do such a thing?"

Again, Lyonshall hesitated. "If she wishes us to reconcile, she may have believed a pair of young lovers might push us in the right direction—even if they are ghostly lovers."

Antonia felt wary, disturbed by the way he had led the conversation back to them. She was in no state to endure more of the previous night's discussion, and she was surprised that he wished to talk about the subject yet again. He had accepted her request to end their engagement with little attempt to persuade her to change her mind, yet now he seemed almost obsessed. She would have thought the blow to his pride—if nothing else— would have made the entire subject unbearable.

She avoided his eyes by turning back to the fire. "I seriously doubt she has any such belief. She told me herself it would be foolish to suppose you would make me a second offer, and she knows very well the idea is—"

"Is what? Repugnant to you?" he demanded when she broke off abruptly.

"Must we discuss this again?"

"Yes. Because you have yet to tell me the truth." His voice was a little harsh now.

Antonia refused to look at him. "I thought you had accepted my wish to have done with this. Your behavior today led me to believe that was so."

He gave a hard laugh. "Indeed? My behavior today,

Toni, was due to your refusal last night. No man with any sensibility could accept with pleasure the look of sick anguish I saw on your face last night. If you wished to hurt me yet again, you certainly did.''

"That was not my intention," she heard herself say, and wondered why she couldn't allow him to believe even the worst of her if it would only drive him away.

"Then what was your intention? You were willing, Toni, we both know that. You came alive in my arms with all the passion I remember so well, and for a moment I hoped . . . But then you refused me, in a voice so cold it froze my heart. What have I done to earn that from you? How can I accept your wishes when I don't understand the reasons for them? Is my desire to make you my wife so unbearable to you?"

Trying to appear calm even if her mask was gone, Antonia held her voice steady. "If you must hear it again, I have no wish to marry you, Richard. I suppose you feel yourself perfectly entitled to your revenge, but—"

"Revenge?" He crossed the room quickly and grasped her arm, turning her roughly to face him. "Is that why you refused me last night? Because you believe I want revenge? What put such a mad notion as that into your head?"

She met his grim eyes as squarely as she was able, though it required a tremendous effort. "It seems obvious to me. In all the months since our engagement ended, you have made no effort whatsoever to heal the breach, or even expressed interest in doing so—why now? Because you suddenly find yourself virtually alone with me and stormbound? No, I think not. You wish to punish me for jilting you. I realized that last night. Why else would you go to such lengths to remind me that I gave up to you what any woman should give only on her wedding night? Why else would you torment me with the knowledge of how—how easily I can be swayed when you touch me?''

A crooked smile curved his lips briefly. ''At least you admit that much. So I wasn't wrong, after all. You do still want me, don't you?''

''Should I deny it?'' she said bitterly. ''What good would that do? You know the truth.''

''I know another truth, Toni.'' His voice was as implacable as it had been the night before. ''You could not feel desire—if you didn't feel love as well. You don't hate me. You might wish to hate me, but you can't.''

It was like being kicked in the stomach, and for a moment Antonia could not breathe. The last of her defenses collapsed into painful rubble. She felt horribly powerless, and her heart ached with its every beat. To love a man she could not trust was bad enough; to know that he was certain of her love was even worse. It was what she had struggled to hide from him—all for naught. Lying now was something she hadn't the strength or will to do.

Finally, in little more than a whisper, she said, ''Then it appears your revenge is complete, doesn't it?''

His free hand lifted to touch her face, and his voice softened to a deep, husky note. ''I don't want revenge, I want you to be my wife. We belong together, Toni, don't you see? Can't you feel that as surely as I do? Give me your love as well as your passion. We can put the past behind us and start again.''

She realized then that the stormy gray of his eyes was a sign of determination rather than anger; he really *did* want to marry her. But that knowledge did little to ease her pain. She loved him, and she wanted him, but she did not trust him not to hurt her again.

She dared not trust him.

''Thank you for the honor,'' she said politely, ''but I must refuse.''

The softened expression left his face, replaced by a hard mask of resolve. His big hands gripped her shoulders, the fingers almost painful as they held her. "Why? This time I mean to get the answer, Toni, and I won't give up until I do. Why won't you marry me?"

She was too tired to avoid the answer, even to spare herself the pain of his lies. "Perhaps it really did mean nothing to you; that is always the defense I hear of gentlemen. But it meant something to me. And even more than that betrayal, you destroyed my trust in you with your lies. How could I marry a man I no longer trusted?"

A swift frown drew his brows together, and she could have sworn his voice was sincerely bewildered when he said, "Lies? What are you talking about?"

"Mrs. Dalton," she replied flatly.

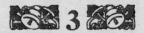 3

"CLAIRE DALTON?" HIS FROWN DEEPENED. "WHAT DO you know of her?"

"More than you intended for me to know, I should say." Antonia smiled thinly. "She was—and perhaps still is—your mistress."

Richard released her shoulders and stepped back. His eyes narrowed, and he spoke very deliberately. "She was. However, since my—arrangement with her ended before I asked you to be my wife, I hardly see why it would concern you."

"If it *had* ended, you are quite right. But it didn't end."

"Toni, I am telling you it did."

Antonia had known it would hurt to hear him lie, and she had not been wrong. It hurt dreadfully. She half-turned away from him, her back to the fire, and she could feel her face harden with aversion. "Of course it did," she said tonelessly. "After all, no lady must ever acknowledge the existence of such a creature. She turns her head away, or makes herself blind to that—unbearable reality."

"Toni—"

"Please, no more lies."

"I am not lying to you."

"No?" She looked at him. "Can you tell me you haven't seen her since our engagement was announced?"

He hesitated, then cursed roughly under his breath. "No, I can't tell you that. If you must have the truth, our relationship resumed briefly—*after* you ended the engagement. But I swear to you, I didn't see her while you were promised to me, nor would I have gone to her after our marriage. I wanted no mistress, Toni, only you."

"I don't believe you." Her lips curved in a painful little smile. "You see? You swear to me, and I can't believe it. You tell me you speak the truth, and I hear lies. I don't trust you, Richard. Imagine the hell you would live in with a wife who called you a liar."

He shook his head slowly, a muscle leaping in his tight jaw. "Why can't you believe me? Who told you about Claire?"

"She did."

"What?" He took a step and grasped her shoulders again, turning her fully to face him. "How came you even to speak to her?"

"Worried about my ladylike sensibilities?" She

laughed without amusement. "I must admit, my mother would have considered my visitor—quite shocking. But Mrs. Dalton found me alone when she came to see me that morning. I was waiting for you, already in the parlor. A housemaid answered the door, and I am afraid she had no idea that the very fashionable lady who wished to see me was nothing of the kind."

His hands tightened on her shoulders. "What did she say to you?"

"What do you think? She congratulated me on our forthcoming marriage. I needn't concern myself with her, she said. She would take up very little of your time. Just as she had during the past months."

"And you believed her? Toni, how could you take the word of a spiteful woman over mine?"

Antonia jerked away from him. She went to her dressing table and opened the jewelry case atop it. Finding what she sought, she returned to Richard and held out her hand. The firelight reflected off the object she held, glinting brightly gold.

"Because *she* had proof," Antonia said raggedly.

He lifted the object from her trembling hand. It was a watch fob, made quite simply; its only decoration was a golden button engraved with the letters AW.

"You have reminded me so often of that day in the stable," she said, her voice still unsteady. "Do you remember? Do you remember how . . . in our haste . . . a button was torn off my riding habit? We laughed about it later. You said you would keep it, as a treasured memento of our first time together. You had this fob made, and you wore it often. Your *mistress* was kind enough to return it to me."

"She had this?" His face was curiously pale. "She told you I had given it to her? Toni, she lied, I swear to you. She must have . . . My house was robbed while we were at the theater together the night before; she must have hired the thief—''

''Please, don't! I have heard enough lies.''

His hand closed hard over the fob, and his eyes darkened almost to black. ''I am telling you the truth. If you had not left London so quickly, you would surely have heard of the robbery—the news was all over town.''

''And was it all over town that we were lovers?'' Tears burned her eyes, and she struggled not to shed them. ''She told me that, as well. How the two of you laughed at my—my innocence. How you compared me to her . . . and found me sadly lacking.''

''*No.*'' He lifted his hand jerkily toward her face. ''My God, Toni, I would never have done such a thing! You have to believe me.''

She backed away, her movements as jerky as his. ''I wish I could. I—I really do. But I can't. Please, just leave me alone.''

His hand fell to his side, and he stared at her for a long time in silence. ''You won't believe me no matter what I say, will you? She poisoned you completely against me.''

Antonia's eyes flicked to the watch fob he still held in his hand, then returned to his face. ''Good night, Richard.''

He must have realized she was a whisper away from breaking down, or perhaps, as he had said, knew that she was simply unable to listen to any more, at least for the moment. Still holding the fob, he went to the open door. He hesitated there briefly, looking back at her with a grim expression, then went out of the room and closed the door quietly behind him.

Antonia's control lasted no longer than that. She found her way to the bed, though it was impossible to see through the flood of tears, and sat down before her legs could no longer support her. She felt that she had turned her back on something infinitely precious, and the grief and pain tore at her as if they were living creatures with talons.

But she couldn't have acted in any other way; she knew that. Without trust, there was no possibility of happiness; eventually, her love would be destroyed by mistrust, and a marriage with Richard would end up worse even than the hollow relationships that passed so often for marriages.

She had no idea how long she sat there, but gradually the tears slowed to a trickle and then ceased. The fire was dying, the room growing chilly—or perhaps that was only a miserable coldness caused by the emptiness inside her. Either way, she realized vaguely that she should go to bed, and tried to summon the energy to do so.

She raised her bowed head, and then went very still as she stared across the room. She was so numb that all she felt was faint surprise and a remote curiosity.

This young woman ghost was neither the fiery-haired enchantress nor the malevolent darker woman. She somewhat resembled the man, with her brunette hair and thin, sensitive face, but her style of clothing seemed to indicate she had lived at least a score of years after him: her gown was simpler in design, with a fuller shorter skirt, which did not trail along behind her, and she wore no cap. She stood in the center of the room, and her gentle, tragic eyes were fixed on Antonia.

"You know I am here," Antonia said slowly, a tiny chill of fright feathering up her spine. "You are . . . aware of me."

The woman smiled and nodded, then stepped back and made a beckoning gesture.

Antonia wanted to refuse, but found herself unable to do so; again, she seemed to be in the grip of a compulsion. She rose and followed as the woman led her out of the room and a little way down the hall. Turning to look at her, the woman gestured again, toward Lyonshall's door. It was a simple gesture, an invitation to enter.

The urge to obey—combined with Antonia's own longings—was so strong she actually took a step in that direction. But then she stopped and shook her head. "I can't," she said in a voice hardly louder than a whisper. "I can't go to him."

The woman gestured again insistently, clearly much distressed, her sorrowful eyes almost pleading.

Though she had thought herself emptied of tears, Antonia felt them stinging her eyes again. "No, I can't. It hurt so much when he lied to me—I am afraid to trust him again."

After a moment of obvious indecision, the woman's hand fell to her side. She moved away from the duke's door and beckoned again.

With a feeling of unreality, Antonia followed. She didn't know where she was being led; though she had explored the castle a few times during her childhood, that had been many years ago when the South wing had been shut up, and she had made no attempt to explore the wing on this visit. The wide corridors were utterly silent, the stone floor chilly beneath her slippered feet, but she kept her gaze fixed on the slightly hazy form of her guide.

Sconces lined only the main corridor where Antonia and the duke were quartered; the numerous other hallways and galleries, unoccupied, were dark. When her guide left the main corridor behind, Antonia had the eerie feeling of being swallowed up by darkness and silence.

"Wait! I can't see you!" She took several hurried steps, more by instinct than sight, then slowed in relief as she saw her guide waiting for her.

The woman had paused at the head of a short hallway

leading to a window, and gestured toward a table against the wall. Gratefully, Antonia lit the oil lamp there, then walked a bit quicker to keep her guide safely within the circle of yellow light as they continued down the hallway. The woman stopped about halfway, and turned to indicate a large portrait hanging between two doors.

Antonia stepped closer, holding the lamp high, and gasped aloud. One of the lovers was beautifully represented, her fiery hair brilliant and her delicate face glowing with life. Formally dressed with her hair piled high atop her small head, she looked almost regal. Her gown was green velvet, the color bringing out faint flecks of green in her big eyes. There was a quantity of lace at her wrists and throat, a heart-shaped patch at one corner of her smiling lips, and an enormous emerald ring glowed on the index finger of her right hand.

Antonia could see the resemblance to herself more clearly in the painting, and for a moment she had the eerie thought that she was the reincarnation of this fragile, doomed creature.

There was a brass nameplate on the frame, and she read it aloud. "Linette Dubois Wingate." She looked up at the face again, then turned to find her guide pointing at another painting directly across the hall. When Antonia moved a few steps in that direction, the lamplight revealed a portrait of the man.

Like Linette, he was dressed formally though his dark hair was unpowdered. His coat was a heavy brocade shot through with gold thread, and both his cuffs and cravat were lace-edged. There was strength in his thin face, honesty in the level gaze of his eyes, and the sensuality Antonia knew him capable of was evident in the curve of his lips. According to the nameplate, his name had been Parker Wingate.

After a moment, she followed her beckoning guide a little further down the hall, and found herself gazing at a portrait of the guide herself. It had obviously been painted when she was a girl on the brink of womanhood, yet the eyes in that gentle face were already shadowed with sorrow.

"Mercy Wingate," Antonia read aloud. She studied the portrait for several minutes, then turned to look at Mercy's hazy form just a few steps away. "You were—their daughter?"

Mercy nodded. She beckoned again, turning back the way they had come, and Antonia followed obediently. When they reached the head of the corridor, she kept the lamp, partly because Mercy went on without pausing. It appeared she was bound for the central part of the castle. Antonia was led to the library on the ground floor, and to a certain area of the shelves.

Her guide pointed to a particular book, then retreated as Antonia went to the shelf and set her lamp on a nearby table. She had to reach above her head, but managed to get the book.

It was a thick volume bound in fine leather and stamped with gold. A book that had been privately printed in the very year of Antonia's birth. She touched the title stamped simply into the cover. *"Wingate Family History.* But—" She turned to speak to her guide, and found herself alone in the huge, silent room.

For a few moments, Antonia stood there questioning herself. It had been real, not a dream, she was sure of it. She *felt* it. She had not walked in her sleep; she had been unaware of the book's existence, so why—and how—would she have dreamed of it? Nor had she known of the portraits, since she had never seen them before; they must have been in storage in the South wing, or else had hung on the walls all the time the wing had been closed off.

No, Mercy had been as real as the ghostly representations of her parents that Antonia—and Richard—had seen during the past two nights. Eerie and strangely compelling in her sorrow and gentleness, she had stepped out of the past because . . . Why? Different from the others, she had been fully aware of Antonia, even communicating with her, however silently. She had been obviously distressed by Antonia's refusal to go into Richard's room, and Antonia had to believe that Mercy had been in some way trying to help them.

Antonia had many questions; she only hoped that the book would provide at least a few answers. She picked up the lamp and, carrying the heavy volume, made her way slowly back to the South wing and her bedchamber.

Weary though she was, the disturbing events and her chaotic emotions made sleep impossible, so she took the book with her to bed and began reading. The writer who had been commissioned to write the history knew his job well; with dry facts gleaned from family records, letters, and journals, he wove together a straightforward narrative that proved to be interesting, often entertaining, and sometimes tragic as he explored centuries of one family's existence.

There was even a family tree, and Antonia studied it for a long time before she went further. She found two shocks there. The date of a death was one. The other was her own lineage: she was a direct descendent of the sad guide—and the lovers. With a better understanding now of her resemblance to Linette, Antonia turned past the family tree and began reading.

Finding herself caught up in the story of the earliest Wingates, she found it difficult to force herself to skip ahead to the previous century, but her curiosity and unease about the young couple was too powerful to deny. She located the correct section dealing with the parents of Parker Wingate, and began reading there.

Theirs was an interesting time, full of historical events as well as the usual details of family life. Antonia enjoyed reading about all of it. As it had been the night before, she remained awake until nearly dawn, finally giving in to sleep still half-sitting up against the pillows with the heavy book across her knees.

Physical and emotional exhaustion had taken their toll; she slept deeply.

Antonia slept through the morning and well into afternoon, waking finally to see her maid sitting peacefully before the fire with a pile of mending in her lap.

"Good heavens," Antonia murmured, sitting up. "What time is it? I feel as if I have slept for days."

"No, milady, only for hours. It is after three."

While Antonia was coping with that slight shock, Plimpton went to the door, opening it just a crack and speaking to someone outside. The conversation was brief, and Plimpton soon returned to the bed. "One of the girls was so obliging as to wait until you should awaken, milady, since I did not wish to leave you. She will bring up your coffee, and you shall have it in bed."

"I have been in bed long enough," Antonia protested.

"Milady, you were worn down yesterday, and spent the better part of the night, I believe, reading that huge book. Her ladyship has been here, and she agrees with me that you should not get up before dinner."

"But—"

"She insists, milady. As do I." Briskly, Plimpton helped Antonia to bank her pillows and offered a damp cloth to wash her face and hands. By the time the coffee arrived, Antonia was more wide awake, and looked presentable enough to receive visitors, should any arrive.

Plimpton, always good company, served her mistress coffee and then returned to her mending, willing to remain silent unless Antonia desired conversation.

It was rare for Antonia to keep to her bed for any reason, but she was glad enough to obey on that afternoon. With no need to keep up her composure for the benefit of probing eyes, she felt much less strained, and she was glad of the opportunity to continue reading the family history—both out of real interest and a desire to keep her thoughts away from Richard.

That wish, however, proved futile. Antonia had fallen asleep last night in the middle of the account of Parker Wingate's early years, and she soon reached the section dealing with his engagement to a young French girl; Linette Dubois was, in fact, his distant cousin, and had come to stay at the castle the previous spring.

The author of the history had obviously found the young lovers' story touching; it seemed he had discovered journals written by both of them that provided him with a wealth of details. No other section of the book was so painstakingly recounted as the brief, tragic love story.

Antonia could not help thinking of Richard as she read. She could not help aching as the lovers' own words about one another recounted a depth of emotion that was so powerful and intimate it had transcended time itself. They had intended to wed just after the new year, but their passion had been too intense to deny; they had become lovers—as noted in both their journals—the week before Christmas.

As Antonia and Richard had witnessed, Linette and Parker had met each midnight hour after the remaining family members were asleep in their rooms, spending the bulk of the night in her room because, as Parker had dryly noted in his journal, it was a much simpler matter for a man to don his dressing gown and slip back across the hall in the silent hours before dawn than for a lady to do so.

Antonia had to smile at that, but then she turned the page and discovered an abrupt, chilling, and inexplicable end to the lovers' happiness. As she read the few remaining paragraphs, she shared the author's sense of grief and tragic waste, as well as his obvious bafflement.

Only the events were known; the actions and results were without the motivations and causes.

"Milady? Do you feel faint?"

She looked up to find Plimpton hovering anxiously, and supposed that she must have gone pale. "I know what happened, and when," she murmured, "but I don't know *why*."

"Milady?"

Antonia shook her head. "Nothing. I am quite all right, really. What time is it? I should dress for dinner."

"We can have a tray brought up, milady—"

"No. No, I had better go down, or Mama will be convinced I am ill."

"Very well, milady," said Plimpton, clearly unconvinced. "I will draw your bath."

Just over an hour later, Antonia encountered Richard waiting at his door to escort her, and felt a pang when she saw that he was wearing the button fob. His eyes were unreadable when they met hers.

"Good evening, Toni," he said quietly, offering his arm.

For an instant, she hesitated, but she seemed to have no more power over her longing to be near him than she had had over the compulsion to follow a ghost through the darkened corridors of the castle.

"I trust you are feeling better," he said as they walked down the hallway together.

"I was not ill, merely tired." Quite suddenly, Antonia had a vision of years to come, of meeting him socially and behaving with this horrible stilted politeness, and her very heart seemed to wrench in pain.

How could it all have gone so wrong?

He might have been thinking similar thoughts. His voice was very even when he said, "As soon as the weather clears sufficiently, I will remove myself. I am sure you don't believe this, but I have no wish to distress you any further.''

Not trusting herself to speak, Antonia merely nodded. She walked beside him, her head a little bowed, and wondered vaguely if the Wingates had always been unlucky in love. It seemed so. It seemed so indeed.

She was never able to recall afterwards how she managed to get through the evening. She remembered nothing of conversations, though knew she must have spoken because neither her grandmother nor her mother seemed to find anything amiss. She recalled only the long, slow walk with Richard back to her room late in the evening, and the stiffly polite good nights at her door.

She changed into her nightclothes and firmly sent Plimpton off to bed. Expecting another ghostly encounter, she didn't go to bed herself, but sat by the fire reading the account of Mercy Wingate's childhood, marriage—and tragically young death. It was not the best of stories to read while alone, and she was actually a bit relieved when a soft knock fell on her door a little before midnight.

It was Richard, of course, and his voice held the same quiet note as before, ''I doubt either of us is in any mood to observe yet another passionate embrace in the hallway, however ghostly.''

Without even thinking of suggesting that he wait somewhere else, Antonia nodded and stepped back, leaving the door open as he entered. She returned to her chair by the fire, torn between her longing to be with him and the pain it caused. What she should have done, she knew, was to have moved to another room long since, but that had only just occurred to her.

''I believe they will both be in this bedroom tonight— at least for a time,'' she said. ''If, that is, they are reenacting the events of their lives.''

"How do you know that?" Richard asked as he came to stand near the fireplace.

Antonia touched the book on a small table by her chair. "I have been reading about them in this book of family history. Their account was based largely on their own journals." She frowned briefly. "I must ask Grandmother if the journals still exist; I would like to read them."

"So would I." He hesitated, then added, "Though, of course, I will be gone soon."

Antonia experienced another sudden flash of memory. It was early in their engagement, when he had taken her to visit the British Museum, and they had scandalized several other visitors by holding hands and ruthlessly criticizing the various works of art. Since both were playfully engaged in trying to outdo each other, their remarks had become so outrageous that one middle-aged lady had sat down plump upon a bench and declared that she had never been more shocked in her life.

Recalling their laughter now, Antonia felt a throb of bittersweet pain. "Richard—" she began impulsively, then broke off when she caught a glimpse of movement near the bed.

It was Parker Wingate, restlessly awaiting the hour of his rendezvous with Linette. They watched as he moved about the room. Richard nodded when Antonia identified him by name.

"Who is the lady?" he murmured.

"Linette Dubois, a distant cousin. And his betrothed."

Antonia had no sooner spoken than Linette entered the room. Parker turned, obviously surprised, and she lifted a finger to her lips in a conspiratorial manner, her delicate face alight with mischief and love.

"I suppose," Richard remarked, "they both consider it less improper for a man to visit a lady's bedchamber than vice versa."

He had read their expressions accurately, Antonia
thought, and nodded in agreement. Then she forgot
everything except the sweet tenderness of the scene they
were witnessing.

Linette went to her betrothed and lifted one of his
hands in both of hers. She rubbed his hand briefly against
her cheek and kissed it, while he stood gazing down at
her bowed head with an expression so filled with love
and desire, Antonia's throat tightened. He said something
to her, and she looked up with a gentle smile before
reaching into the pocket of her dressing gown.

A moment later, she placed a gold, heart-shaped locket
into his hand. She opened it and showed him the curl of
her fiery hair lying inside, then closed it again and stood
on tiptoe to put the chain around his neck. She kissed
him very tenderly. He held her close for a long moment,
then lifted her into his arms and carried her from the
room.

"Toni, love, don't," Richard said huskily, and only
then did Antonia realize she was crying.

"You don't understand." Huddled in her chair, she
felt overpowering grief, for them and for all lovers torn
apart. "Tomorrow is Christmas Eve. That is when it
happens, tomorrow night." She covered her face with
her hands, unable to hold back a jerky sob. "Oh, God,
how could it go so wrong for them? How could it go so
wrong . . . for us?"

He made a rough sound and came to her, grasping her
arms and drawing her up from the chair. "Please don't,
sweetheart, I can't bear it. I have never seen you cry
before." His voice was still husky, and the arms that
held her close were gentle yet curiously fierce.

Antonia couldn't stop; she sobbed against his broad
chest in a storm of grief. Gradually, however, she became
aware of his murmurs, the hard warmth of his body, and
the strength of his arms around her. She was still aching,

but instinct warned her that she had to withdraw from him before her churning emotions sparked another kind of storm.

Finally, she was able to raise her head, but before she could speak he surrounded her face with his hands, thumbs gently brushing away the last of her tears.

"Toni . . ."

He was too close. His face filled her vision, her heart, her soul. The tenderness in his eyes was her undoing. She tried, but there was no force, no certainty, behind her murmured plea.

"Please . . . please just go."

At first, it seemed he would. But then his face tightened, and his head bent toward hers. "I can't," he whispered just before his lips touched hers. "I can't walk away from you again."

Antonia couldn't ask him a second time. The first touch of his mouth brought all her senses alive, and though some tiny part of her consciousness whispered of regrets, she stopped listening. The sadness of the tragedy awaiting the ghostly lovers had made her own painful love more acute than ever before. She would take what she could, if only for a night.

He kissed her as if he felt the same desperate need, his mouth slanting over hers to deepen the contact and his arms drawing her even closer to his hard body. She felt the thick silk of his hair under her fingers, and realized only then that she had slid her arms up around his neck. A fever of desire rose from the core of her, spreading outward until all she knew was heat and yearning.

She was kissing him back and, just as in that snug stable so many months ago, she forgot she was a lady and knew only that she was a woman.

She murmured a wordless protest when his lips left hers, but shivered with pleasure at their velvety touch on her neck. His hands untied the ribbons of her dressing gown, and she shrugged the garment off blindly.

"Toni . . . let me love you, sweetheart . . ."

She didn't answer him aloud, but when his lips returned to hers he didn't have to ask again. His tongue slipped into her eager mouth and stroked hers, and his hands moved down her back to cup her bottom, the fine cambric of her nightgown providing a soft friction between her flesh and his. Antonia could feel her entire body molding itself to his as if it were boneless, and the hardness of his arousal made her achingly aware of the emptiness inside her. Her breasts were pressed to his chest and they were throbbing, swelling with the need for his touch.

She wanted him to touch her, wanted to feel his hands on her naked flesh. It was an overpowering desire, a necessity so intense that nothing else mattered to her except the satisfying of it. She felt him lift her, carry her a few steps, and then the softness of the bed was beneath her.

Her eyes still closed and her mouth fierce under his, she pulled impatiently at his dressing gown until he wrestled the garment off. For a while then, she didn't know who was doing what, only that her nightgown vanished and she felt the sensual shock of his flesh against hers.

In the stable, they had not completely undressed; the shortness of their time together and their haste to have one another had made that a luxury they could ill afford. But now they had the night and assured privacy, and Antonia wanted to cry or laugh aloud at the glorious freedom.

A little moan escaped her when he trailed his lips down her throat, and she forced her eyes to open. He was looking down at her naked body, his eyes dark and on his hard face an expression of wonder she had seen only once before.

"Toni . . . Oh, God, you're so beautiful . . ."

Antonia felt no embarrassment, and not even a hint of shame, no matter what the whispery voice of her ladylike upbringing insisted. She was glad he found her beautiful, glad that her body pleased him. Her hands touched his broad shoulders, the strong column of his neck, and then her fingers slid into his hair as his head bent to her again.

His lips trailed over the satiny slope of her breast, and then she felt the burning pleasure of his mouth closing over her tight nipple. She cried out in surprise, her body arching of its own volition, stunned by the waves of sensation washing over her. His hand was stroking and kneading her flesh, his mouth hungry on her nipple, and she knew he could feel, perhaps even hear, the thundering beat of her heart.

Heat built in her, burning, and she couldn't seem to hold her body still. His hand slid slowly down her belly, making all her muscles quiver, and when he touched the burnished red curls over her mound her entire body jerked at the shock of pleasure. Her legs parted for him, and his hand cupped her, one finger probing gently.

Antonia moaned wildly, all her consciousness focused on his hand and mouth, and the surging response of her body to his skilled touch. He was caressing her insistently, stroking her damp, swollen flesh until she didn't think she could bear another moment of the coiling tension. It was pain, yet it was pleasure, and she shuddered at the vast, engulfing sensations.

"Richard . . . please . . . I can't . . ."

She heard her own thin voice as if from a great distance. Mutely, she tugged at his shoulder, and almost sobbed when he immediately shifted his weight to cover her tense, trembling body. She felt the hard, blunt prodding of his manhood, and then the shockingly intimate sensation of her passage stretching to admit him.

It was . . . not quite . . . painful. She had taken him inside her only once, months before, and he was a big man; it was almost like the first time. She felt smothered for an instant, and tremors shook her as her body accepted him. The stark closeness was shocking, but her intense satisfaction when he settled fully into the cradle of her thighs pushed everything else aside. She could feel him, deep inside her, and his heavy weight on her was a pleasure beyond words.

His arms went underneath her shoulders to gather her even closer, and a shudder shook his powerful frame. ''You feel so good, sweetheart,'' he whispered, and his jaw tightened when she moved slightly beneath him. ''God, Toni—'' His mouth took hers hungrily, and he began moving.

Antonia was lost, and didn't care. She held him, moved with him, her body matching his rhythm with female instincts as old as the caves. The tension wound tighter and tighter, gripping all her muscles while the rising fire burned her senses. It was like being in some desperate race she had to win no matter what the cost to her pounding heart and striving body.

She heard her voice moaning his name, and she thought she kept telling him she loved him over and over, but she was kissing him so wildly that she wasn't sure the words were anywhere except in her feverish mind. There was an instant of something like terror when she lost all control in the helpless wash of feelings. Then even that was submerged beneath waves and waves of pulsing ecstasy. She whimpered into his mouth, her eyes opening as her body carried her far, far beyond herself, and pleasure exploded everywhere.

Crying, she kissed him wildly and held him with the last of her trembling strength as he groaned and shuddered with the force of his own release.

In the stable, the aftermath of their loving had been cut short because of the groom's expected return, but there was no need for haste now. Antonia lay close beside him, in his arms, the covers drawn up over their cooling bodies. The fire was dying in the hearth, but the lamps were still lit, and a soft glow filled the room.

She looked at her hand resting possessively, trustingly, over his hard chest, saw her fingers move caressingly in the thick mat of springy black hair—and she had never felt so confused in her life. What had she done? Swept away by desire for the second time in her life . . .

"Toni?"

"Hmmm?"

"I love you."

She tilted her head back and found him gazing at her steadily, his eyes so tender it made her heart ache. There was only one response she could give him, because there was nothing left except the truth. "I love you, too," she said simply.

He touched her cheek, then shifted slightly, raising himself on one elbow so that he could see her face more clearly. "Don't say it like that, sweet—as if it hurts you to love me."

The conflict within her was plain in her voice. "It did hurt me once. It hurt me so much I can still feel the pain. That hasn't changed, Richard. I'm afraid to trust you."

There was something a little bleak in his eyes now. "All I can do is give you my word that she lied, Toni."

"I know." She didn't have to say it aloud, that his word wasn't enough. They both knew. She had to feel trust, and nothing he could say would repair what had been shattered.

He was silent, gazing down at her, stroking her cheek. "When you told me that morning it was over, all I could think, all I could feel was the shock and pain. You were suddenly a stranger, so filled with hate and bitterness that every word you spoke was like a knife. I didn't know what went wrong, but I could see you were unwilling to talk about it. So I did as you demanded."

His mouth twisted. "I didn't expect you to leave London immediately, nor stay away so long. And when you refused to see me, when my letters were returned unopened . . . What was I to do, Toni? Make a fool of myself by chasing after you like a lovesick boy?"

"No, of course not," she murmured, admitting that he had been put into an impossible situation. With the gawking eyes of society fixed on him, he could hardly have done anything except what he had done—behave like a gentleman.

He bent his head and kissed her, very slowly and thoroughly, until she felt more than a little dizzy. When he drew back at last to look at her, she had to fight the urge to pull him down to her again. The first tingles of feverish need were stirring in her body once more, and it was difficult to think of anything else.

"You avoided me for so long," he said huskily. "Then my father died less than two months later, and I barely had time to think for nearly a year. Settling the estate seemed to require all my time and energy. At least it kept me too busy to feel very much. But I couldn't forget you, sweet. The scandal had died down, and I hoped there was still a chance for us. I dared not try to see you alone, but I knew we would attend many of the same parties.

"So we did, at the beginning of this season. You at least spoke to me—however stilted and formal those conversations were. And I knew, by then, that you had refused several offers after our engagement ended. But you treated me like a stranger. We were never alone long enough for me to even begin to ask you what had gone wrong."

"Is that why you accepted Grandmother's invitation to come here?" she asked.

He hesitated, clearly trying to decide something. He choose his words carefully. "I came here because it seemed the last chance to heal the breach between us. And because Lady Ware was certain you still loved me."

IT WAS NOT, PERHAPS, AS GREAT A SHOCK AS IT MIGHT have been. Antonia had long since begun to wonder about her grandmother's motives.

"She told you that?"

Richard nodded. "Her letter was—rather extraordinary. Very blunt and quite assured. She said that she was utterly convinced you were still in love with me, and that if I wished to repair—her term—our relationship, the holidays would present the best opportunity in which to do so."

Almost to herself, Antonia murmured, "How did she know? She left London shortly after I did, and I saw her only a few times afterward. She seemed disgusted by my—my want of conduct, but never inquired into my feelings."

"Perhaps she didn't need to. You may have given yourself away, love, without knowing. Lady Ware is very wise, I think, and unusually observant."

"So she took matters into her own hands." Antonia was not comfortable with the idea of another's hand steering her fate, and her feelings were plain in her voice.

He smiled. "I am afraid I can feel only gratitude to

her. She gave me the opportunity I wanted so badly. Toni . . . take a chance on me, please. Let me prove to you that you can trust me. Marry me.''

Antonia stared up at him, biting her bottom lip. She was still afraid to marry him, shying away from her own mistrust, and with that realization came the true enormity of what she had done. ''Oh, God,'' she whispered.

Obviously trying for lightness, he said, ''I don't believe a proposal calls for divine assistance.''

She laughed, but it was a sound of controlled desperation. ''How could I have allowed this to happen? I have behaved like a jade, a—a whore.''

Richard's smile disappeared. ''By giving yourself to a man you love?''

''By giving myself to a man I won't marry! A man who lied to me, hurt me . . .''

His lean face tightened. ''We always return to that, it seems. What can I do to atone for this betrayal you believe me guilty of? Do you want to hear me beg, is that it?''

''No, I don't want to hear you beg.'' She would have turned her face away, but his hand held her still. ''But I can't pretend a trust I don't feel. Nor can I believe the result would be anything but unhappiness if I married you without trust.''

He hesitated, then said ruthlessly, ''This is the second time you have lain with me, Toni. What if I have gotten you with child? Will you still refuse to marry me then?''

She closed her eyes. The possibility had already occurred to her. She couldn't help remembering the week after their engagement had ended—the longest week of her life—when she had waited anxiously to discover if their lovemaking had resulted in a child. It had not happened then, but there was every possibility it had happened now.

''Toni, look at me.''

Entirely against her will, she met his gray eyes. "I don't know," she whispered. But she did know. If she became pregnant, she would have no choice but to marry him. She would never bring such shame to her family as to bear an illegitimate child—and he would never allow his child to be born without his name.

"*I* do know." His eyes were glittering strangely, and his voice was grim. "I don't want to force you, and if I believed you would be truly unhappy with me, I wouldn't force you no matter what. But I don't believe that, Toni. We love each other, and that love *may* have created a child. If nothing else will persuade you, then that possibility should. You will marry me. If I have to remain in this bed with you until every soul in the castle knows it, then I will."

In an instinctive movement, she tried to pull away from him, but he held her firmly. "No! Richard, you wouldn't—"

"Wouldn't I? There is nothing I can say to make you trust me; very well, then—I will forego trust for the present. In time, I shall prove you can trust me, if it takes me years to do it. But I won't sacrifice those years. We belong together."

Fighting against his determination was a losing battle, and Antonia knew it. He meant what he said; she could see that in his eyes. He wouldn't hesitate to compromise her, and if he did, her grandmother would escort them to the altar with no loss of time, regardless of Antonia's feelings. She would be the Duchess of Lyonshall before the new year.

"I wish I could hate you," she whispered. "It would be so much easier if I could hate you."

His expression softened, and he bent his head to kiss her. "But you don't hate me, sweet," he murmured against her lips. "And if you would only realize it, you *do* trust me. You could never have lain in my arms a second time without trust.''

Before she could examine the suggestion, his mouth began working its magic. Her body heated and began to tremble, and she was kissing him back helplessly. She couldn't seem to think of anything but the building pleasure of his touch. Rational thought vanished beneath overwhelming sensation.

Still kissing her, he found the end of her braid and removed the ribbon, and his fingers combed through her thick hair until it was spread out on the pillow like a shower of fire.

''I have dreamed of you like this,'' he said huskily, lifting his head to gaze at her burning eyes. ''Your beautiful hair unbound, your face soft with yearning, your lovely body trembling with desire. We were always a good match, but never more so than in passion.''

Antonia caught what was left of her breath and tried to think straight. ''You—you are attempting to seduce me,'' she accused unsteadily.

For some reason, that amused him. Warm laughter lit his eyes and a crooked smile curved his lips. Gravely, he said, ''It would take a ruthless man to seduce a woman against her will. Are you unwilling, sweet?''

She might have forced herself to say yes, but since one of his hands cupped a throbbing breast just then, the only sound she was able to make was a whimper. His long fingers caressed her tingling flesh, stroking and kneading, while his gaze remained fixed on her face.

''I wish you could know how beautiful you are in passion,'' he murmured, his voice husky again. ''How soft your skin feels when I touch it. How the warmth of your body entices me.'' He lowered his head to tease a tight nipple with his tongue, drawing back before she could do more than gasp, then looked at her again as his hand slid down over her belly.

"Are you unwilling, my darling?" he repeated, just as his probing fingers found her wet heat.

Antonia couldn't answer him. She was staring into his fierce eyes, yet her own were unfocused. Her body had remembered pleasure quickly, and now it was demanding more of it. Of him. She arched upward, offering, pleading. She felt the quickening waves of throbbing pleasure.

He bent his head again and took a nipple into his mouth, wringing a broken cry from her. She was out of control, out of herself, lost somewhere and completely dependent on him to bring her safely back again. It was the most incredible feeling she had ever known, of vast helplessness combined with a strange freedom, as unrestrained as pure madness.

She pulled at his shoulder, moaning, but he resisted, lifting his head again to look at her as his fingers caressed her insistently. She wanted to beg him to stop tormenting her, but then the sensations swept over her with a rush, swamping everything, and she cried out wildly. His mouth captured the sound, taking hers possessively, and a moment later his body covered hers.

Antonia felt him come into her while the spasms of pleasure still rippled through her flesh, and the sensation was so incredibly erotic she cried out again. He took her from one peak of pleasure to another, to the most profound fulfillment she had ever known or imagined was possible.

There was no abrupt dividing line between mindless delight and the return of sanity. When she came back to herself he was still with her, his powerful body heavy on hers with a weight that brought another kind of satisfaction. The muscles of his back and shoulders were damp beneath her hands, and she could feel the faint aftershocks in both their bodies. She could also feel a slight coolness in the room since the covers had been kicked away from them, but she wouldn't have wanted to move even if she had been freezing.

She rubbed her cheek against his without thought, and when he lifted his head she was smiling. It felt strange, that smile, unfamiliar and yet not at all wrong.

He kissed her very tenderly. "God, I love you so much," he said in a low, rough voice. "I will be like your ancestor—even death won't stop me from loving you, wanting you."

There was still a tug of resistance in Antonia's mind, but the pull of him was far greater; she knew that she had surrendered. Being his wife could bring her vast happiness or agonizing pain, but she had no choice except to take the risk. Not because she might have conceived his child, but because the thought of living without him was more unbearable than the possibility of pain could ever be.

She lifted her head from the pillow and kissed him. It was the first time she had ever done that, and she saw the flash of hope in his eyes. It moved her, and made her feel pang of hurt. For him. In that moment she truly believed that he loved her.

"You did seduce me," she murmured, smiling.

His mouth curved in an answering smile. "Were you unwilling, love?"

"No." She brushed a lock of dark hair off his forehead and linked her fingers together behind his neck. "I suppose I must be utterly shameless."

"Never say such a thing about my future wife." He was still smiling, but she felt the tension in his body.

She hesitated. "Richard . . . I can't promise to put the past behind me. I don't know if I can do that. But I will try not to let it ruin the future—"

He stopped her hesitant words with kisses that held more love and tenderness than triumph, and his eyes glowed down at her. "My sweet, I swear you will never regret it."

She almost believed him. "Do you still intend to marry me before the new year?"

"Would you mind that?" His question was serious. "Your grandmother has informed me there is a small church nearby with an obliging vicar."

"Has she, indeed." Antonia's voice was dry.

He smiled slightly. "If you wish, we will announce our engagement for the second time and be wed in London with all the accompanying pomp and ceremony. I own I would prefer a more quiet wedding—and an extended honeymoon. We could travel abroad, perhaps."

Innocently, she said, "Fainthearted, Your Grace?"

His smile turned a bit sheepish. "Well, I admit I would find it less—taxing—to reappear in London next season after the *ton* has had time to become accustomed to our marriage. By then, some other choice morsel of gossip will no doubt command their attention."

Antonia knew how his pride had suffered from the scandal she had caused, and she was grateful to him for not making her feel more guilty about it. He really was a gentleman to the core, she thought—and the first tiny seed of doubt was sown in her mind.

Would a man of such honesty and character have been capable of the magnitude of his betrayal? To not only keep a mistress during their engagement, but also to discuss her and their lovemaking with that woman? To give his mistress a fob he had gone to the trouble of having fashioned from a button torn from his future wife's clothing?

And would *that* man have been so willing, even determined, to offer up his pride in an attempt to woo the lady who had spurned him?

It made no sense, Antonia realized with a jarring shock. The picture painted of him on that bleak day nearly two years before simply did not match what she knew of him—and what she saw of him now.

"Toni, love, if you wish to brave the *ton* in a stupendous London wedding, I am more than willing."

She blinked up at him. "What? Oh—no. No, I would much prefer a quiet wedding. Really."

He frowned slightly. "Then what is wrong? For a moment, you were very far away."

Antonia knew there was an answer, but she had to find it for herself. Only then would she have a chance to rebuild the shattered trust.

She smiled. "I just realized how cool the room has become. One of us should find the blankets. Or . . ."

"Or?" His eyes were darkening.

Antonia moved slightly beneath him, and felt the first feathery pulse of renewing need. "Or," she murmured, and lifted her face for his hungry kiss.

It was the sense of his absence that woke Antonia hours later, and for some time she lay with a drowsy smile on her lips as morning sunlight slanted through the window. Just like Parker Wingate, Richard had apparently slipped back across the hall to preserve his lady's reputation. Having won her acceptance of his proposal, he was gallant enough not to expose their intimate relationship to the entire castle.

He would have done so, however, Antonia acknowledged wryly, if it had best served his purpose.

Her attention was drawn by the soft sounds of Plimpton entering the room, and a sudden realization caused Antonia to sit bolt upright in bed, the covers clutched to her breasts. Her naked breasts. She looked wildly around, and discovered that both her nightgown and dressing gown lay crumpled on the floor, several feet apart. And far out of reach.

She knew her hair was tumbled about her, the curls unruly from Richard's passionate fingers. Just as the bed was tumbled, one of the blankets having been kicked to the floor and never reclaimed. And both pillows bore clear imprints, which made it blatantly obvious that Antonia had not slept alone.

Antonia's face felt very hot, and she had not the faintest idea what she could possibly say.

Plimpton stood stock-still in the center of the room, her thin form erect and her face expressionless. She looked at the abandoned clothing, then examined the blanket on the floor. Then her thoughtful gaze studied the two pillows. Finally, she looked at Antonia.

To her astonishment, Plimpton's prim lips curved in a smile of immense satisfaction.

"I won five pounds," she said.

Antonia was speechless. She watched as Plimpton gathered up the nightclothes and carried them to the bed. "I beg your pardon?"

Calmly, Plimpton said, "The castle staff placed wagers, milady, on whether you and His Grace would patch things up. Only His Grace's valet and myself were of the opinion that you would. He said by the new year. I said before Christmas."

Antonia eyed her maid severely. "You did, did you? And what made you so certain, pray tell?"

"I knew you loved him."

That statement deprived Antonia of speech for a second time, but she recovered quickly. "It is highly improper for you to be placing bets on my virtue!"

"So it would—if we were speaking of anyone other than your betrothed, milady."

Silenced a third time, Antonia decided somewhat wryly that discretion might well prove the better part of valor. In a haughty tone, she said, "I would be obliged if you would hand me my nightgown."

"Certainly, milady," Plimpton replied. "And I will fetch your hairbrush as well."

Antonia had to laugh. She was still a great deal astonished by Plimpton's approval of her scandalous conduct, but it was certainly a more reassuring reaction than shock and disapproval would have been. And since she had implicit faith in her maid's discretion and loyalty, she was not worried about offensive tales being spread below stairs. In fact, she knew very well that Plimpton would not claim her winnings until Richard and Antonia announced their intention to wed.

While she drank her coffee and prepared to face the day, Antonia considered her doubts of the night before. In the bright light of day, those doubts were even stronger, but she could still reach no resolution in her own mind.

If indeed Mrs. Dalton had set out to deliberately destroy Richard's engagement . . . But it was all so farfetched! *Would* she have gone to such lengths as to hire a thief to break into his house? And how had she known about the fob if he hadn't told her? As far as Antonia knew, only the two of them had known of its significance; anyone else would scarcely have noticed that the fob had been fashioned out of a button.

And how had the woman known Antonia and Richard had been lovers?

She might have guessed, or merely assumed, perhaps. If Mrs. Dalton had found the same pleasure in Richard's arms that Antonia had . . .

Antonia pushed that thought violently aside, feeling a little sick. Just the idea of another woman sharing that with him was almost unbearable.

Antonia's gaze fell upon the book of family history, and she felt a pang of guilt. She had actually forgotten what was to happen tonight, on Christmas Eve. Remembering now, she brooded about it as Plimpton finished dressing her hair, then rose from the table and went to get the oil lamp that still sat on a table near her bed.

"I have to return this," she murmured.

"I can do that, milady."

"No, I will on my way downstairs." She wanted to take another look at the paintings.

She encountered no one, and despite the fact that her previous viewing of the paintings had taken place in almost total darkness, Antonia was able to find the short hallway. The window at the far end let in enough light to see clearly, so she left the lamp on the table.

The portraits looked different in natural light, even more alive somehow. Parker and his Linette seemed to gaze longingly at each other across the hall, their eyes locked. And Mercy seemed less haunted and sad, more at peace, than she had in the dark watches of the night.

Antonia stood gazing at the paintings. For the first time in her life, she was aware of her own connection to the past. The roots of a family went deep, she realized, bonding each person to those who had come before—and to those who would follow.

Perhaps that was why Mercy had appeared to Antonia, she thought. Family responsibility. Perhaps she had somehow sensed her descendant's unhappiness, and had sought a means of helping her. She might have believed that the story of her own parents' tragedy would help Antonia to avert one of her own.

"But it isn't complete, Mercy," Antonia murmured as she gazed at that gentle face. "I still don't know *why*."

"Toni?"

She half-turned, a bit startled, but smiled as Richard reached her. "Hello."

His slight tension disappeared, and he drew her into his arms for a long kiss. Antonia responded instantly; she had burned her bridges, and there was no resistance left in her.

"Hello," he said, smiling down at her. "What are you doing here all alone?"

"Looking at them."

He kept one arm around Antonia's waist as he turned to study the representations of the two ghosts he had seen.

"What are they doing in this hall if their rooms were ours?" he murmured.

"I don't know. I suppose Mercy might have moved them here because her room was in this hall."

"Mercy?"

Antonia pointed. "There. She was their daughter. The other night, Mercy led me here, and to the book of family history in the library."

"Why, do you suppose?"

"I was wondering about that just now. She was . . . different, Richard. She saw me, and even managed to communicate without saying anything. She was so sad. I think perhaps she knew I was unhappy, and wanted to help me. She . . . uh . . . wanted me to go into your room."

He lifted an eyebrow at her, his eyes gleaming with amusement. "But you, of course, stubbornly refused."

"Well, yes. So she led me here, and pointed to the paintings. Then she led me downstairs to the library, and showed me the book. After that, she vanished."

Still holding her close to his side, he studied the painting of Mercy again. "She looks like her father more than her mother," he remarked. "So they did marry after all."

Antonia hesitated again. "Actually, they didn't."

He looked at her, then back at the portrait. "Mercy Wingate," he read.

"She married a third cousin who was a Wingate, and who eventually inherited the title. I am a direct descendant." Antonia sighed. "Her maiden name was officially Wingate; Parker's father persuaded the local vicar—somehow—to swear there had been a deathbed marriage between Parker and Linette, so it was officially recorded in the parish records. But a ceremony never took place.''

Reaching a logical conclusion, Richard said slowly, ''Because Parker died? How?''

Antonia hesitated. ''*How* makes no sense, because the *why* is missing. But if they are reenacting what happened then, we may discover the *why* tonight. It happened on Christmas Eve.''

He was silent for a moment. ''Then we will wait until tonight. Will we see a mystery solved?''

''The author of the history didn't know what happened, and I don't believe the family did either. Linette's journal had no entry for Christmas Eve—or any date after that. According to other family members, she never spoke of what happened. She died when her daughter was only a few months old.''

''How did she die?''

''The doctor called it a decline.'' Antonia kept her voice steady with effort. ''Parker's mother was convinced that Linette survived him only long enough to bear their child—and then just made herself die.''

''What do you think?''

Antonia looked up at him. ''I think so too.''

''Love is . . . a very demanding master,'' Richard said softly.

She rested her cheek against his chest. ''Yes,'' she agreed. ''It is.''

Various members of the castle staff may have been bowled over by Richard's announcement over breakfast of his and Antonia's forthcoming marriage, and Lady Sophia was certainly so astonished she nearly swooned, but the Countess of Ware merely offered a satisfied smile.

''You planned this to happen,'' Antonia accused her.

''Only fate arranges the affairs of mortals,'' her grandmother replied. ''I merely presented the two of you with an opportunity to reconcile and left the matter up to you.

I am, however, pleased that you both had the good sense to mend your differences. You obviously belong together.''

"Thank you, ma'am," Richard said politely, while Antonia could only stare at her grandmother in surprise.

"Oh, dear," Lady Sophia murmured, her expression still shocked. "I never imagined—that is—Of course, I am delighted for you, darling, if it is truly your wish to marry His Grace." She gave Richard such a doubtful look that he grinned at her.

"I will send word to the vicar," Lady Ware announced. "He has expressed himself perfectly willing to perform the ceremony at whatever day I should care to choose."

Antonia regarded her wryly. "Only fate arranges the affairs of mortals? Am I not to be allowed to set my own wedding day?"

There was a hint of genuine amusement in the countess's normally frosty eyes. "Certainly, Antonia."

Antonia and her betrothed had discussed the subject on their way downstairs, but she saw no need to explain that the duke had gotten his own way. He had stated that he would marry her before the new year, and he would settle for nothing else. So she merely said, "December 31st then."

Lady Sophia was flustered all over again. "Here? Do you mean *this year*? But darling, an announcement! And the banns—"

"I have a special license, ma'am," Richard told her. "We won't need to call the banns."

After an obviously stunned moment, she said sternly, "You were very sure of yourself!"

Richard grinned again. "No, ma'am—merely very hopeful."

Lady Sophia, much ruffled, turned to her amused daughter. "Still, darling—so quickly!"

Glancing at her betrothed, Antonia said dryly, "Mama, I would really prefer *not* to attempt to word an announcement to the effect that the engagement of Lady Antonia Wingate and the Duke of Lyonshall has been resumed."

"Oh, dear! No, I suppose people would think that very odd, indeed. But a spring wedding, darling—"

This time, Antonia very carefully avoided looking at her intended. Considering that they were lovers, a delay even of weeks could prove to be unwise. "We would prefer not to wait so long, Mama. Recall, if you please, that we actually became engaged more than two years ago. Even the most censorious of our acquaintance must surely forgive our impatience now."

"But you haven't even a gown!" Lady Sophia wailed.

"Yes, she has." The countess looked steadily across the table at her granddaughter. "My wedding gown has been perfectly preserved, Antonia, and would fit you quite well, I believe. If you wish . . ."

Antonia smiled. "I do wish, Grandmother. Thank you."

From that point on, Antonia found the day to be a full one. With the wedding set for just days away there were arrangements to be made which required lengthy discussions. Lady Sophia had to be gently soothed by Antonia and charmed by the duke into accepting the hasty wedding. Antonia's efforts met with little success, but when Richard stated that he firmly intended Antonia's mother to live with them at Lyonshall, she was so pleased and moved by his obviously sincere desire that much of her awe of him deserted her.

Since he had found a moment alone with Antonia to make the suggestion to her earlier, she was in perfect accord with this scheme. She and her mother had always gotten along well, and Antonia had no fears about the arrangement.

With the wedding details more or less agreed upon, attention turned to the last remaining preparations for Christmas day. The castle tradition was to celebrate the holiday with a large midday meal and the exchange of gifts—the latter being something of a problem for Antonia. She had gifts for her grandmother and mother, naturally, but she had not expected Richard to be here.

So, while the remaining decorations were put into place and the appetizing scents from the kitchen reminded everyone of the meal to come on the following day, Antonia grappled with her problem. She found it unusually difficult to concentrate, partly because Richard had developed the knack of catching her in doorways underneath the mistletoe, where he took shameless advantage of that particular Christmas tradition.

She discovered early on that his composure was unshakable no matter who happened to observe a kiss or embrace, and that he apparently didn't mind that he so clearly wore his heart on his sleeve. She also discovered that her certainty of Richard's earlier betrayal was growing less and less sure. He was the man she had fallen in love with in the beginning, and she could not reconcile this man with the one who had hurt her so deeply. They might have been two entirely different men—or one man wrongly accused.

She continued to worry over the matter at odd moments, but had reached no certain conclusions by the time they retired to their rooms that night. Obviously mindful of Plimpton's presence in the room, Richard left her at her door with a brief kiss. Antonia nearly told him he needn't have bothered to be so circumspect, but in the end kept her maid's knowledge of their night spent together to herself.

"Did you collect your five pounds?" she asked dryly.

"Yes, milady."

Smiling, Antonia sat at her dressing table while

Plimpton brushed her long hair and braided it for the night as usual. Almost idly, she opened her jewelry case and looked over the contents. She had been unable to think of a gift for Richard. He would, no doubt, say that her agreement to marry him was all the gift he wanted— but she knew very well he had a gift for her, because she had seen it under the tree, beautifully wrapped.

Snowbound in a castle in Wales, she could hardly drive to the nearest shop to find something appropriate. Therefore, she had to make do with what was available.

She thought of Linette's locket, a gift from the heart. Antonia had no locket she could give to Richard, but she did have a lovely old ruby stickpin that had belonged to her maternal grandfather, who had worn it in his cravat. Richard often wore a jewel in the same manner when in evening dress, and she knew he favored rubies.

Antonia used a small, carved wooden box in which she usually stored her earrings apart from the rest of her jewelry to hold the stickpin, and a colorful silk scarf with which to wrap the box.

By eleven, Antonia was alone in her room and dressed for bed as usual. Her gift for Richard lay on her dressing table, to be taken downstairs in the morning and placed under the tree. With that problem solved, she found her thoughts wholly occupied with what would happen to the lovers tonight.

It had been in the back of her mind all day, producing a small, cold anxiety. There was nothing she could do, her rational mind insisted. Whatever would happen— already had. Still, she could not help worrying about it.

Outside the castle, the day's cold wind and overcast sky had finally given way to another bleak winter storm, and Antonia shivered as she stood by the fireplace and listened to the wind wail in the night. She was not expecting anything to happen until nearer to midnight, but at a quarter past eleven it began.

She was standing by the fireplace when she caught a glimpse of movement near the door, and when she turned her head a chill went down her spine. It was the dark woman with the curiously fixed expression who had shown herself only once before. She had come into Parker's room.

She stood just inside the door, gazing toward the bed. When Antonia looked in that direction, she felt a faint shock to discover that Parker's bed of a century before was exactly where Antonia's present-day bed was—perhaps it was even the same bed. She couldn't help feeling peculiar at the thought that he might have returned from Linette's room each dawn and crawled into bed with herself.

He was lying there now, wearing his dressing gown as if he had meant to rest for just a few minutes. But he seemed to be asleep. He didn't stir as the dark woman moved slowly to the bed and stood gazing down at him. She was dressed—or partly dressed—in a nightgown so sheer that her body was clearly visible beneath it. She glanced toward the table by the bed, and an odd smile curved her thin lips.

Antonia looked as well, and saw the hazy shape of a mug on the table. She returned her gaze to the woman, puzzled and uneasy. What was the significance of the mug? And why was this woman in Parker's room?

As she watched, the woman bent over the sleeping man and seemed to be searching for something. A moment later, she straightened, a heart-shaped golden locket dangling from her fingers.

"No," Antonia murmured, shocked. "Linette gave that to him. You have no right!"

Like the lovers, the woman showed no awareness of a flesh and blood intruder. She put the chain around her own neck and looked at the locket, then very deliberately opened it and removed the curl of Linette's fiery hair, dropping it to the floor with a scornful expression and then moving as if to grind the token underneath her slipper. She looked back at Parker for a moment, a frown drawing her brows together as he moved his head restlessly.

"Wake up," Antonia murmured, hardly aware she had spoken aloud. She felt a cold, awful foreboding. "Please wake up and stop her."

He continued to move in a sluggish way, his eyes still closed, and Antonia was suddenly sure that the mug had contained something to make him sleep. She was feeling colder by the minute as she watched the woman's nimble fingers untie the string of the sheer nightgown and draw the edges of the material apart to bare full breasts almost to the nipples.

With her dark eyes fixed on the sleeping Parker, the woman moved slowly. She released her hair from its braid and combed it with her fingers, deliberately disarranging it. Her upper body seemed to sway, the gold locket shifting between her pale breasts, and she braced her legs a little apart. Her hands left her hair to slide slowly down her face and throat to her body.

Antonia felt sickened as she watched, feeling the woman's unbalanced hunger so acutely it was as if it were a living thing loose in the room. If the lovers' emotions had been tender and passionate, this woman's need was a dark and twisted thing. And it shocked Antonia on some deep level, so that she had to look away.

She didn't want to look back, but after several long minutes her gaze was pulled entirely against her will. And she felt a little sick, still deeply shocked. The woman was languidly stroking her body now, and even as hazy as she was, it was clear she wore the sleepy-eyed, sated look of a woman who had just experienced the utter pleasure of a physical release. Smiling, still caressing herself, she turned away from the bed.

Antonia glanced at Parker once, seeing him move even more restlessly and open his eyes, but she didn't wait to see if he would get up. Instead, she followed the woman.

It was eleven-thirty.

The woman made a movement as if to open the door, then passed through it. Antonia quickly opened it in reality, but stopped before she could do more than cross the threshold. The woman was directly in front of her, half-turned to face Linette's room across the hall.

Her sheer nightgown gaped open, revealing most of one breast and all of the other, the locket dangling between them. Her hair was tumbled, her heavy-lidded eyes and puffy lips glistening. Her smile was filled with a purely female satisfaction.

To a seventeen-year-old girl who had experienced passion herself, there was no doubt this smiling, sated woman had just come from the arms of a lover. And there was no way Linette could have known that the dark woman had been her own lover. She was standing in the open doorway of Parker's room, from which she had just stepped, and the conclusion was a tragically obvious one.

"No," Antonia whispered. "Oh, no, don't believe it."

But Linette did. Her lovely face was dazed with shock and agony. Her hands lifted in a strange, lost way, and her mouth opened in a silent cry of anguish. Then she stumbled into an unsteady run, heading, not toward the stairs, but toward the other end of the wide corridor.

Antonia spared one glance behind her and saw that Parker was struggling up from the bed. Then she raced after Linette, as unaware of her own cry as she was of the fact that she had passed through the hazy form of the dark woman.

If she had been thinking clearly, Antonia would have realized the uselessness of her action. What she had watched happen had occurred a century before, and no mortal hand could change the outcome. But she was completely caught up in the tragic drama, the players as real to her as they had once been in actuality, and it was sheer instinct that drove her to try to stop what was going to happen.

She thought she heard Richard call out her name as she ran, but her eyes were fixed on Linette's form ahead of her. The distraught young woman might have been running blindly, but Antonia knew she was not. She was running toward the widow's walk.

It was a remnant of the original castle or a fancy of some distant Wingate—Antonia didn't know which. The crumbling stone wall around the small balcony might once have been a parapet designed to protect soldiers standing guard, or it might simply have been a rather plain, low balustrade built to prevent a casual stroller from pitching over and falling to the flagstone courtyard far below. In any case, it had begun to deteriorate more than a century before, and though the wing had been renovated, that exterior balcony had been left to crumble.

A solid wooden door, locked once but now merely barred, gave access to the balcony from the corridor. Linette paused for only a moment, seemingly struggling to open the heavy portal, then passed through. Antonia paused barely as long, desperation lending her the strength to lift the stout wooden bar and open the door.

She had forgotten the storm, and the blast of icy wind was shocking. Snow swirled wildly in the air and crunched beneath her thin slippers as Antonia hurried out—and almost immediately lost her balance.

The balcony was only a few feet in width, though it ran along the castle wall for nearly twenty yards. Snow had piled up against the castle wall in a deep drift, and it was that which caused Antonia to stumble and lose her balance. Two steps out from the door the balcony had been swept clean of snow by the wind—but earlier sleet and freezing rain had coated the rough stone in a sheet of ice—and because its support had been crumbling for a century, the outer edge of the balcony had a slight downward tilt.

Antonia tried to stop herself, but the icy stone gave her no purchase. Her own momentum was carrying her in an inexorable slide toward the low wall.

In a fleeting moment that seemed to stretch into infinity, she saw Linette to one side, collapsed against the wall in a heap of grief and pain. The young woman might have meant to throw herself over the wall; it was impossible to know for sure. She huddled against the rough stones, her frail shoulders jerking as she sobbed.

Then Antonia saw Parker stagger out, his unsteadiness clear evidence of the lingering effects of the drug the dark woman had given him. He called out something, shaking his head dizzily, and lurched toward Linette.

It must have been storming that night too. Parker seemed to slip and slide across the few feet of stone, his arms windmilling. It was clear he was trying to get to Linette, but either his drugged reflexes or the blinding storm made him misjudge the distance and angle. He was moving too fast, sliding wildly toward the wall, and he couldn't save himself.

Linette looked up at the last minute, and what she saw must have haunted her all the remaining months of her life. Her lover hit the wall only a couple of feet from her, and it was too low to save him. He pitched forward, and vanished into the darkness.

Antonia saw all of that in a flashing instant. Then she felt the bite of the wall against her upper thighs, and her momentum began to carry her, too, over the crumbling stone.

"Toni!"

His arms caught her and wrenched her back with almost inhuman strength. For a moment it seemed they would both go over, and Antonia could feel the shudder of the parapet as the old stones began to give way. But then, somehow, Richard dragged her from the edge and onto the relative safety of the balcony nearest the castle wall, where the deep drifts surrounded them.

The snow blew angrily around them, but Antonia was conscious of nothing except the loving safety of Richard's arms.

And the tragedy of two people destroyed by a twisted, evil woman.

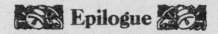 **Epilogue**

"Here it is." Sitting on the edge of the bed where Antonia was, at last, warm, Richard held the family history book open on his lap. He had been searching for a particular reference, and had finally located it.

"Who was she?" Antonia asked quietly.

He read in silence for a few moments, then looked up at her. His face was still somewhat drawn; Antonia's close call on the balcony had shaken him badly. But his voice was steady when he replied to her question.

"Her name was Miriam Taylor. She's included in the book only because she grew up in the castle, and because she was the ward of Parker's father. You were right—the author of this history had no idea she was responsible for what happened to Parker and Linette. Apparently, no one did. Linette must have taken that secret to her grave.''

"And Miriam wouldn't have told anyone, even if she believed it was her fault.'' Remembering what she had seen, Antonia shuddered. "She was . . . sick, Richard. If you could have seen her in this room, what she did . . .''

"I didn't even see Linette in my room, not this time. It wasn't yet midnight, but I was about to come over here because I couldn't stand not being with you a moment longer. Then I heard you cry out. By the time I reached the hall, you were nearly at the widow's walk. And Parker was only a few steps behind you.''

"You didn't see Miriam?''

"No. And, until you told me, I had no idea what had happened out there. All I saw was you.''

His voice remained steady—now. But he had sworn at her frantically when he had carried her back to her room little more than half an hour ago. He had been too anxious over her shivering to be much interested in anything except getting her warm again. But once she was tucked into the bed and no longer so pale, he had heard the whole story from her.

Antonia fumbled one hand from beneath the covers and reached out to him, smiling when his fingers instantly closed over hers. "You saved my life,'' she said gravely.

His voice roughened. "Don't remind me of how nearly I came to losing you. Never, as long as I live, will I forget the terror I felt when I saw you hurtling toward that wall.''

"I know it was foolish,'' she admitted. "But somehow I couldn't think of that. It was all so heartbreaking—and such a tragic waste for all of them. I wanted so badly to stop it, change it . . ."

"Yes, I know. But it happened, sweet. No one can change it now."

"If only Linette hadn't run. If only she had faced Parker and asked him to explain."

Richard hesitated, then spoke very deliberately. "If she had, Parker might not have died. But their love would have been changed forever by suspicion. It was, after all, his word against Miriam's that what Linette saw was a lie. He had no witness, no one to step forward and call her a liar. Linette might never have been able to forgive Parker. For his betrayal."

Antonia's grave eyes searched out his every feature as if she had never seen them before. She was still trying to reconcile two disparate men—and the only way she could do it was to accept the possibility that one of those men had been a lie, a creation.

Who was to say that a woman might not go to extremes in order to get—or keep—the man she wanted? Miriam had. And in so doing, she had caused Parker's death.

Claire Dalton might well have done all in her power to keep Richard Allerton for herself. She might have hired a thief to break into his house, out of greed or revenge because he had turned away from her. Finding the fob could have been pure chance, and since the button had been engraved with Antonia's initials, it would not have been difficult to figure out that Richard had fashioned himself a memento.

A woman might even have guessed how that button had come to be lost.

After all, what did Mrs. Dalton have to lose by her lies? If Richard really had ended their arrangement, she might have believed there was a chance he would return to her once his betrothed was out of the way—and she might have guessed that a young woman such as Antonia would likely break the engagement in a burst of emotion and flee. Richard might have returned to his mistress in anger.

There was really, Antonia realized suddenly, no other logical reason why Mrs. Dalton would have visited her, or said the things she had—except for spite or the desire to reclaim something she had lost. If her relationship with Richard had been as solid as she had said it was, she would never have jeopardized it by going to Antonia. The result, as anyone of reason might have guessed, had been scandal and a severe blow to Richard's pride— neither of which was a thing any man would thank his mistress for inviting into his life.

"Toni?"

She realized that she had been silent for a long time, and that he was watching her intently. "I have said a great deal about broken trust, haven't I?" she said. "But the truth is, if I had trusted you as I claimed to, I would have at least listened to your side of the story. I'm sorry, Richard. I should have listened—and I should have believed you."

"Do you believe me now?"

Antonia nodded, and the resistance inside her was gone as easily as that. She believed him because she loved him and accepted his honesty. And because, after what she had witnessed tonight, she knew the folly of trusting her own eyes and ears to tell her . . . all of the truth. Sometimes, only the heart could know that.

"Yes. I do believe you."

She went into his arms eagerly, pushing the bulky covers away so that she could feel the hard strength of his body against hers. He kissed her with intense desire, a little rough because the fear of having so nearly lost her was still with him, and she responded to his passion as she always had.

It was a long time later when Antonia lay close beside

her duke in the warm bed. As sleep tugged at her, she thought of a question left unanswered. "Richard? In the book—does it say what happened to Miriam?"

He pulled her a bit closer and sighed, stroking her tumbled hair. "Yes, it does. Six months after Parker's death, she threw herself from the widow's walk."

Antonia wasn't much surprised by the information, and gave it only fleeting attention. Her thoughts turned to Linette and Parker, and to their daughter Mercy. Perhaps those three had been doomed to short lives and anguish, but all of them had known love. And all of them refused to completely let go of life. Was that a testament to love? Tragedy? Family?

She didn't know. But she was deeply grateful that she had been given the opportunity to learn something from an old tragedy, and even more grateful that her own mistaken belief in betrayal had not demanded so high a price from the man she loved.

Unlike Linette, she had been given a second chance. And she intended to make the most of it.

"Merry Christmas, love," Richard said, pressing a tender kiss to her forehead.

Antonia had a flashing vision of future holidays filled with happiness, laughter, and the delighted cries of children. Perhaps, she thought, the sounds of life and love would fill this castle one day. She meant to make sure of that, because now the castle felt like home to her. Besides, she and Richard had a debt to repay. Perhaps only the contentment of their descendants would lay the restless spirits of the Wingate family to rest.

Perhaps.

Snuggling up to her betrothed, Antonia wondered sleepily how many Wingates had occupied this bed over the years, and if any of them might visit it from time to time. It would be unnerving to wake up with a ghost in one's bed. But Antonia wasn't particularly concerned about the possibility, and it seemed too much trouble to worry about—or to warn Richard.

"Merry Christmas, darling," she murmured.

HAPPY HOLIDAY WISHES
from . . .
KAY HOOPER

I am single, in my thirties, a scorpio if that matters. I'm prone to collect things (currently it's dragons): I love books, animals, old movies, and baseball. I live with two cats in a very small town (three caution lights, a bank, and a post office) and there's nothing in the world I'd rather do than write.

To me, Christmas has always seemed a magical time filled with possibilities, a time when the ties of family are felt more strongly than ever before. So it seemed fitting to me to tell a story about a pair of lovers teaching their descendant a lesson about the tragedy of mistakes.

Anything is possible at Christmas. Even ghosts.

Gifts of Love

Shannon Drake

Prologue

TWENTY-FOUR ...

Kaitlin carefully scratched the number into the hide of the teepee. Twenty-four. It followed her other numbers, a series that began with the number three, and was arranged like the numbered days of a calendar.

As she finished scratching out the number, tears sprang to her eyes. She wiped at them furiously. She hadn't cried when she'd scratched out all of the other numbers, but this one was different. Twenty-four. The month was December. It was Christmas Eve. And tomorrow would be Christmas. At home, in their small town, people would be caroling in the streets. For the first time in her life, she would have celebrated Christmas in her own home.

Shane had given her that.

She would have decorated the house with evergreen boughs and holly, just as she had promised Francesca she would. She could still remember the little girl's eyes growing round with wonder when she had told her about Santa Claus.

"Well, he is really Saint Nicholas, you see," Kaitlin

had told her with a wink, as they had shaken out a bed sheet. "He was a bishop hundreds and hundreds of years ago and he was kind and generous, the patron saint of children, and he loved to give out gifts. To the Dutch people who came to live in New York, he was 'Sinter Klaas.' So for us now, he is Santa Claus! And he comes every Christmas to bring gifts. A minister named Mr. Moore described him in a poem back in 1823—before I was even born—and he is wonderful, Francesca, truly wonderful! He dresses in a red suit with white trim, and he is this huge roly-poly bear of a man, so kind, so very wonderful."

And she could still remember looking up to see that Shane was watching her from the hallway, his gaze speculative and curiously soft. He'd caught her arm when she would have fled. "Thank you."

"For what?"

"For giving her Christmas."

And she had nodded, needing to flee the warmth of his touch. She'd given him so little. He'd given her so much. But she had built the walls that lay between them, and Shane had seemed more than determined to stay on his own side of them. He could be so hard. Their battles, perhaps her survival, depended on his being that way.

But then he had touched her cheek. So gently. "You're just like her, you know. A child deprived of Christmas." And his voice was soft, so soft. "This year, we will have Christmas. We'll drink mulled wine before the fire. I'll chop down a fir tree and we'll decorate it with angels and stars. And we'll all put gifts beneath the tree. You will have Christmas, Kaitlin."

She'd had to pull away. Knots had tied within her stomach, her heart had seemed to lodge tight within her throat. How did he know her so easily, so well? How could he touch upon those places in her heart that were the most vulnerable?

"I have no money of my own," she had told him. "I shall have no gift for you."

That glittering gaze of his, hot, too-knowing, taunting, wicked, and wise, had come sweeping over her and she had heard the sound of his laughter, a sound that touched her up and down the spine. "Oh, but, my love, think of it, you do, you do."

Her cheeks had grown hot. She wanted to slap him then and there.

She wanted to fall into his arms . . .

She'd had a chance to do neither. He had pulled her close to him. Yet for all the rough carelessness of his touch, there had been a note of true and painful longing in his voice when he spoke. "A son, Kaitlin, give me my son."

And she had pulled away from him once again. "You'll have to speak to God on that, sir, since I seem to have no choice in the matter."

"But you do. You run. You fight me," he told her. His voice was too soft. His eyes too searching. He was coming so very close to the child who had always missed Christmas, to the woman who was still so terribly afraid.

"I don't seem to run fast enough," she informed him primly, which brought laughter to his lips, but something else to his eyes. He wanted things from her. Things she couldn't give.

Things she was too afraid to give.

"What is it, Shane? Is something wrong?" Francesca asked worriedly. Poor little thing. She was just ten, and she sometimes seemed very old. Life had given her a too-acute awareness. She had been passed from relative to relative, and now she was concerned that she might be the cause of the troubles that lay between them.

"Wrong?" Shane said to his niece, lifting the little girl into his arms. "When I live with two of the most beautiful women in the West? Never! We were just discussing Christmas, Kaitlin and I. And Santa Claus is coming this year.''

"He never came before,'' Francesca said.

"Well, he's coming this year. Right down the chimney.''

"He'll singe his rump!'' Kaitlin advised.

"Never. Santa Claus is invulnerable to fire.''

Francesca laughed. ''Will he come for us both, for Kaitlin and me?''

His eyes had touched Kaitlin with a curious light of understanding as he answered Francesca. ''Oh, yes. Santa will come for you. And for Kaitlin.''

But Santa could not come. Not here, to this teepee in the wilderness where all those who surrounded her did not believe in Christmas.

The tears grew hot behind her lashes. She blinked hard, not willing to let the first one fall.

She hadn't cried yet. No matter how frightened she had been, no matter how despairing, she had never given way to tears. She was strong, her will was strong, her spirit was strong. Shane had said so. It was one of the things that he admired about her. Watching her with that cool expression in his eyes, his hands on his hips, his head just slightly cocked at an angle, he had said so. She could still remember the deep timbre of his voice as he had spoken to her after the first Indian raid. ''Well, you've courage, my love. And a will of steel.''

Perhaps the implication had been there that she was lacking other things, but she did have courage.

Kaitlin leaned back against the tough hide of the teepee, closing her eyes, continuing to fight the overwhelming urge to cry.

You were wrong, Shane! she thought. So very wrong. Some of the other things were there. I did love you, but I was lacking the courage to tell you.

She had almost told him. She had almost done so on

that fateful day when she had etched her first number into the hide of the teepee. A three . . . for December third, 1869.

That was the day when they had fought so furiously because she had disobeyed him.

Genevieve had disappeared into the far north field. She was a small, part-Arabian, part-wild horse, and she was precious to Kaitlin. She wasn't just the only horse Kaitlin had ever owned, she was fine and beautiful, and so affectionate. She gave Kaitlin so much love.

So when she had disappeared, Kaitlin had gone after her, riding old Henry, the plow horse. She hadn't found Genevieve but Shane had found her. And he'd very nearly dragged her back, calling her a fool over and over again, and warning her that he didn't have time to keep going after her. It was going to prove to be a brutal winter for those living at the foot of the Black Hills.

"I didn't do anything—"

"Tell it to the Blackfeet when they find you the next time!"

"I'm not worried about the Indians. Chancey told me that they're a distance away."

"They're right on our border!"

"Living their lives. While we live ours—"

"Don't fool yourself, Kaitlin! The Blackfeet were the most warlike tribe in the area!"

"Yes, and they killed a lot of whites, and the whites killed them. But that's because the whites were infringing on their fur trade. And now we *buy* the furs from them and—"

"And that's supposed to make everything all better?"

"But the Indians don't come in this close—"

"The hell they don't! Ever since that fool trapper disappeared with Black Eagle's boy, the Blackfeet have been coming in closer and closer. All kinds of rumors are going around, of Indian war, real, horrible, disastrous war. Damn you, Kaitlin, I know Black Eagle! I know him well. You stay the hell out of the north field and the north woods!''

''But Genevieve—''

''Genevieve is an Indian pony now. There aren't any finer horse thieves in the world than the Blackfeet. If only you'd really cared for any living thing around you, she might not have disappeared!''

To Kaitlin, that had been it. She had promptly assured him that he was the only living thing around her that she didn't care about.

''I pulled you out of a New Orleans sewer. Maybe that's where you belong!''

She struck him. And suddenly she was being dragged across their room, and tossed on their bed. ''I've seen the fire in you,'' Shane said angrily. ''I've seen you smile, and laugh. By God, it's there. It was there for Daniel Newton.''

''Daniel's a gentleman—''

''And a half-assed fool. And he isn't for you. But damn you, Kaitlin, the fire is there. Within you.''

''Maybe you haven't the spark to light any fire within me!'' she replied furiously.

And he had gone still. Dead still. ''Oh, but I do,'' he had assured her. ''Oh, but I do!''

She had leapt up, suddenly feeling very afraid. But she was determined that he not see it.

She wanted to run—she couldn't. He had planted his hands on his hips, blocking the doorway. ''Well, you've courage, my love. And a will of steel. But that won't help you now. Not one bit. Whether I wooed you or won you, Kaitlin, I made you my wife. And you agreed to the terms. And I'll be damned if I'll let you try to cast me out one minute longer. You want a spark, Mrs. McAuliffe? I'll light a boxful of matches, and so help me, we will find the fire within you.''

His voice had thundered, deep, harsh, determined. Sitting in the teepee, Kaitlin could still hear the thunder of it in her mind. Remembering, she felt a trembling in her fingers, and the trembling seemed to spread. She couldn't forget what had followed. She had relived it time and time again, here in desolate captivity in the wilderness.

There had been more that afternoon. So much more.

Even now, the thought of all that had happened could bring a crimson flush to her cheeks. There had been so much more . . .

There had been his hand on her arm and the startling iron-hard grip of his fingers. She had gazed at that hand detaining her, and some sharp retort had sprung to her lips. But then she had met his eyes. Hazel eyes, with sparks of glimmering gold. Eyes that commanded, eyes that held her fast. Eyes hotter than the glitter of the sun, alive with anger, with determination, with fire . . .

And with desire.

Oh, yes, there had been more. The violent force of his kiss, the rent and tear of fabric. Her fists had flown in protest, pummeling against him. And then . . .

Then there had been the magic. Things whispered in shadows of their bedroom. Intimate things. A touch, a brush, his hands, his caress, so knowing. Demanding here, so tender there. The feel of his naked flesh against her, and a burst of the fire-hot gold of his eyes entering her so that a flame was ignited within her, stirring her, arousing her, taking her places she had never been before, until showers of ecstasy had burst upon her like a honeyed rain from heaven . . .

She'd been tempted to cry then, too. For the words should have come. She should have whispered them, she should have made him believe. She should have had the courage to risk ridicule; she should have been able to give to him at last.

But she had been so afraid that he would shove that gift aside . . .

And so she hadn't spoken, and he had risen, and she had turned her back on him. "I'm sorry, Kaitlin. No, damn you, I'm not sorry. You're my wife. And I want you to be more than a cook. I'll not be stopping at Nelly Grier's when I've a black-haired beauty at home, even if she has emerald eyes flashing nothing but hatred my way."

Kaitlin didn't respond. If he hadn't been so fond of the industrious Nelly Grier, she might not have longed to be the ice princess he liked to call her.

"Black-haired, and black-hearted," Shane whispered softly, and it was then that she spun on him.

"No! No! It's not me, Shane MacAuliffe. You prove time and time again that you prefer the company at Nelly's to that at home—"

"Damn! I prefer a spark of warmth!"

What had she just given him, she wondered, feeling lost. And why did he seem more violent and furious now than ever before? She had thrown the pillow at him in a sudden fury herself, and she had cried out that she hated him . . .

And he had stared at her. Hard. He had almost spoken, but he had not. He had turned on his heel, and left her, slamming the door behind him.

"No, no, that was a lie!" she whispered, but she spoke to a closed door. "I love you, Shane." And she did love *him*. Not the beautiful home that he had given her. Not the closet full of dresses. None of the things that she had married to possess really meant anything at all, not when she compared them to that look in his eyes when she had insisted that she hated him.

She had to tell him. And she had to make him believe in her.

And so she washed quickly and hurried out of the house. She ran to the stables he had built on the edge of the wilderness. Chancey, Shane's old sidekick and now master-of-all-trades, was there, whistling as he rubbed oil into a harness. "Chancey, where's Shane?"

"Why, I think he rode off to the north field. Said there was supposed to be some good hunting up that way."

Forgetting everything Shane had said to her about the north field and disregarding all of Chancey's protests, she had saddled old Henry. "I have to find Shane," she'd said urgently.

And she had ridden out.

And she quickly learned just how wrong she had been, for she had barely reached the north woods before she had heard the cries. She had turned, terrified to see them. A war party. They were in winter gear, dressed in fringed deer hides, beaded jackets, and fringed breeches. Feathers had danced from the bands at their heads.

Their cries, their whoops and calls, had sent panic spiraling through her.

She might have made it safely back to the ranch on Genevieve, but not on old Henry.

She had tried to run the horse. But she had barely started off before the first of the warriors had come upon her.

She waited to feel an arrow or a tomahawk pierce her back. Strong arms wrapped around her instead. She was drawn onto the Indian's mount. The wild ride that followed was almost as frightening as the first sight of the Indians.

But she hadn't cried. She'd refused to be cowed.

Even when the Indian had pushed her from his horse to the ground.

Even when she had realized that the Indians seemed

to think that old Henry was a greater prize than she was herself.

Perhaps not, for she quickly realized that she was to be the property of that first warrior, who had led the party, and swept her from her horse.

He was tall, nearly as tall as Shane, and had long, straight, ink-black hair. His face was deeply bronzed, with hard, high cheekbones and deeply set dark eyes. If she weren't so terrified, she might have said that it was a noble face.

She could not think of it as a noble face for long because when night fell the Indian came to the teepee where she had been brought. Quickly she had realized that he meant to have white property indeed, for he had barely finished the meal provided for him by an Indian woman before he had reached for her.

She had fought. Valiantly, she thought. But there had never been any contest. The Indian had laughed, finding her struggles amusing. He had wrested her to the floor, his dark eyes claiming her, his lips curled into a smile. Then suddenly his fingers had moved over her ring.

Her wedding ring. There had been no proper band of gold when Shane had wed her. Her wedding ring was his signet pinkie ring, set upon her middle finger, made to fit her with long lines of thread.

All her struggles had done nothing.

One look at that ring, and the Indian had drawn away.

Then she discovered that the Indian she had been calling all manner of names spoke English, and spoke it very well.

"This is MacAuliffe's ring. What are you doing with it?"

"I am MacAuliffe's wife," she had said, her heart seeming to have ceased to beat.

And that had been that. The Indian had risen. "MacAuliffe's wife."

He had walked out of the teepee.

And Kaitlin had scratched the number three into the hide of her curious prison.

December third . . .

So long ago now! And she hadn't been hurt. They had dragged her back when she had tried to escape, but other than that, they had been kind enough to her.

Shane had told her that he knew Black Eagle. Knew him well. She didn't know how, but apparently, there was some kind of bond between them, for the Blackfoot chief respected her husband. Why, she wasn't sure.

Yes, she was. Because Shane was always honest, he kept his word. Because he was determined, and honorable. Because he was brave. Because he respected his Indian neighbors, because he saw them as human.

There were so many wonderful things about Shane.

And she had just discovered them too late. She'd been so wrapped up in her desperate need to find happiness that she had let it slip right through her fingers.

And now it was nearly Christmas. How foolish her pride had been. Now that it meant so little, she could so easily have thrown it all away. She closed her eyes tightly. She should have been home. With the fir branches and the holly. With the decorated tree. With the mulled wine before the fire . . .

No, the decorations didn't really mean anything. Shane meant everything. She should have been with him. She should have been able to sit on his lap, put her arms around his neck, and whisper into his ear. *"Shane, I have a gift for you . . ."*

But Christmas would come and go. Christmas would be the number twenty-five etched into the hide of the teepee. There could be no help for it. Black Eagle's tribe of Blood Blackfeet so far outnumbered the white settlers in the region that no one could come to her rescue. As Shane had said of Genevieve, "She is an Indian pony now," so they must all be saying of her, "She is an Indian's woman now." If they assumed that she was still alive.

No great posse could come riding to her rescue. No one could ride to her rescue. No one at all.

Kaitlin started suddenly as the teepee flap, closed against the cold of the season, was suddenly thrown open. Black Eagle, tall and menacing in his buckskins and winter furs, stood before her.

He reached down a hand. "Get up, Kaitlin."

She stared at him uneasily. She had been here for what seemed like a very long time now. She felt that she knew Black Eagle fairly well herself, for she had talked with him many times.

But he had never come to her like this, demanding that she come with him. Not on a day when the winter snows piled up high outside and a vicious wind swept down upon them.

"Kaitlin, get up!" he repeated.

She didn't dare to refuse him. She let him take her hand and pull her to her feet.

He threw a heavy fur over her shoulders and led her out where the wind blew strong and wickedly and snowflakes swept wildly through the village of teepees.

And then she saw him.

No one could come to her rescue. Any white man who rode into Black Eagle's camp now had to be mad, for Black Eagle was furious with the whites, and the Blood Blackfeet were known for their skill at warfare, torture, and death.

But Shane had ridden in.

He was mounted on Diablo, the fine black stallion that had taken him safely through years of war, wandering, and peace. He was very tall in his saddle, just as he had been the day she first met him back in New Orleans.

He was clad against the severe cold in his high hunting

boots, a black wool cape with shirted shoulders, black leather gloves, and a low-brimmed hat. Wisps of his sand-colored hair escaped the hat in the wind. Beneath the brim of his hat, she thought that she saw the glitter of his eyes. Gold, challenging, never wavering as they met the coal-dark stare of Black Eagle.

Kaitlin's heart seemed to slam against her chest. He could not be there, not really. She had been thinking of him so poignantly that she had caused this mirage to appear. This was not really happening . . .

But it was.

"This is your wife?" Black Eagle asked, holding tightly to Kaitlin.

"Yes, that's her," Shane replied easily enough.

"Then we will talk," Black Eagle said. His grip remained tight on Kaitlin's shoulders. As Shane dismounted from Diablo, Black Eagle spoke softly to Kaitlin. "MacAuliffe is a brave man. We will see how brave. Perhaps he will leave with you. Perhaps he will die at the end of my hunting knife."

Her knees were trembling. She was going to fall.

"Go back to the teepee," Black Eagle commanded. "I will meet with him elsewhere."

She shook her head ferociously. "No! I—"

"I will talk with him elsewhere!" Black Eagle repeated.

Once again she shook her head. "Please, just a moment!"

She didn't wait for an answer. She didn't believe that Shane had come here, that he had risked nearly certain death.

For her. She had to tell him to go.

She broke free from Black Eagle's hold and started to run. The snow was deep on the ground and she had to flounder through it.

"Kaitlin, stop! Go back to him!" Shane ordered.

But she didn't obey him, she couldn't. She had nearly reached him and she stumbled through the last of the snow, vaulting into his arms.

He felt so good. She raised her eyes to his. God, they were so gold. As gleaming as the sun. As startling, as powerful.

She had never expected to see him again. The handsome, hard-chiseled features of his face. That jaw that could clench so determinedly. She had never expected to feel his arms around her, feel the soaring heat within their protection.

"Shane! Go!" she said, her lips trembling, her teeth chattering. "Go, while you can. He likes you, you know. He admires you. If you just leave him alone and go home, back to Francesca—"

"MacAuliffe!" Black Eagle thundered.

Shane shook her. "Stop it, Kaitlin, now! Go back to him, and leave me to talk."

"He could kill you!"

"It's a gamble," Shane admitted.

"Then—"

His lips twisted in a wry grin. "Ah, but it always seems to be a gamble, doesn't it, Kaitlin? It was a gamble that we met, the flip of a card that we wed. Well, I am a gambling man. Leave me to play the game."

Black Eagle was nearly beside them. Shane was going to hand her back, until they played this game of chance between them, whatever it might be. It filled Kaitlin with dread.

"Shane, I love you!" she cried out suddenly, passionately.

His arms tightened around her. They were nearly brutal. "Damn you, Kaitlin, don't say things like that just because I've come here for you!"

"No, it's true!" she whispered urgently.

His eyes, fierce and golden, met hers. I have loved

you for such a long time, really! she thought. But she couldn't tell him that now. She couldn't begin to explain it.

"Don't gamble your life!" she pleaded.

But his eyes left hers and met Black Eagle's. He shoved her back to the Blackfoot chief.

"You are a fool, or an extremely courageous man," Black Eagle told him.

"It's nearly Christmas," Shane said. "A very great holiday for my people. We exchange gifts on that day. I've come to ask for my wife back for Christmas. She would be your gift to me."

"I am not white but I know all about Christmas. Why should I give you such a gift?"

"Because I have a gift for you," Shane said. "If you will just come with me . . . ?"

"Alone? Why should I trust you?"

"Why should you not? When have I ever betrayed a trust?"

"If I am not pleased with your gift, I will kill you, no matter how well I know you," Black Eagle told Shane.

"You will try. I will defend myself," Shane said.

Black Eagle smiled. "It will be as you say." Abruptly he turned to Kaitlin. "Go back to the teepee as I have commanded, or I will call the women to be sure that you do so. You will be one man's gift this night, either mine or his. For if he is slain, I need not, by any man's honor, respect his wedding vows."

Her knees were buckling again. She meant to obey him, though, for she knew that the Blackfoot women could be far worse than the men when they took hold of a hostage.

But Shane was still there . . . with his blazing eyes upon her, filled with some emotion. Passion, hatred . . . love?

She knew not which.

"Please . . . !" she whispered.

And Shane moved. Against his own better judgment he took a step through the deep pile of snow. He took her into his arms for a moment, and his kiss seared her lips with a startling force and heat. She would fall because of the fierce pounding of her heart . . . because of the way her blood was streaming through her veins.

"Go back," he told her.

"Shane—"

"It's a gamble, Kaitlin." He touched her cheek, smoothed back her hair. His breath was a cloud against the cold of the day. "And I'm a gambling man. You know that well."

He turned, thrusting her away from him, leaving her. Kaitlin felt the tears stinging her eyes with a vengeance now. She started to stumble back to the teepee through the snow. There was nothing that she could do.

But wait.

She fell to her knees in the teepee. Tears flooded her eyes.

She looked up and saw the numbers she'd scratched on the hide of the teepee.

The last number.

Twenty-four.

It was Christmas Eve. The last day she might ever see Shane.

She closed her eyes again.

And suddenly, all she could do was remember the first day she had seen him, the very first.

Funny.

It had nearly been Christmas then, too.

1

Christmastide 1868
Vieux Carrée—the French Quarter
New Orleans, Louisiana

KAITLIN STOOD IN THE SMOKE-SHROUDED HALLWAY OF
Madame de Bonnet's Wine and Ale House, staring
blankly at the man named Jack Leroux.

He was seated at one of the tables. His game tonight
was poker.

Thank God for poker.

The game had taken Leroux's attention from her, and
if she could just gather her wits about her, she could find
a way to escape Leroux. Did she really need to escape
him? She hadn't yet legally committed herself to him,
he had no right to hold her!

But from the moment he had seen her at the station,
he had begun to laugh, a laugh of pure pleasure.

The last thing she had felt like doing was laughing.
The fear that had consumed her on her journey all the
way from eastern Georgia swiftly became horror.

Whatever had possessed her to answer an ad for a
mail-order bride?

Life, she reminded herself bleakly. Not that it had ever been really good. Her father—God rest his soul—had been a drunkard. Once he had done well enough with his gambling to acquire an attractive spit of land. Enough to convince her aristocratic mother's folks that he would be a fine catch.

But the land he had acquired was slowly sold off acre by acre. Kaitlin's mother had died when she was barely five, leaving behind a beautiful portrait of herself and nothing more. There had been years of struggling to get enough to eat, to make ends meet. And there had been Jemmy, her brother, a year younger than her, her only salvation.

But the war had come. And the war had taken Jemmy. And when it was over, the war had taken even the meager roof over her head.

She had tried. She had tried so hard. Although he'd been a drunkard, she'd loved her father, and she was the only one left to care for him. She'd taught children to read and to write, but the war had taken the money from the aristocrats, too, and left behind the carpetbaggers and a world that was merely a ghost of what it once had been.

Then last year Pa had finally died and she had looked around at the devastation of Georgia, and she suddenly decided that it was time to leave. In the West, in Montana and Arizona and South Dakota, there were new worlds. Worlds unravaged by Sherman and his troops. Worlds where little children didn't go hungry.

She had wanted a taste of that world.

And so she had begun to read the papers, and at long last, she had found the perfect advertisement. A Mr. Jack Leroux was seeking a bride. He was a businessman of means, French by descent. He was tall, young, handsome, and amiable, and seeking a lovely young lady to brighten up his days.

He had sent her a picture of himself, and asked for

one in return. She had sent him one, and soon after, she had received the passage money.

It was a wild idea. But there was nothing left for her at home, and the idea of meeting this Frenchman in New Orleans was exciting. His property was in Montana, but he often traveled to New Orleans. It would be a fine place to meet and marry a bride.

From the first moment she had seen him—awaiting her in his carriage—she knew that she had made a dreadful and horribly naive mistake.

He didn't begin to resemble his picture. The tintype had shown the slender face of a lean young man with dark hair and a luxuriant mustache.

Well, this Jack did have dark hair and a mustache, but that was where any similarity ended. Jack Leroux was a big man, broad in the shoulders, paunchy at the middle. Kaitlin didn't care about that. She hadn't expected to fall in love. All that she wanted was something tangible out of life. A house with a good roof. Clothing that wasn't mended on top of the mends. Food other than onions and potatoes. Simple things really. And the man in the letter had promised so much more. Silks and satins and so forth.

What horrified her about Jack Leroux was his eyes. They were nearly jet black and small.

And they were evil.

She had barely felt his fingertips on her own when she realized what a fool she had been. What a naive fool. Jack Leroux had not been looking for a wife. Or perhaps he was—perhaps he married many women. But she knew—knew!—as soon as his gaze raked over her assessingly that he had other plans for her that didn't involve any homestead in the West.

She tried to keep her smile in place as his hands touched hers. She excused herself discreetly, saying that she needed to look for her luggage.

And then she had tried to run. She didn't know where to go. Or how she would manage once she got there. She had spent Leroux's money on the passage. Did that mean that she was indebted to him? Did he have a legal claim to her?

She was afraid, even, of the law, for Reconstruction had brought with it a horde of procurers, and thieves and scalawags, and it didn't seem to matter if there was a title before a man's name or not..

It didn't matter because as she tried to run away she wasn't caught by the law. She was caught by two of Leroux's thugs, who promptly returned her to their boss. He had rudely informed her that he had a game to attend, and that she might as well spend her first night in New Orleans getting accustomed to her new station in life. According to Jack, she was indebted to him. To the tune of fifty dollars in gold.

"You can't force me to marry you!" she had told him, as the carriage lurched forward.

When he had laughed she had known that he didn't care in the least about marriage.

"You'll get used to your new life soon enough, my precious. But you are a beauty, quite a prize! You'll pay me back in no time."

"I'll not!"

"I hope you're not thinking of trying to run away from me again, my dear."

"And I'll not do anything for you, either!"

"I know men who like a feisty woman."

"I'll manage to kill you somehow, I will."

That had sent him into further gales of laughter. "Another Rebel boast! Well, Miss High and Mighty, your side lost the war, remember?"

She spat at him. He pulled out his snow-white handkerchief and mopped his face. "I'll see that you pay for that later, *ma chérie*. Right now, open your eyes. Take a look around. You've the beauty to make money. Real money. Think about it.''

When the carriage stopped in front of the alehouse Leroux and his thugs had forcibly escorted her inside. Then Leroux had walked away, leaving her in the hallway. It didn't matter. The place was filled with his people. He was confident that there was no way that she could run.

But she had to, somehow!

And it was nearly Christmas. The season of peace, of good will toward man!

There were decent folk in New Orleans, Kaitlin was convinced of it. War or no war, carpetbaggers or no. If she could just manage to elude Jack and his men.

The poker game seemed a godsend. Jack was seated at a table, leaning back in his chair. The lights were very dim, and the smoke was heavy. There were other women in the place. Blondes, brunettes, and redheads in strange, scanty outfits. They moved about with various parts of their indecently exposed bodies jiggling as they served drinks to the men.

The players were drinking straight whisky.

The stakes were high.

With nothing else to keep her panic at bay, Kaitlin began to study the players. Beside Jack there was another big fellow. He was as round as a cherub with a little bow mouth and a clean, bald head. He must have been very wealthy, for he threw gold piece after gold piece on the table. Beside him, in contrast, was a reed-thin fellow with sallow dark cheeks and long stringy hair.

Next to him was a younger man. He wore a low-brimmed hat, even at the table. He would probably be tall when he stood, Kaitlin thought, and he was built well, with fine broad shoulders and a narrow waist. He was clad in a long railway frock coat, and he appeared to be a friend of the fellow sitting to his right.

That fellow was a young man who had caught Kaitlin's attention.

He had beautiful blue eyes. Soft as clouds. Kaitlin knew because he had looked right at her as she stood in the hallway. His features were very fine, and his hair was so light that it was nearly a platinum color. He smiled at her, and she felt her heart thud against her chest. He was wonderful. If only he had been the man to advertise for a bride . . .

But surely, such a man would have his pick of respectable young women. He wouldn't need to advertise. She had been such a fool.

At his side, his friend nudged him. The blond man said something, and his neighbor looked up at Kaitlin.

And she saw his face clearly.

Brilliant eyes, hazel eyes that gleamed like gold, fixed on hers with amusement and speculation. He chewed idly upon a straw and looked her up and down in a fashion that seemed to make her blood steam. She wanted to crawl beneath the table.

It's not my fault that I'm here, and I'm not that kind of woman! she wanted to scream. Damn him. There was so much mockery in his golden gaze. So much speculation. Something cold, and something hard. And something so curious, too.

She gritted her teeth. He was a very handsome man— lean, taut, and bronzed, at once both rugged and elegant. But his manner disturbed her and she stared at his friend again.

Hope was suddenly born in her chest. When the time seemed right, she would throw herself on the mercy of the blond man. Surely, he could not be part of Jack Leroux's party!

"Come on, Leroux, put your money on the table!" the blond said.

"And don't pull out another ace," the man with the golden eyes warned.

"You're accusing me of cheating!" Leroux was suddenly on his feet.

"I'm not accusing anyone of anything," the man said. He was calm, he was smooth. Those gold eyes assessed Leroux. "I'm just suggesting that you don't pull out another ace."

"Why, you—" Leroux began, and from behind him, two men appeared with guns.

There was the roar of a firing gun. Kaitlin was certain that she cried out.

The man with the golden eyes had pulled out his guns and disarmed the men who had aimed at him.

He hadn't killed them. He had shot them both in the hands. The gun hands.

"*Jesu!*" someone gasped.

"You want to put your money on the table?" the reed-thin man asked Leroux.

Leroux sat very still, staring at his cards. Then he stared at the pile of gold on the table.

"I haven't got any more gold."

"Then you're out of it," the man with the gold eyes said.

"No, no, I'm not." Leroux grinned broadly. "I've got something better than gold. A Christmas gift, gentlemen."

Suddenly he pushed back his chair and rose. Turning, dramatically, he swept an arm in Kaitlin's direction. "A prize far greater than gold, gentlemen. Miss Kaitlin Grant, my fiancée." He drew papers from his pocket. "Her indebtedness to me, gentlemen. She can be yours." He threw the papers down on the table.

Kaitlin gasped. She stared at the men seated at the table. The thin man had a lean, hungry look about him. It was not reassuring.

The fat man looked at her as if she were a steak and mashed potatoes and apple pie, all rolled into one.

"But I'm not property!" Kaitlin protested.

Jack Leroux ignored her. "Are we on, gentlemen?"

The handsome blond man with the blue eyes and his golden-eyed friend were both watching her, too.

The blond, kindly.

The golden-eyed man—more speculatively than ever. Well, she belonged to Jack Leroux, it seemed. She must appear to be a whore.

"I am *not* property! I don't owe anything to any man! I'm trying to get hold of a sheriff or a constable or the law in some shape or form—"

"Shut up!" Jack said, walking toward her. "Shut up, or I'll see you black and blue—"

"The lady's fate is on the table," a voice interrupted sharply. It belonged to the man with the golden eyes. "Don't touch her. Show your hand."

Jack swore in bastardized French. But his two henchmen were still moaning about their bullet-torn hands, and he didn't seem to relish the idea of testing the fast-drawing stranger again. He sat down and flipped over his cards.

Kaitlin couldn't see them. She was afraid to breathe.

Quickly, one by one, the rest of the men flipped over their cards.

The handsome blond gave a glad cry. Jack swore again, partly in English, partly in French. The fat man looked deflated.

The stranger with the golden eyes shrugged. "Seems to me like you're done, Leroux."

Kaitlin heard no more, for the blond man was up and out of his seat, hurrying toward her. Before she knew it she was picked up and spun about. Then, laughing with a wonderful boyish humor, he set her down again.

"You're saved, princess!"

She smiled in return, certain that he had won the game.

"Let me introduce myself. I'm Daniel—"

"Daniel, watch out!"

Daniel turned, sweeping her with him, just in time. Jack Leroux had risen, a small but razor-sharp knife glittering in his hand. But before he could use it, the sound of a shot exploded in the room. Leroux screamed, the knife clattering to the floor.

The man with the golden eyes had made another perfect shot.

"Maybe we'd best take our winnings and get out of here, Shane," Daniel said.

"I think I agree."

The golden-eyed man, the one called Shane, was on his feet, having collected the gold from the table. He was wary, his eyes on every man there as he backed toward the hallway.

"Bastard!" Jack hissed at him.

"We're leaving, Leroux. Don't let anyone lift a hand to stop us. Next time, I'll shoot to kill. And I'll be aiming right at your heart."

Kaitlin looped her hand around Daniel's arm, following as he led the way out. The man named Shane stayed behind, covering their exit.

A minute later they were out in the street. A breeze was wafting in off the Mississippi. It lifted Kaitlin's hair, and seemed to caress her cheek. Excitement was bringing a flush to her cheeks; relief was making her giddy.

Don't be a fool! she tried to warn herself. She had trusted in Leroux's letters enough to endure a rough journey through several states only to find out he'd wanted to turn her into a waterfront harlot.

And there had to be something to the mail-order debt. The men had all been willing to play for it.

Or for her.

But this Daniel . . .

He was so good-looking, and so very kind. She couldn't help but laugh with him, couldn't help but feel wonder in his presence.

"We took him!" Daniel exclaimed. "We took that Frenchie bastard, Shane!"

"Yes," the one named Shane said, his hat brim pulled even lower now. Still, Kaitlin felt his eyes. She couldn't really see them on her, she just felt them. Watching her. Wondering about her.

Condemning her?

They had found her with Leroux.

"Instead of standing around here cackling, I think that we'd best get a move on," Shane said. "We're too close to the river here, and not a good section of it."

Daniel mentioned the name of a hotel. "It's very proper, we can make arrangements for our princess here—Kaitlin. Kaitlin Grant. That's what he said your name is, right?"

She opened her mouth to reply.

Shane answered for her. "If he was giving us your real name."

"What other name would I use?" Kaitlin demanded. If she had hackles, they would be rising. Just like those on any hunting dog when it knew that a dangerous beast was nearby.

Maybe not a beast quite so wicked as Leroux, but dangerous nonetheless.

"I don't know," he said bluntly. He shoved back his hat, and those golden eyes studied her from head to foot. "What exactly were you doing with him? How long have you been with him? Were you making big money for him?"

Kaitlin gasped.

Not even Yankees spoke like that!

Quick as a trigger, she reached out to strike him.

He was quicker, catching her arm.

"Shane!" Daniel protested, distressed. "Shane, look at her dress! It's obvious that she's a lady. Let's hear her out!"

He still held her arm. Her teeth were gritted, her eyes were blazing. "Get your hands off me!"

The sound of her voice was cutting. She had lost her mother years ago, but she had never, never forgotten her. Never forgotten the things that a lady should do, the way that a lady should act. She knew very well how to don a cloak of dignity that few people could breach.

Nevertheless, she was somewhat surprised when this man released her.

However, she still didn't like the mocking smile on his face.

"Perhaps we bested Leroux. Perhaps she's besting us."

Kaitlin wasn't even going to speak with him any longer. She turned to Daniel. "Every member of my family is dead," she said softly. "My brother died in the war, my father just a year ago. There was nothing left. I had to get out. I had to. If you could see the way that they're running the place—"

"The Yankees?"

She hesitated. "I met a few Yankees who weren't so bad," she went on quietly. "They tried to leave me something of a roof, and something to eat. They were tired soldiers when they came through, just like my brother might have been a tired soldier up in the North. It wasn't soldiers who came in afterwards. It was trash like Leroux. So I had to get out."

"So you sold yourself to a man like Leroux," Shane interjected dryly.

"No! Yes! I didn't think that—oh, never mind! You won't understand no matter what I say!"

Shane grunted noncommittally. Daniel took her arm. "Come on, Shane. She's shivering something awful.

Let's go to the hotel and have some dinner."

Shane shrugged. "But I've got to head back in the morning. No matter what."

"I don't—" Kaitlin began.

Daniel tugged lightly on her arm. "Please let's go to the hotel." he said.

They walked quickly through the streets. There were sailors out, and probably thieves, pickpockets, and whores. Daniel had thrust her between himself and Shane as they moved along the street. She swallowed hard, aware of the hard body of the man on her left. She didn't want to allow him any grace at all, he was so cutting and so rude. But to his credit, she realized, he had no intention of letting anything happen to her.

And she couldn't forget just how quickly he could make the pistols in his gun belt blaze.

As they walked, the atmosphere of the city gradually changed. Not so many sailors seemed to roam the streets. Handsome carriages began to roll by.

The women had a different look, and a different air.

Then Daniel paused before a set of heavy wooden doors with the words "The Saint Francis" emblazoned above them. He opened the door and ushered her in.

The hotel was beautiful. Kaitlin didn't think that she'd ever seen anything like it, even before the war. Dark, rich velvets covered an array of chairs and love seats. Brass chandeliers with glittering crystals hung from the ceilings. The lobby was papered in an elegant beige with barely discernable embossed white flowers. The reception stand was made out of the deepest, darkest wood.

"I'll make arrangements," Shane said, leaving Kaitlin with Daniel in the center of the lobby where a circular seat was set beneath one of the grand chandeliers.

"Why is he so mean?" Kaitlin asked Daniel.

"Shane? Well, he's not exactly mean. I guess he's just not too trusting of folks anymore, that's all." He wasn't going to offer more. He seemed more perplexed with Kaitlin and the circumstances in which she found herself.

"You've no home to go to?" he said.

She shook her head. "And I'm sure that you've won my indebtedness. I can make it up to you, I promise. I teach. I can teach almost anything. Reading, geography, history, piano."

"But you intended to be a mail-order bride?"

She nodded, feeling color seep into her cheeks again. Did this man intend to marry her? Excitement rippled through her veins. It would be just right. He was so attractive, and so kind. She could easily manage marriage to him. She didn't love him, of course; she barely knew him. But she hadn't been expecting love any more than she had been expecting white-trash vermin like Jack Leroux.

People were watching them, she realized suddenly. She had drawn the attention of any number of masculine eyes. No one walked into the room without glancing her way. It made her uncomfortable.

"Well?" Daniel persisted. "Are you still willing to be a bride?"

Was he asking her to marry him? "Yes," she said softly.

"And you teach? Can you cook?" he asked.

She glanced into his eyes. He had such a beautiful smile. She nodded, smiling, too. "Yes. Rather well, actually."

"You'd be so good for Francesca."

She frowned, but then she realized that he wasn't really talking to her.

The man named Shane had come up behind her. She didn't know how long he had been there, or how long he had been listening. She didn't really care.

Shane grunted.

Daniel went on talking as if she wasn't there anymore. "She has to be the most beautiful creature I've seen in my entire life. She cooks and cleans and teaches—"

"So she says. Maybe her true talents lie in those eyes, or maybe even when she's on her back—"

"And just how bad would that be?" Daniel demanded.

"That is it!" Kaitlin exclaimed.

Daniel caught her arm. "Please! I apologize for him! He hasn't met a lady in so long he just doesn't know how to behave!"

Shane ignored him. "You think she should be a bride?"

"What could be lost?"

Then Shane was staring at her with those gold eyes of his. They seemed to blaze right through her. They seemed to undress her, right there in the lobby.

Then he smiled again, mockingly, but the mockery was addressed somehow toward himself. "Hell, yes, you're right, just what could be lost! Well, Miss Kaitlin Grant, there could be no love match here. But let's hear it from your lips. Are you ready to face a land that's nearly raw wilderness? The Indians still think that it's theirs. You'd get a house and a home. And a fair amount of riches, I think. But there are terms to a marriage like this. The wilderness can also offer a hard life. And a house must be taken care of. It's a lonely place at times. And a husband has to be taken care of, too, Miss Grant, if you understand my meaning, which I'm quite certain that you do."

She felt a spark of fire racing to her cheeks again. If she could just hit him really hard, just once, she would feel so much better.

But she couldn't, not standing in the elegant lobby, not with the very kind and gentle Daniel awaiting her answer.

Why was he letting this Shane ask all of these questions? Well, when she married Daniel, she wouldn't let Shane run his life a minute longer.

"Leroux was right about one thing, sir," she said tightly. "You certainly are a—a *bastard*."

"Those are the terms, lady."

"*Your* terms."

"My terms," he echoed flatly. "Oh, yes. You do appear to be a very beautiful woman, Miss Grant. There's nothing beneath the fabric that would mar that beauty, some fault we should know about?"

"Shane!" Daniel protested.

The nerve of the man! He should know, didn't he have her practically undressed with his eyes, right there in the lobby?

"No faults, sir," she snapped.

"Well, do you agree to the terms?"

She gazed at Daniel. He wanted to make things so much easier for her, she could see it. She swallowed hard. The intimate part of marriage was going to be hard no matter what. But she had accepted that when she had agreed to Leroux's proposal.

"I understand the bargain, sir," she said coldly to Shane.

"Then maybe we can solve this now. Tonight," Daniel said gleefully.

"Why not?" Shane said. "Excuse me. I'll see if they can help us at the desk."

Once again, Shane walked away. Kaitlin felt numb. So much had occurred in one day.

She turned and looked around the beautiful hotel. Someone had laced the windows with holly branches and the tiny red beads of holly were bright and beautiful. A string of brightly colored Christmas angels hung over the paneling behind the desk, where Shane now stood.

It was nearly Christmas. How wonderful. For Christmas, she'd be receiving a husband—Daniel.

"I imagine we could go up to the suite," Daniel said, smiling. "Ah, here comes Shane now!"

He was striding toward them again, so tall in that long railway frock coat of his. He should have been incongruous in the elegant lobby. But he was not. He cut an imposing figure, striking and commanding.

And mean, Kaitlin thought. She cast her eyes trustfully upon Daniel.

"I've spoken with the manager, and he was very understanding of the—er—delicacy of our situation. He'll be up immediately with a friend, a Father Green of Saint Paul's. Shall we go? Suite 204, Daniel, right up the stairs."

Kaitlin wished that those golden eyes of his wouldn't blaze so intently into her own, nor flicker with quite so much amused challenge.

Daniel took her hand, and led her up the stairs. She was startled to feel Shane's touch on her shoulders, pulling at the simple cotton fabric of her dress.

"You'll need a whole new wardrobe," he commented. "Expensive."

She swung around on him, arching a brow. "Maybe my husband will find me worth it."

He laughed softly. "Maybe."

"Ah, here's our suite!" Daniel said.

Shane fit a key into the door and pushed it open. They entered an elegant little parlor with several dark wood side tables and richly upholstered chairs. On a sideboard was a beautiful cut-glass decanter full of brandy and snifters at its side.

There were two doors in the parlor. One leading to a room on the left, and one leading to a room on the right.

"Would you like to freshen up?" Daniel asked Kaitlin. "I'm sure there's water in the bedroom—"

"We can order up a bath for her, once this thing is over," Shane said curtly. "Brandy?" he asked Daniel.

Then he looked to Kaitlin. "Miss Grant? Perhaps you feel the need for one. After all, you are about to sell your soul to the devil."

"No, thank you," Kaitlin said sweetly. "I don't feel that I'm selling my soul to the devil at all."

"No?" he replied, arching a dark honey brow. His eyes were glittering.

There was a knock at the door. Two men came in: Mr. Clemmons, the manager, and a kind-looking old white-haired soul in robes who was introduced as Father Green, an Episcopal minister.

"Well now, I understand that the circumstances here have been a bit peculiar." Gentle gray eyes looked down upon Kaitlin. "Ah, lass, a beauty is what you are, and lured into a den of thieves, as it were! Well, let's thank the Lord that this kind gentleman intends to make an honest woman of you, give you his name, and all the earthly possessions he holds. Step forward now, and hear the words of our Lord!"

Kaitlin moved forward. She closed her eyes and listened as Father Green read from his prayer book.

To have and to hold, to honor and to cherish.

She was about to be married. Legally wed. And she would leave behind all that was familiar to her, leave behind her beloved but tattered South, and travel on to a new life. She had been saved from the grasp of Jack Leroux by a wonderful man who was now making her his wife.

"Do you, Shane Patrick MacAuliffe, take this woman to be your lawfully wedded wife—"

She heard no more. Her eyes flew open and she looked to her side.

She wasn't marrying Daniel. She was marrying Shane!

"You!" she gasped, interrupting the minister.

"Well, what did you think?" Shane demanded in exasperation. "I won your debt papers."

No! she thought with dismay. No! "But I—"

He leaned close. "Daniel is married already, Miss Grant. His wife's back home in the Black Hills," he informed her in a whisper for her ears alone.

"Is something wrong?" Father Green asked.

"Everything is wrong!" Kaitlin said.

Shane drew her aside. "What difference does it make?" he said in a low voice, his face unreadable. "It's a bargain, remember? I suggested that you might be selling your soul to the devil, but you seemed willing all the way. And the devil himself might be an improvement over Leroux, and you agreed to give your life to him."

"I did not! I explained—"

"Yeah. Sure."

"Oh, how dare you—"

Father Green cleared his throat loudly. "If there is a difficulty—"

"No!" Daniel called out from the sidelines. He stepped forward. "Shane, we can't just leave her here!"

"I can make my own way—" Kaitlin began.

"Both of you, think about it!" Daniel pleaded. "You can both give each other what you need! Think of Francesca, Shane. And Kaitlin, you'll be safe!"

"Do I go on?" Father Green asked.

"Yes!" Daniel answered for them.

Shane pulled her back to their place in front of the minister. Her fingers were cold. So cold. She heard the ceremony go on. And on. Then Father Green asked her to vow that she would love, honor, and obey Shane Patrick MacAuliffe.

And she heard her own broken whisper. "I do."

He slipped a ring on her finger. It was too big, she had to clench her fingers together to keep it on. She glanced down at it. It was a signet ring with the initials SPA.

"I now pronounce you man and wife. You may now kiss the bride, Mr. MacAuliffe."

It was done.

Kaitlin didn't give Shane a chance to kiss her. She bolted for the sideboard and the brandy bottle.

He followed her, his mocking gold eyes upon her. "So you've sold your soul to the devil. Regrets already?"

"I can keep a bargain," she told him coldly.

"Can you?"

"Mr. and Mrs. MacAuliffe, there are papers to sign," Father Green reminded them.

Kaitlin signed the papers. Then she wasn't sure what happened. She was so numb. They all had brandy. Then Father Green and Mr. Clemmons were gone. A roast beef dinner had been brought up for the three of them: her, Daniel—and her husband, Shane MacAuliffe, who had ordered up a hot steaming bath for her.

And then Shane was setting down his brandy glass. "Perhaps you'd like to prepare for your bath, Mrs. MacAuliffe."

She nodded stiffly.

He swept her a courtly bow, his arm outstretched to indicate one of the doors. "Madame, to your left." He grinned sardonically. "Our room."

Her knees were buckling. She was going to fall.

No. He wanted her to fail in some way. He had married her, but he seemed to despise her.

Well, she wouldn't falter, and she wouldn't fail. She'd never fail in her duty.

But she wouldn't give him a thing more. Ever. She swore it silently to herself.

She had just been married.

She had just gone to war, she thought woefully.

Somewhere a clock chimed.

Shane started to laugh. Startled, she looked at him.

"Merry Christmas, my love," he told her. His gaze held her and he swallowed more brandy. "Oh, yes, Merry Christmas! What wonderful gifts we have given one another!"

SHE WAS, SHANE DECIDED, THE MOST BEAUTIFUL woman he had ever seen.

He had thought so long before the strange twist in the poker game. From the moment he had first seen her in the hallway, standing against the wall, looking so bewildered, he had felt the most curious fascination.

Any man would find her beautiful. She had hair blacker than ebony, almost blue in its richness. Small tendrils curled about the oval frame of her face and large, gem-green eyes while the long bulk of it was drawn from her face with pins to cascade freely down the length of her back. Her mouth was generous, the lips full, promising a wealth of sensuality. Her cheekbones were classical— they might have graced a statue of Venus in a museum. Her nose was fine and straight, her ink-black brows were beautifully arched and slim. She was of medium height, but even in her worn and mended and somewhat voluminous garments, her form was anything but average. She was small, and she was slim, but there seemed to be the most extraordinary curves to her body.

But she had been with Jack Leroux. His experience with women hadn't left a trusting taste in his mouth, and he was still wondering if he hadn't been taken for the biggest fool in the Western world.

She had thought that she was getting Daniel.

The laugh was on them both, perhaps.

"Well then, Merry Christmas, Mr. MacAuliffe!" he toasted himself. He sat alone at the bar, but he had suddenly decided—just minutes after the ceremony—that he had had enough of his brand-new wife for the moment. He'd needed to escape the suite for a while. To sit by himself.

To brood?

Well, hell, yes, it was Christmas. He drummed his fingers on the fine oak paneling of the hotel's bar. He should have been at home with Francesca. She shouldn't have been left alone. She was so fragile these days. Her father, Shane's brother, had died in the first days of the war when she had been nothing but a babe in arms. Her mother had succumbed to the smallpox a year later. Francesca had gone on to spend the next few years with her mother's sister, but then Deidre, too, had died of a frightening fever.

Shane himself had been with General Kirby-Smith. They hadn't surrendered with Lee, they had fought right on into May, and it had been near November of '65 when Shane had made it home at last.

Well, to what was left of his home.

Jeannie was gone. She hadn't been killed by any accidental fire in the war, and she hadn't succumbed to any disease, unless the disease had been greed.

New Orleans had fallen quickly. And a number of the big homes outside the city had simply been taken over.

Well, from what Shane heard, Jeannie had figured that if the Yanks were taking over the place, she was going to take over the Yanks.

When he first heard about it, he had wanted to kill her. Her, and the infantry colonel she had chosen to spend her time with. He was far away fighting, though, and all that his anger managed to do was make him careless. Somewhere, in the midst of some battle, he had decided that he just wasn't angry anymore. He had some of the right connections, and he sued for a divorce.

It seemed to take the rest of the war to get his divorce, but he did. He never had to see Jeannie again. He was glad. He was afraid that he would have been tempted to strangle her and the colonel, and since the war was over, they probably would have hanged him for it, and that wouldn't have been fair.

He'd ridden on home, a sharpshooter, or ex-sharpshooter now, who had been raised to take on the working of a major plantation. Only it seemed that there just weren't any plantations left, major or minor.

One look at what had once been his family home just north of the bayou country in southern Louisiana had convinced him that it was time to move onward. In that aspect, he'd been lucky. At Shiloh he'd managed to save the life of a man in his company, and that man had just happened to have one damned smart father—a fellow who didn't turn against the South to invest in Yankee dollars, but who had managed to hold tight to his gold and holdings by dealing in Europe. He'd been determined to reward Shane, and he'd done so, gifting him with a large parcel of land out in the Black Hills of South Dakota. It was still rather raw country, and not too long ago there had been really violent Indian activity. But the Indians were being constantly forced in a westwardly direction, and there had been very little trouble in a long time now.

The nearest town was a place called Three Mills, and an amazing quantity and range of goods could be found there, along with a fair amount of society. At least, that was what Shane had been told. And as he walked among the ruins of what had once been his home, it was something he was determined to believe. The war was over. He was going north.

He'd been there a little more than a year when Francesca had arrived. She'd been sent on a steamer up the Mississippi, then she'd been shuffled onto whatever railroads were available, and brought by stage the rest of the way. He'd never seen a more forlorn creature than his little niece when he'd arrived in town to pick her up that frigidly cold afternoon in February. Her little face had been pinched, there had been tears near-frozen on her cheeks, but her chin had been high and her eyes . . .

Her eyes had nearly broken his heart. They were old eyes in such a young face. They were a beautiful velvety brown, but they mirrored an awful loneliness, and a worse fear of rejection. For years, people died on her. And then those who remained shunted her from place to place. The death of her grandmother on her mother's side had brought her here now. Looking at that little woebegone face, Shane had sworn that if he managed nothing else in life, he would make up to Francesca all that she had lost in her younger years. He was quick to discover that he loved the little girl very much. And though she was slow to come around, he knew that she loved him. Trusting was difficult for her, and Shane could easily understand why. Each time he thought of his niece's eyes . . .

Eyes.

Francesca's were a deep, rich, haunting brown. While his new wife's were that shimmering green. But like Francesca's, they seemed haunted. They drew him in. There was something so stark in them, so anguished, so . . . well, haunting. More than her beauty, that look in her eyes had led him to his decision to make her his wife.

Wife. What a strange word. He hadn't thought to use it again in relation to himself.

He drank down a tumbler of whisky, rolling the word around in his mind. Jeannie had been wife enough for several lifetimes. Shane had decided that anything he wanted from a woman could be obtained at Nelly Grier's. After all, Three Mills was no fly-by-night town. Nelly ran one classy establishment with lovely, talented, and vivacious little creatures who made few demands upon a man.

And he in return, expected nothing from them. Nothing but the laughter and entertainment of the moment.

What the hell had happened? Now he had a wife again. Just when things were starting to go really well. He had nearly a thousand head of cattle. Chancey, who had been with him in the war, acted as foreman to the hired hands. Francesca kept house. Well, more or less; but he'd been a soldier, and soldiers became accustomed to looking after themselves. It was a good life. He worried a bit about Francesca, and he was heartily sorry that he wasn't with her now, for Christmas, but he'd had to come to New Orleans to settle some old family disputes. Property that had been stolen was being returned, and Shane had decided that it was necessary to have his land back. He might never give a damn if he saw the East or the Old South again, but one day, Francesca would want to know where her father had come from.

He drummed his fingers on the bar. Well, at least he could tell Francesca, when he returned to Three Mills, that he had done something for her for Christmas. His fingers wound around his glass. He'd have to have a long talk with the hostile beauty upstairs. He didn't care if she regretted her bargain from this night until the day she died, but she was going to make life pleasant for Francesca. She had said that she could cook. Dinners were going to become far better. She could keep house. Well, his clothes had best be kept clean and neat, his parlor in shape.

But none of those things really mattered. There was only one thing his new acquisition needed to do, and that was to care for Francesca in a manner that Shane could not himself.

He glanced toward the stairway. Had he just been taken in by one of Jack Leroux's best whores?

And did it even matter? As long as she had a heart, heart enough for Francesca?

He tossed a coin on the bar and stood, looking toward the stairs. It was Christmas, and he now had a wife. A woman who was exceptionally beautiful, and one who had married him agreeing to his terms.

Maybe it was time he found out just a little more about her.

He took the stairs two at a time, suddenly feeling a hot surge of both anger and desire shoot through him like volcanic lava. He burst through the doorway to the suite and found the parlor empty.

Where the hell was Daniel? Were he and the new Mrs. MacAuliffe together somewhere?

He ground his teeth, wondering why he was allowing his thoughts of her to make him mistrust a good friend. Still, the question remained with him. He strode silently across the parlor to the door on the left side of the room and quietly opened it.

She was there. Alone. Stretched out in a big tin bathtub. Her eyes were closed, her head was tilted back, the luxurious length of her hair lay over the rim of the tub where her head rested, the ends just dusting the floor.

Bubbles surrounded her. Lots of them. Even though they hid her body, they merely enhanced that feeling of fire that grew within him. Fire that burned, and fire that brought . . .

Warmth. A warmth he didn't want to feel. She looked very tired, and defenseless. The porcelain beauty of her face had never been so evident. Then her eyes opened, and she started violently. She had heard him.

For a moment—so brief a moment—he thought that he saw fear within her eyes. But then they were flashing, emerald and glittering, and very hostile.

He walked into the room, casting off his coat and his gun belt. She watched him all the while, her lashes fluttering as her gaze fell on his gun belt.

"I'm not going to shoot you," he told her. Then he paused for a moment in reflection. "Not yet, anyway."

She glared at him. He smiled and shrugged innocently.

"You're awfully good with them," she said.

"Yes, I am."

"And you're humble."

"It isn't a matter of being humble. I spent four years of my life using them almost daily. Yes, I'm good with them," he said wearily. He sat down on the bed, and took off his boots. She seemed to jump a mile when they thudded on the floor. Her eyes met his. They stayed captive there as he unbuttoned his shirt, button by button. Then he pulled the tails from his jeans and let the shirt fall casually to the floor. He stood. Once again, there was that look of panic about her. A pulse that beat like wildfire at the very beautiful base of her throat.

He walked closer to the tub. Then he knelt down beside it. Maybe that had been his mistake. The smell there was soft, a mingling of roses and clean femininity. Something twisted inside him. He itched to touch her, to wrench her from the tub, to have her then and there and look to the subtleties later. He ground his teeth again, determined that it wasn't going to be that way. Maybe she was one of Jack Leroux's sluts. Maybe, hell. Probably. But she was his wife.

He dangled his fingers in the water, just above her breasts. She hadn't moved. Just that pulse at her throat, and then the rampant rise and fall of her chest.

"Having second thoughts?" he inquired.

Her eyes met his. She shook her head. He smiled. She was plainly longing to hit him. Longing to really hit him.

"Think you've been in that bathtub long enough?"

She shook her head again. "If you'll just go away for a few minutes—"

He laughed out loud. "No, I won't just go away. We made a bargain. You're not trying to squirm out of it, are you?"

"No! I am not trying to squirm out of anything. Yes, I made a bargain! And I intend to keep every painful promise that I made!"

"Painful promise?" Shane said indignantly. "I beg to differ. I haven't ever had any complaints."

"The lamps are burning, I've no decent gown—"

"You certainly don't need a gown—"

"But the light! No decent folk would think of doing— what you're thinking of doing—with so much light—"

"I'm not so sure that we are decent folk, Mrs. MacAuliffe. And I just acquired a bride under very unusual circumstances. I intend to inspect every single inch of my new acquisition."

Her eyes went very wide, and suddenly he could take it no longer. Heedless of the denim breeches he still wore, he reached into the tub, plucking her from it, bubbles and all. He lowered her onto the bed, sprawling halfway over her. A startled scream began to escape her lips and he covered them with the palm of his hand.

"You musn't start shrieking with pleasure yet," he warned her sarcastically. "We've company. Daniel. He's probably sleeping by now. Alas, my love! And you thought that you'd be sleeping with him. Sorry, it's me!"

Fury flared in her eyes again, hot and green. Shane felt as if those flames ripped into his loins, and tore through the length of him. He had recognized her beauty so quickly. He had known that he was falling into some prison in the haunting emerald of her eyes.

He hadn't realized that he could want her this way. So damn desperately. That the flames inside him could burn and soar more brightly than the wicked tempest of a forest fire.

She bit his hand. He gave a muffled curse and pulled it back.

"I'm not about to shriek with pleasure," she assured him.

"Perhaps you will," he taunted. Her hands were pressing against his chest. "Then again, maybe you do want to renege."

"No! Get on with this wretched business!"

For a moment he paused, staring down into her face. It was Christmas. Let her be. Seek some peace.

No. It was Christmas, and they had formed a strange bargain. And it would probably be best if she knew from the very start that he had not taken a wife for her ornamental value, that she would fulfill every aspect of her bargain.

"I shall try to make it the very least wretched that I may," he told her softly.

There might have been a hint of tears in her eyes. The softest hint. Then she closed them.

And then he could truly wait no longer.

He kissed her eyelids. Lightly. The tip of her nose. Then he found her lips. Found the resistance within them. But he kissed her anyway. Her mouth was closed against him. Prim. He let his tongue tease and caress the softness of her lips until they began to part. He caressed the more tender, inner flesh. And when she began to give, he allowed passion and desire their free rein, freely, fully, forcefully knowing the secrets of her lips and teeth and tongue, and feeling the ever-expanding thunder of desire within his own loins.

Her fingers no longer pressed against him. He rose quickly, baring the whole of her body to his eyes as he stripped off his breeches. She was instantly on the defensive again, eyes growing very wide as she looked at him, her fingers groping for the covers.

"No!" he told her hoarsely, catching her hand and pausing for a minute.

There were no flaws on her anywhere. She was shaped like a goddess, with firm, full breasts, peaked with dusky rose nipples. She had a miniscule waist, softly rounded hips, and long shapely limbs. She was so stunning that he stared at her. Stared at her so long that her temper and defiance flared and her distress disappeared.

"Shall I stand, shall I walk around?" she demanded furiously.

Shane laughed. "Madame, I wouldn't mind one bit!"

"*Oh!*" she gasped, but he allowed her protest to go no further, sweeping down upon her, and covering her nakedness again with the bulk of his body. He caught her lips again, and kissed her until she surrendered to the kiss.

Then his lips left hers, and traced a slow steady pattern over the length of her body. His mouth paused at the soaring pulse at her throat. It played where the dusky rose nipples rose so hard and tempting before him. He listened to the catch of her breath, felt the twist of her body beneath him, and went on, burying his face against the sweet flat plane of her belly.

Her fingers tugged at his hair. She murmured some protests. He ignored them, twisting her body suddenly, stroking the length of her spine with his touch, and following that touch with the hot moisture of his tongue. He flipped her again and found her eyes on his. Her breasts rose and fell quickly. Perhaps she wasn't shrieking with pleasure, but she was trembling fiercely. So fiercely.

He smiled, and feathered his fingers over the length of her again, softly stroking over her breasts, her belly, and below. He pressed his lips against her flesh once again. Lower and lower. She cried out in protest, but he gave her no quarter, touching, stroking, caressing. When he rose high above her, her head was tossing against the pillow. He caught it, held it still, and met her eyes.

Dear Lord, but there was passion within them! If only he could draw out the warmth and the fire. She was trying so desperately to hold against him.

She was his wife.

He parted her thighs, his desire at a fierce and hungry peak.

Yet he held tempered that desire swiftly when he felt the barrier, heard the sharp intake of her breath. He met her eyes again and they were shimmering with moisture. ''You weren't one of Leroux's whores.''

''I told you who I was!'' she cried. Her arms were on him now, hands that grasped his shoulders, bracing against the pain. He could stop, he could pull away. But the damage would be done.

And she was his wife. They were bound now. And she had assured him that she would do her ''wretched'' duty.

He held very still, then moved slowly. So slowly. And he began to feel the subtle change in her body, felt it give, felt it accept. Once again, the force of his desire tore through him. Surged and swept. The scent of her, the feel of her, even the emerald of her eyes, all swept into the force of his need.

She moved. He had touched something within her. Maybe he hadn't found the deep searing passion within her, but he had touched something. A soft sound escaped her lips. Her body moved beneath his.

The depth of his own hunger seized him. Shattering, volatile, it tore through him until it burst within him, and swept into her. The aftermath kept shudders raking through him as he eased his weight from her, coming to her side. She tried to pull away from him, choking, embarrassed.

"No," he told her softly.

"No, what! I've already fulfilled my bargain."

"That 'wretched' bargain!" Shane said. Damnit. He wanted to slap her. He knew that he had given her something. "Mrs. MacAuliffe, this has been one night. We've a lifetime ahead of us."

"But you—"

"I enjoyed this 'wretched' bit tremendously. Especially since I discovered . . ."

"That I wasn't one of Leroux's whores?" she demanded.

He stared at her; her ebony hair was a wild mane about her fine features. "Yes," he said.

She tried to pull away. He caught her arm, wishing that he hadn't begun the relationship with so much hostility. What relationship? he asked himself. He barely knew her.

He had mistrusted her from the beginning.

Hell, she was still an adventuress.

Maybe that wasn't so bad. Maybe they were all damaged shells that had once been people.

If nothing else, he figured, he had a tempting bed partner.

Fires could build and burn within him again so swiftly . . .

He held back, gritting his teeth. He had married her. He was going to make it work.

"Let's call a truce for Christmas," he said softly.

"What?"

"It's Christmas, Kaitlin. The season of good will, peace and all. Let's call a truce. We'll act like man and wife until tomorrow afternoon."

"Tomorrow afternoon?" Her beautiful green eyes narrowed suspiciously and he laughed.

"Yes, you'll appreciate this, I believe. I'm going to head back home without you."

The startled pleasure in her eyes was downright close to insulting.

"You have to have some clothing made, and New Orleans just might be the right place to have it done. I've got to get back. I've left Francesca, and a very big herd of cattle. You can follow as soon as you've acquired everything that you may need. You might want to look for household items, too. Buy some pots and pans that you might like. And draperies."

He wasn't sure what impression he had made, allowing her free rein on purchases. She studied him gravely as he spoke, then asked, "Who's Francesca?"

"My niece. She lives with me. She's almost ten."

"Oh," she said simply.

Anger, irrational perhaps, suddenly seized him. He rose over her, straddling her on the bed. "You can bear any hostility toward me that you want, Mrs. MacAuliffe, but don't you ever show it before her! And don't you ever raise a cruel finger to that child, do you understand?"

Emerald fire lit her eyes. "I shall be entirely grateful for her company over yours!" She stared at him in defiance, and then she seemed to realize his position, and their mutual nakedness. Her lashes lowered. "Honestly. I love children. Will you really leave in the morning?"

"Yes. It will probably be April before you see me again, by the time you'll be able to travel."

Her eyes opened wide to his. She nodded gravely. "That will be fine." She could be so damned prim at times. "I shall be very careful with your money," she said.

"You don't need to be so careful. You need to buy what you want, and what you need. I've managed to become a fairly wealthy man," he said. He thought that her eyes widened again. "The bargain is not such a one-sided one, Mrs. MacAuliffe. I think you'll like your new house. It's very gracious. Like I said, buy anything at all that you want."

Her eyes met his. "Thank you."

"Have we a Christmas truce?"

"Yes." It was barely a whisper.

"Then lie back, Mrs. MacAuliffe, for I see cold and lonely months ahead for myself—when I have just acquired a wife."

She swallowed hard. Then she wound her arms around him, and pressed her lips to his.

In his amazement, he stiffened and pulled back. "Is that for the clothing?" he asked her bitterly. "Or for the house?"

"Oh!" she cried out, and tried to twist away. "It was for neither! It was for Christmas."

He was sorry, so sorry. No matter what it had been for, she had made a tentative move in his direction.

And he did want her. His fascination with her had become something that beat within him, driving him. He wouldn't be able to get her out of his mind once he had left her. Not for a minute. He was sorry for his promise. He couldn't begin to foresee the months ahead without her.

"Kaitlin!"

She had rolled to her side beneath him. He caught her shoulder, pulling her back. "Kaitlin, I'm sorry. Come. Come love me for Christmas."

Those eyes of hers met his. Brilliant, beautiful.

She made no overtures toward him again, but neither did she fight him.

Well, she had said that she was determined to do her duty.

And still . . .

He made love to her slowly, completely. And his need

for her reached peaks that startled him, they were so strong.

He touched something in return. Something. He knew that he didn't hurt her, that he gave to her. But she held back. No matter what emotions and feeling escaped her, there was something that she held back.

Maybe it didn't matter. Maybe it would come. Yet it left him with a sense of loss, of deeper hunger.

He had to have it.

That would be the future.

For that early, early Christmas morning, he slept with his new wife in his arms.

Christmas truce.

3

KAITLIN DIDN'T ARRIVE AT THREE MILLS UNTIL THE end of May.

Shane and Daniel left in time to avoid the most wicked weather of the season. By the time that Kaitlin should have been on her way, the winter had become so harsh that Shane had sent a telegraph advising her to hold off her travel plans for a while.

Kaitlin had stared at the telegraph for a long time, wondering if he wasn't sorry about the whole thing already. He'd left her on Christmas day.

It hadn't been that terrible a Christmas. She'd awakened to find him gone from the room, and a box beside her bed. *Merry Christmas*, the tag read. And inside of it had been a beautiful dress of red velvet and silk, a Christmas dress. There had been a note embedded in the folds, too. *The fit may not be perfect, but it will get you through to do your own shopping.*

It had seemed rather difficult to rise and to walk that morning. Her body was sore, but still so warm!

And just thinking of the night, she could flush so easily. She had told herself that it would be wretched, but that she had resolve, she was strong, she could endure.

But in the end . . .

The night just hadn't seemed so wretched. Maybe there had been Christmas magic around them. Something warm, something very giving. It should have been so horrible.

It was remarkably pleasant. It made her think of her new husband in an entirely different light. There was something in his touch . . .

Whatever it was, one minute it had made her dread to see him again and long to do so the next. For one, their leave taking hadn't been in the least romantic. She had tried to thank him, not so much for the dress, but because he'd given her a Christmas present. It had seemed like forever since she had received one.

But by morning, in the light of the day, the gold eyes had seemed shrewd and assessing once again each time they fell her way. "I'd hardly have my wife in rags," he told her bluntly.

"Nevertheless, thank you," she'd said primly. "I— I don't have a gift for you."

His smile was wicked, taunting. "Last night was quite a present in itself."

She turned from him quickly, feeling as if bristles rose at her nape. He knew she'd never been one of Leroux's women. But he still seemed to condemn her for the fact that she was there to begin with.

She had begun to feel more than anger or fascination toward him. More than the startling electricity that had seemed to surround them last night. He was giving her what she wanted. A home. A family. A different world. And he was a unique man. He was . . .

Handsome. Wonderfully strong, powerful. He was built beautifully, tight and lean, with rippling muscles that were whipcord-hard and vibrant. That night, even when he had merely left the room, she had found herself remembering the feel of his arms, the heat of his flesh next to hers, the encompassing breadth of his shoulders. To her amazement, she didn't dread his touch at all anymore. She had slept absurdly sweetly with his sheltering arms around her.

But she couldn't let him know. He would think she was a whore and be all the more convinced that she should have stayed with Jack Leroux.

He could be kind enough. He could also be as hard as rock. She had to be careful, so careful, of what she gave. The war had taken too much from her. She just couldn't be hurt anymore. She wouldn't allow anyone to do so. She would be a good wife—she would just keep a careful distance. She certainly wouldn't fall in love with him.

And still, that Christmas day, in the hotel suite, was far more than she might have hoped for. Shane ordered up a Christmas goose, and she and he and Daniel sat down to it. And if Shane was quiet, his eyes hard on her the entire meal, Daniel was charming. She laughed and chatted with him throughout, trying to ignore the golden gaze upon her.

Then it was time for the men to leave. Shane had arranged for Kaitlin's board at the hotel, and she was supplied with steamship passage along the Mississippi, railway tickets once she reached the North, and stage fare from there.

She didn't think that her new husband was going to kiss her good-bye at all. But he did. Down in the street. He suddenly swept her into his arms, and she was startled by the strength of the fever that encompassed her with his touch. Startled, and frightened. She didn't want to care too much; it was dangerous to do so.

He set her down, and met her eyes. There was something almost gentle in his for a moment. "I'm sorry that this is your Christmas."

Her eyes widened. It had, in fact, been a wonderful Christmas. He just didn't know what her past Christmases had been. "It was fine."

"No tree, no decorations, no reading of Mr. Dickens' 'A Christmas Carol' with the family warm by the fire."

"I . . . I'd like such a day. Surely."

"Next Christmas. Next Christmas, I swear. For Francesca. For you."

Then he was gone, and Kaitlin had been left to wonder after a while if any of it had really happened.

Then the weather had become so severe, and soon after that she'd received his telegraph warning her not to attempt to travel until some of the snow cleared. Then she began to wonder if he really wanted her to come at all, if he wasn't regretting his rash marriage with all of his heart and mind.

At the beginning of May, though, she'd received another telegraph. She wasn't sure how he had managed to pack so much anger into so few words. *You'd best arrive soon.* Then Kaitlin imagined that he was thinking her one of Leroux's women of the very worst kind, the type who would take payment and give nothing in return.

It made her angry, and it brought chills along her spine. She had to go. They hadn't made so simple a business deal. She was his wife.

And so she arrived in the spring. The mountains rose majestically, beautifully in the distance, the grass was endlessly green, and the small town was bustling. She had barely emerged from the stage before she saw all this, and more, for there was Shane, waiting on the steps of the Three Mills Travelers' Inn, a young girl before him.

At first, Shane drew her entire attention. There had been so many endless days and nights when she had both dreaded and anticipated their meeting again.

He was taller than she had remembered. Leaner, his skin more bronzed.

But she had remembered his eyes just right. Gold eyes that were touched with the most extraordinary fire.

She tore her gaze from his and looked at the little girl. Wide, hesitant eyes met hers. Big, beautiful brown eyes. Wary ones. The little girl had a lovely face, her features fine and delicate. Francesca was frightened of meeting her, Kaitlin thought. People hurt people so frequently, and Francesca knew it.

Kaitlin shivered, remembering her new husband's fierce warning about his niece. He didn't really care what else she did, as long as she was good to Francesca.

He needn't have warned her about such a thing, she thought indignantly. She'd never hurt the little girl. Never.

They hadn't stepped toward her. The stationmaster had handed her down from the coach. A sense of panic seized her. He'd been so cold, and then so angry. Was there really any kind of a welcome here for her?

He had promised her Christmas this year, she thought. Christmas, for her and Francesca.

She stepped forward.

''Well! She's come! She's made it!'' a voice called out. And Daniel Newton, leading a tiny and pretty and very pregnant woman on his arm, came bursting out of the hotel doorway. He didn't seem to realize that no one had really greeted anyone else and he left his wife's side to give Kaitlin a warm embrace, swinging her around. "See, she's here, Shane, Francesca. Oh, Kaitlin, this is my wife, Mary. She's been dying to meet you—and she's thrilled to have another woman near! We're quite a ways out from town, by you."

"Naturally," Mary said, extending her hand, smiling warmly. "Your husband gave us our property. It adjoins yours."

Kaitlin shook Mary's hand. "I'm truly delighted," she said. Then she turned to Francesca. "And I am truly delighted to meet you, too, Francesca."

The little girl blushed pink. She was pleased. "Thank you," she said softly.

"Well, come on, come on!" Daniel said. "Let's go inside and have something to eat. It's been an awfully long trip for Kaitlin. And we've got well over an hour's ride back home tonight, too!"

Daniel led the way with Mary, slipping his arm through Francesca's to urge her along.

Kaitlin felt as if a cold wind touched her. She met Shane's gaze again. She tried to smile. "You haven't greeted me yet, Shane." Her stomach was pitching. She felt as if her words sounded hollow. "Aren't you—aren't you glad that I've come?"

"Oh, indeed, I'm very glad that you've come. And don't worry. I'll greet you at home, Kaitlin."

Sizzles touched her spine. He took her elbow, and they followed behind the others.

They'd come into Three Mills with a big wagon, knowing that Kaitlin would be bringing goods from New Orleans. And she had a number of trunks with her, filled mostly with household goods. She had tried to go very sparingly on buying personal items. Shane eyed all the packages and trunks as they stowed them, but he didn't say a word to her then.

The trip out to his house was not so bad, or at least

it wouldn't have been if Kaitlin hadn't been so nervous about going home with Shane. To distract herself, she thought about her other companions. Mary was a sweet, wonderful woman, one who really seemed to belong with Daniel, they were both so friendly and lighthearted. And Francesca . . .

Francesca watched her. Much like her uncle did.

The home that Shane brought her to might have been in the wilderness, but it was beautiful. It was a large, sprawling, two-story house that had been whitewashed and trimmed in a deep forest green to match the surrounding foliage. Her eyes were on it from the minute the wagon came to a halt. Her eyes remained on it when he lifted her down from the wagon.

"Did I keep my side of a bargain?" he asked softly.

"Yes," she replied.

"Then you keep yours," he told her.

Again, her stomach catapulted. She escaped his hold and turned to the little girl. "Francesca, would you show me the house, please?"

Blushing again, Francesca stepped forward. Tentatively, she took Kaitlin's hand. And then she led her in.

Inside, the house was beautiful too. There was a huge parlor, and an indoor kitchen and a wonderful large dining room. Up the stairs there were four bedrooms. "Here is mine," Francesca told her proudly, leading her into the first. And she should have been proud. There was a beautiful white knit comforter on the bed, which was covered with a fairy-tale canopy. Her furniture was painted white, and all in all Kaitlin couldn't imagine a more perfect room for a little girl.

"It's lovely," she said, smiling.

Francesca's lower lip quivered. "It is, isn't it? It's the first bedroom that I've ever had all to myself."

Kaitlin came down on her knees before her. "This house is really the first that I've ever had," she told her.

Francesca hesitated, then put her arms around Kaitlin and hugged her tight. Kaitlin held her, and gently smoothed her hair.

At length Francesca pulled away. "Come on, let me show you your room!"

"My room?"

"Well, yours and Shane's!"

Yes, hers and Shane's. She followed Francesca down the hallway, and found her room. Most of her bags were already there. Shane and Daniel and Shane's foreman, Chancey, had already been bringing things up.

Shane's room, she thought. It was a masculine room. The furniture was all deep mahogany, untouched by doilies or dust ruffles of any kind. The two armoires in it were large and heavy. The room wasn't that big. There were two more rooms down the hall . . . She met his eyes.

He must have been reading her mind. He smiled, and slowly shook his head.

She tore her gaze from his, her thoughts scattered. Daniel and Mary were still there. Chancey was a fine man with a warm handshake. She had already made friends with Francesca. There was a festive mood about the place. She had her own home. Her very own home. She was going to ignore Shane, and enjoy the celebration.

She wasn't quite able to ignore Shane then, for he invited her out to the barn. They weren't alone, for the others followed. He introduced her first to Jimmy and Jane, the harness horses, then Diablo, his own big black stallion, and then he brought her to a stall where she saw the prettiest horse she thought that she had ever seen, a mare with a deep dish nose and high flashing tail. "Genevieve," he told her. "I picked her up for you last week."

"She's—mine?" Kaitlin asked. She could barely imagine owning such a creature. Horses had become so precious in Georgia during the end of the war. She hadn't thought she'd even see anything like Genevieve again. "Mine?" The present seemed incredible. The mare nuzzled her, pushing against her chest. Kaitlin touched her warm, velvety nose and a rush of affection swept through her. "She—she's wonderful. Thank you."

Shane shrugged. "You need a good horse out here." He turned his back on her. She wondered what she had done wrong. Then she decided that she would enjoy the night, and enjoy her new life, no matter what. She was going to ignore Shane.

She did. Chancey had done his best with a meal of venison and summer vegetables, and Daniel—being Daniel—had supplied the champagne. They had a wonderful meal. And when it was done, they sat in the parlor, sipping coffee laced with just a touch of brandy.

Kaitlin sat on the love seat, and Francesca fell asleep with her head in her lap.

But then it was time for Daniel and Mary to leave, to go onward to their own home. And Shane lifted Francesca into his arms to take her up to bed. And finally there was nothing left for Kaitlin to do but go up to her own room and await her husband.

She'd bought a new flannel gown that buttoned all the way up to her throat and it was in that gown that she awaited him, in the darkness, in their bed. She thought about pretending to be asleep, but then she decided not to bother. And in a matter of minutes he was there with her. He opened and closed the door and leaned against it in the darkness.

"Time for that 'wretched' business again, eh, Mrs. MacAuliffe?"

"If you're going to make fun of me—"

"I'm not going to make fun of you. That is not my intention at all."

It wasn't. In seconds he was across the room. And the flannel gown was on the floor.

And suddenly, all the dread and anticipation of all the long months were with her. His kisses were hot and fevered. They did incredible and wonderful things to her. In the darkness, it seemed that the Christmas magic was there once again, the magic that had touched them when they'd wed. She could have returned his every touch, his every caress. She could have returned his passion. She fought so hard to hold back. She was so very afraid to give to him completely.

Yet later, it seemed that he was the one to withdraw. He didn't hold her but lay on his own side of the bed. She was suddenly certain that he could see in the darkness with those gold eyes of his.

But he said nothing to her. "Shane?" she asked softly.

He grunted. "Go to sleep. Sometimes it can be a hard life out here."

Perhaps it was a hard life. The next morning at five she was awakened with a firm hand upon her rump. Before she knew it, she was out of bed; and barely dressed and half-asleep, she was proving that she could cook by complying with his orders for a hearty breakfast. He was testing her, she thought irritably. She'd failed him somehow, and this was his way of having her make up for it. Well, she wasn't going to fail him. She could cook, and she did.

And she could keep house, and she did so. By the end of her first two weeks in Three Mills, she had changed everything about the place. Though the house was big and adequately furnished, it had lacked the little touches that only a woman could provide. Kaitlin gave the place those little touches. Now there were sunny yellow curtains at the kitchen window over the sink and water pump. There were beautiful draperies with valances in the parlor. Needlepoint pillows rested cozily upon the sofas in the living room.

And Francesca had become almost talkative.

The hour-long ride into town kept her from any regular schooling, but she was a very bright little girl. And Kaitlin had discovered that if she could dare to love anyone in this life anymore, it would be Francesca. She taught her far more than reading and writing and mathematics. When they finished with two hours of such basics every morning, Kaitlin went on with her, teaching her everything she could remember about etiquette, just the way that her mother had taught her. They would have tea, and laugh together as Kaitlin dramatically overdid the proper way to hold a cup. It was fun.

And busy. There was so much to do. It was a large house to keep clean. There were soap and candles to be made, linens to be washed, chickens to be fed, floors to be swept. And Kaitlin was determined to excel at it all.

For Shane noticed. Every move that she made, he noticed. He seldom commented, though, unless she asked him. "Do you like the parlor?" Or "Does the kitchen suit you?"

His grunts she assumed were by way of approval.

Except when he saw her with Francesca. Then he watched her very thoughtfully.

And then there were the nights . . .

The first two weeks were exactly the same. He came up to bed at ten, looked at her without expression, and took her into his arms.

And as the nights passed, she discovered herself more and more fascinated with her husband. Excitement stirred her blood as he came near her, wonder filled her at his touch. But she held back, so carefully, determined that she would not dare put too much trust into him, nor would she give him any opportunity to deride her.

Usually he stared at the ceiling when they were done, then eventually fell asleep.

But one night the end of May, he did not. He abruptly turned to her.

"In what way have I failed you?" he demanded. "You've come halfway across the country to a new life. You've my name, and my house. Why won't you uphold your part of the bargain?"

Kaitlin gasped, pulling away. How had she failed him? Had he found some fault with her? Did she simply do everything wrong?

"I've kept my part of the bargain!"

"No, no, you haven't!" he told her. His hands were on her shoulders. Though shadows crept between them, she could see him then. See the passion and the strength in his face. "Are you still in love with Daniel?"

"I was never in love with Daniel!"

"He was the man you wanted to marry."

"He didn't accuse me of awful things!"

"Well, I did find you in a whorehouse and gambling establishment."

"I told you—"

"Yes, you told me," he said wearily.

"I was a lady! Always!" she cried.

"Oh, yes, always. With your pinkie up as you sip your tea. It's wonderful. Just wonderful."

"If there's something wrong with me—"

"No, no, Kaitlin, there's nothing wrong with you. Even Chancey says he's never seen a more perfect or beautiful woman. You're a princess, Kaitlin. A damned princess. Ice princess!" he added softly.

She felt as if she had been slapped, and she turned away from him, fighting tears. "I don't know what you mean," she told him indignantly.

His fingers feathered down her back. "Don't you? Never mind. Go to sleep, Kaitlin."

She wasn't sure exactly how things changed after that. Perhaps she'd had a chance at happiness, and perhaps she had thrown it away.

Maybe it was just summer, and the Christmas magic was all gone.

Perhaps it was the situation with the Indians.

Whichever. But on the first of August, Shane was leaving. There had been confrontations with the Blackfoot Indians and since Shane had once signed his own individual treaty with Black Eagle, he promised the sheriff and the people of Three Mills that he would go speak with the chief once again.

Her heart seemed to be in her throat the day that he rode away. She was terrified that she would never see him again. She wanted to tell him that she . . .

That she what?

That she wanted him to come home, that she needed him. He had become her life. She cared for him.

That morning she discovered that she loved his eyes. Those gold eyes that could stare at her so shrewdly, always searching. She loved the planes of his face, the wry curl of his lips. She loved his shoulders, and the warm feel of his bronze flesh. She loved sleeping with him.

But there wasn't time. No time to say all of these things. War drums were sounding, and Francesca was at her side. And bright tears were in Francesca's eyes. Shane was staring at her, daring her to be anything other than perfect.

His perfect ice princess.

So she waved to him when he left, when he rode away, and she held tight to Francesca.

The days seemed longer. She didn't teach Francesca so long in the morning. The two of them started taking morning rides over to see Daniel and Mary. Kaitlin loved riding Genevieve. And she was grateful for the company, and glad to be there for Mary, who was very nearly due. The days she could manage.

The nights she slept alone. And waited.

"I wouldn't worry about Shane," Daniel told her one day. "He's seen Black Eagle often enough in the past."

"I'm really not worried," Kaitlin lied.

She had barely said those words before Mary called out suddenly to them. The baby was coming.

Daniel, completely disconcerted, had to be reminded that he needed to ride into town for the doctor. Kaitlin, scared silly herself but determined that Mary not realize it, tried to remember all the proper things to do. They needed all kinds of clean linen and scissors for the cord, and the worst of it was that she needed to sit with Mary.

For the first two hours, Mary seemed to be fine. Then she cried and screamed out, and no matter what Kaitlin tried to say to her or do for her, nothing seemed to help. Mary was soaked with perspiration. She fell asleep several times, only to wake screaming once again.

Kaitlin walked to the window, watching for Daniel to return with the doctor. They didn't come. It began to dawn on her that things were going badly, very badly, and that there was no one there but herself.

She gritted her teeth, and waited some more. The ride into town was at least an hour. And an hour back out. The doctor would still come.

But two more hours passed. Then three. And Kaitlin realized in panic that the baby was going to come.

"I'm going to die," Mary said softly, looking up at the ceiling.

"You're not going to die! I simply won't let you. I'm not going to live out here without you," Kaitlin told her fiercely.

And I'm not going to live out here and have a baby, ever! she decided. It was too frightening, too dreadful, after all she'd been through already.

"Oh, Kaitlin, the baby is coming!"

The baby was coming. Kaitlin assured herself that she was capable, and she kept thinking of all the things that she must do. She had to deliver the baby.

And she did. The tiny head appeared in her hands first, and she urged Mary to push again. Then came one shoulder, and then the next.

And the baby seemed to pop right into her hands, and to her great relief, let out an ear-piercing cry, filling its lungs.

"Oh, Kaitlin! What is it?"

"What?" Kaitlin stared at the miracle in her hands, for even if it was a bloody mess, Mary's infant was a miracle.

"A boy!" Kaitlin said. "A boy!"

It was just minutes later that Daniel and the doctor did arrive. The doctor came in to see to Mary, and Kaitlin walked out into the hallway with Daniel.

"What happened? What took so long?" Kaitlin demanded. Perhaps she shouldn't be so rough on Daniel, she scolded herself. He looked as if he had just been through hell himself.

"When I went by the Thompson place, they told me that there was some worry about an Indian attack on white riders down the main road. I thought that I had best ride around the long way."

"Oh," Kaitlin said simply. She walked down the hall, her knees trembling. She did love Daniel—she loved him like she loved Mary. They were both good people.

But she was certain that Shane would never have left her in such a position. He would have ridden through every pack of Indians in the West to see that his child was safely delivered.

Except that she was never going to have a child. She was determined about it. Not after today.

Exhausted, she walked down the stairs and sank into one of their parlor chairs. She leaned her head back, just meaning to close her eyes, but she fell asleep. Sound asleep.

She was startled when a male voice awoke her. "Kaitlin. Kaitlin."

She opened her eyes, vastly disoriented. Then she realized that Shane was standing above her. He was back.

"Shane!" For a moment a wide smile lit up her face and she nearly leapt to her feet to greet him. He was back.

He seemed to be looking at her with a rather tolerant smile. "Yes. And I hear I've married rather a heroine. You delivered Mary's baby."

"I wasn't a heroine. I didn't mean to deliver the baby."

He kissed her forehead. "Maybe not. But he's beautiful. Big and beautiful. And wonderful. With any luck, maybe we'll soon have a son."

The smile faded from her lips. No. No, she didn't want to have a baby.

But he didn't see her expression at the moment. He was talking to Daniel, telling him about his meeting with Black Eagle, the chief of the Blackfoot tribe.

"I think that he'll call off his warriors. As long as we keep to our side of the bargain."

"I don't think that he can be trusted," Daniel was saying. "He's a heathen! Why, no man was more warlike before. Remember the Petersons? How they were killed?"

"Black Eagle's wife had been killed by that stupid trapper, Johnson, right before!" Shane said.

"You're defending him."

"I'm not defending him. I know him. He'll kill if he thinks it necessary. He promised that he'd even kill me if I disturbed him on his own ground again. But there is something about him . . ."

"What's that?" Daniel asked.

"He's always willing to listen."

Kaitlin was drifting off to sleep again, when she suddenly felt strong arms around her. Blinking, she met Shane's golden eyes.

"I'm taking my wife home, Daniel. Congratulations on your boy."

Kaitlin didn't ride home on her own horse. Shane held her on the saddle before him, with Genevieve trotting behind them on a lead.

By the time they reached their own home, she'd fallen asleep in his arms.

Shane looked at his wife a long while, then swallowed down his expectations for the night. He carried her up the stairs, and laid her down on their bed.

She was so beautiful. And strong, and courageous.

Maybe he'd been too hard on her. Maybe he owed her more. His bitterness over his first marriage had tainted his second. Yet when she had first seen him tonight, there had been something wonderful in her eyes. As if she had waited for him. As if she wanted him.

As if she loved him.

He smiled. Maybe he hadn't realized it, but perhaps she had been the best Christmas present he had ever received.

He didn't disturb her, but let her sleep. Her face was like porcelain, her skin ivory, her cheeks blushed a perfect rose.

He leaned down to kiss her forehead, not intending to wake her. She was very tired, and he was weary himself. And he was suddenly determined that he was going to woo her. Make her fall in love with him.

And maybe there he would find the warmth and the passion he sensed beneath the barriers she cast against him.

But as his lips touched her flesh, she opened her eyes. And she sat up quickly, as if she were suddenly frightened of him.

"What's the matter?" he asked.

"I'm—I'm tired. I'm so exhausted. Please . . ."

"Please what?" he demanded, aggravated.

She flushed and her lashes fell. "Please don't—er, force anything on me."

He gritted his teeth. "I didn't know that I did force things on you."

She rose from the bed. "I can go in the guest room and not bother you—"

"Get in here," he told her harshly. "I *will* force *this* upon you—you can sleep in your own bed. I never intended to touch you, Kaitlin. Not tonight. I *know* you're exhausted, what with the baby—"

"That's just it," she whispered. "I . . ."

"What?"

"I don't want a baby."

"What?" he said again, blankly.

"I don't want a baby. We—we have Francesca. I don't want to have a child out here in the wilderness where you can never reach a doctor—"

"Kaitlin, I would have reached a doctor."

"And children are so delicate. Look at what happened to Francesca. Look how she was passed around. Life can be so very cruel to children."

"Was it so cruel to you? My lady with her pinkie flying so elegantly in the air?"

"I grew up in a cabin with a drunkard for a father. Is that what you want to hear, Shane? The one good thing in my life was my brother, but the war took care of him. I was never Leroux's woman, but I was never a great belle, either. Are you happy? Whatever, it doesn't matter. I don't want a baby!"

A baby? Or his baby? Shane narrowed his eyes. "Well, we're in a sad state of affairs here, aren't we? I do want a baby."

She went very pale. He tried to remember his resolve to woo her. So what if unimaginable fires seemed to burn inside him when he was lying beside her? He wasn't going to force anything. Not for a while, anyway. She was tired. Upset. Maybe she just didn't see him as the charming, docile man she saw Daniel to be.

"Get in bed!" he roared. "I won't touch you. Not tonight."

Her green eyes luminous, she complied.

And lay beside him, her back to him.

His Christmas present . . .

Yes, but there was next Christmas. And it was coming soon, very soon.

For some reason, he felt a shiver race down the length of his spine.

4

THANKSGIVING CAME, AND IT WAS A WONDERFUL DAY for Kaitlin. The house was warm and comfortable, there was a light snowfall, and Shane, ever-watchful in the background, seemed willing to let her have her way with everything.

Once filled, her table was nearly ostentatious. She'd cooked a huge turkey, a generous-sized ham, and a tender, spit-roasted side of beef. Their guests were Daniel and his wife and the baby, Kevin Richard Newton, and the Reverend Samuels and his wife, Jemimah—a wonderfully short and round woman with the most delightful smile Kaitlin had ever seen—who came out from town. All the day before, Kaitlin and Francesca baked and prepared, and the next morning, they started with all their meat dishes and fresh vegetables.

In the soft glow of the candles, the dining room was beautiful. Kaitlin was pleased to overhear the reverend telling Shane that he had indeed brought a beautiful and talented wife into the wilderness, and later she was doubly glad to hear Daniel telling Shane that he was one lucky fellow, Kaitlin was just amazing.

The pity was that she was entirely certain that Shane didn't find her amazing in the least, and lately it seemed more and more that he had grown very weary of her.

He hadn't been coming home until very late at night. Often past midnight. And she'd heard that there was a certain place in town, as establishment called Nelly Grier's, where ranchers were known to congregate.

Kaitlin wasn't quite sure why, because she *did* realize that she'd asked him to leave her alone and that that was exactly what he was doing, but she was furious with him.

Maybe it was because she didn't really want to be left alone anymore.

Or else she didn't want it to be so easy for him to leave her alone. She had wanted to make up, she just didn't really know how to do so. And once Mary had let it slip about Nelly Grier's place . . . well, then she'd been just too stubborn and angry to even think about trying to make things right with Shane.

Maybe he just just didn't care at all anymore. That thought made her miserable, but it didn't really change anything. Night after night, they lay there, their backs to one another.

But then Thanksgiving came, and Kaitlin was determined to prove her worth, and it seemed that she was able to do so. The meal was delicious. Conversation flowed easily around the table—until the reverend mentioned Black Eagle and the Blackfeet who were really so very near Shane's property.

Shannon Drake

"You know the Indians attacked three riders just last week, Shane," Reverend Samuels said, pausing with a portion of turkey halfway to his plate.

Kaitlin glanced at Shane. He hadn't mentioned Black Eagle lately. In fact, he'd really said very little to her about his visit with the Indian. But then, they'd scarcely been talking since that night.

Shane shrugged. "So I heard. But I also heard that a fool trapper named Nesmith raided one of Black Eagle's camps and kidnapped one of his sons. If that's true, we might well have a major war on our hands very soon."

"Oh, dear God!" Mary Newton cried, hugging her baby close to her. "Are we in danger?"

Shane shook his head. "Not yet, at any rate. Except maybe . . ."

"Maybe what?" Kaitlin demanded.

"Maybe in the north woods, and the north fields. Black Eagle feels the roadway just beyond it was built on his land. He can be dangerous. Unless that little boy is found and returned to him quickly." He looked at Mary and smiled gently. "Don't be afraid. There hasn't been any real Indian trouble here in a long, long time."

Kaitlin's festive party had grown rather somber. She stood up. "Pumpkin and apple pies, coming right up. And we'll have coffee and brandy here at the table. Gentlemen, you are welcome to your cigars right here. We are not going to part ways on a holiday with the men going one way and the women another!"

She was very busy for some time then, collecting the dishes, putting out the pie plates and the coffee. But a little while later she had some time, and she insisted on taking little Kevin Richard Newton from his mother. She and Shane were going to be godparents and she was delighted. The little boy was an adorable little bundle of love and all the fear and uncertainty she had felt when he was born was fading away.

While she held him, she was startled to find Shane staring down at her. She looked up, feeling guilty. "He's beautiful, isn't he?" she said.

"There's only one thing wrong with him."

"What's that?"

"He isn't ours."

Kaitlin's cheeks burned. "Well, Shane MacAuliffe, heaven knows you could have half a dozen children, from what I understand," she whispered, walking away from their guests, to the other side of the room.

"Really? And how do you understand this?" he asked, following her.

"Well, you've disappeared far more than half a dozen nights."

"I didn't realize that I was missed. And I didn't seem to have any reason to hurry home."

"As long as you seem so determined to visit Nelly's, you don't have any reason to hurry home. And as long as I have a choice—"

"You don't have a choice, my dear, lovely—*amazing* little ice princess! Just bear that in mind, and stay on my good side. And bear in mind this fact, too. This state of affairs is not going on forever!"

It didn't go on forever. It was stopped that very night, for some fever had swept into Kaitlin's system, and she was determined to cause him some heartache.

Perhaps it was because of her own.

But when all the guests were gone, when it was time for bed, she found that she was not really ready to lie down. Nor did she dress in anything prim or made of flannel, but chose an ethereal white gown of soft silk. And she stood before the window, watching the moon, brushing out her hair, certain that he would prove his point that the choice was not really hers at all.

He ignored her until her hair had been brushed at least two hundred times. Then he had told her irritably that he had a great deal of work the next day, even if she didn't.

Rejected, furious, she crawled into bed.

And then he let her simmer until she was just at the boiling point before he suddenly and forcefully pulled her into his arms.

She opened her mouth to yell at him, but he stopped her words with a kiss. Then, within minutes, the urge to stop him had disappeared.

Each time he touched her, the magic came more sweepingly upon her. And when it did seem to skyrocket through her at last, she buried her face in a pillow, determined that she would not cry out at the intense pleasure he'd given her.

She was not one of Jack Leroux's women, nor one of Nelly Grier's tarts.

No, she certainly was not, for in the morning, he apologized offhandedly for his tough treatment of her.

And in the evening, he came home very late.

Kaitlin wanted to rip him to shreds. She wondered why it hurt her so very badly, like knives tearing into her soul. Then she knew. It had happened slowly. It had happened for many good reasons.

She had fallen in love with her husband.

But love was a brutal emotion, one she didn't dare trust in. Once again, she decided that her best defense was to ignore him. It was incredibly difficult when he slept beside her, but she told herself that he wasn't getting anything from her again, anything at all.

Still, it was almost December. And she had a home this year, a beautiful home. He had given it to her. She could decorate as she chose, she could do anything she wanted.

And there was Francesca. Francesca who had learned so very little about the mysteries of Christ and Christmas and Santa Claus and caroling.

"It there a Santa?" Francesca asked her excitedly just a few days after Thanksgiving.

"Well, he is really Saint Nicholas, you see," Kaitlin said, winking. She and Francesca had done the laundry, and were now making the beds. "He was a bishop hundreds and hundreds of years ago and he was kind and generous and the patron saint of children and he loved to give out gifts. To the Dutch people who came to live in New York, he was 'Sinter Klaas.' So for us now, he is Santa Claus! And he comes every Christmas to bring gifts. A minister named Mr. Moore described him in a poem back in 1823—before I was even born!—and he is wonderful, Francesca, truly wonderful! He dresses in a red suit with white trim, and he is this huge roly-poly bear of a man, so kind, so very wonderful."

She heard a noise. It was early, but Shane was home. He was standing in the doorway, watching her.

Kaitlin finished the bed, and tried to walk on past him. He caught her arm. She gazed at him, waiting.

"Thank you."

"For what?"

"For giving her Christmas."

He touched her cheek. She was startled by the tenderness in his fingers. "You're just like her, you know. A child deprived of Christmas." And his voice was soft, so soft. "This year, we will have Christmas. We'll drink mulled wine before the fire. I'll chop down a fir tree and we'll decorate it with angels and stars. And we'll all put gifts beneath the tree. You will have Christmas, Kaitlin."

This kindness from him almost brought tears to her eyes. She pulled away. "I have no money of my own. I shall have no gift for you."

He laughed huskily. "Oh, but, my love, think of it, you do, you do."

And then the laughter was gone, and she was in his

arms, held there so hard. "A son, Kaitlin, give me my son."

She pulled away from him. "You'll have to speak to God on that, sir, since I seem to have no choice in the matter."

"But you do. You run. You fight me."

"I don't seem to run fast enough," she informed him, her flashing eyes reminding him of the night so long ago when she had teased and taunted . . .

And he had won in the end.

He started to laugh, but then Francesca was suddenly there, looking worriedly at them both.

"What is it, Shane? Is something wrong?"

"Wrong?" Shane lifted her into his arms. "When I live with two of the most beautiful women in the Western world? Never! We were just discussing Christmas, Kaitlin and I. And Santa Claus is coming this year."

"He never came before," Francesca said.

"Well, he is coming this year. Right down the chimney."

"He'll singe his rump!" Kaitlin advised.

"Never. Santa Claus is invulnerable to fire."

Francesca laughed. "Will he come for us both, for Kaitlin and me?"

"Oh, yes. Santa will come for you. And for Kaitlin." He smiled at Kaitlin, his golden eyes afire. "Will he come for me, do you think?"

"I hardly know," Kaitlin said sweetly. "I hear it on good authority that you have not been a very good boy this year." And with that she swept by him.

At dinner that night Chancey came in with news and they heard that one of the ranches had been burned to the ground. The rancher and his wife had been spared, but Black Eagle's warriors had forced them to watch the destruction, and Black Eagle himself had said that they must warn the whites that there might be worse to come.

Shane came into the kitchen as Kaitlin was washing dishes. "It could prove to be dangerous here. I'm thinking of sending you and Francesca down south until this is over."

She dropped her dish and spun around. "No! I'm not going anywhere. We're going to have a family Christmas. We've—we've promised Francesca."

"Kaitlin, listen—"

"Please, Shane!"

He sighed, watching her. She wondered what lay behind the glitter of his eyes. Then he spoke softly. "Well, you've courage, my love. And a will of steel." He stared at her hard. "Yes, I'll grant you that."

Then he was gone.

It was the next day when Genevieve disappeared.

Kaitlin decided to ride into town. She didn't need the buggy because she wasn't going to make any major purchases, but she did want ribbon; red ribbon and green ribbon. She and Francesca were going to begin to decorate. Thanksgiving was over, they were into December. Perhaps it was a bit early, but Francesca was one child who had really had just too little Christmas in her life.

Maybe Shane was right. Perhaps Kaitlin was also a child who had really had too little Christmas in her life.

She was determined to make up for it.

But when she had brought Genevieve out of the stall to brush and saddle her, she had been distracted when Daniel had ridden by. He always had such a nice smile for her. She had stopped to talk. And when she had turned back, Chancey was just warning her that the wayward mare had broken loose and gone running off.

Right for the north field.

Kaitlin didn't really remember any of Shane's warnings. She was just desperate to find her affectionate little mare. Old Henry the plow horse was still in the barn and so she saddled him quickly and rode out. Chancey was shouting behind her, but she ignored him.

She rode straight for the north field. And she searched and searched, calling to her, but she didn't see a sign of the little mare.

Then she did see Shane, riding toward her on Diablo. He was furious. "What the hell are you doing out here, you fool!"

"I'm just—"

"You're just getting back to the house. Now!"

"I'm not your prisoner, Shane—"

"No, you're a damned idiot! Get back there, or *I'll* get you back there!"

She rode ahead of him, urging old Henry into as quick a pace as he could manage, and she and Shane fought all the way back. When they reached the barn she leapt down from old Henry and started for the house. She meant to reach it before he could yell anymore.

But his hand was on her arm.

"Dammit, Kaitlin, listen to me—"

"I didn't do anything—"

"Tell it to the Blackfeet when they find you the next time!"

She wrenched away from him. He didn't stop her. But as she started for the house, he was right behind her. And when she realized that he was following her into the kitchen, she headed for the stairway.

He followed her there, too. And when she would have slammed the bedroom door, he pushed it open and then slammed it shut behind him.

"I'm not worried about the Indians!" Kaitlin said sharply. "Chancey told me that they're a distance away."

"They're right on our border!"

"Living their lives. While we live ours—"

"Don't fool yourself, Kaitlin! The Blackfeet were the most warlike tribe in the area!"

"Yes, and they killed a lot of whites, and the whites killed them. But that's because the whites were infringing on their fur trade. And now we *buy* the furs from them and—"

"And that's supposed to make everything all better?"

"But the Indians don't come in this close—"

"The hell they don't! Ever since that fool trapper disappeared with Black Eagle's boy, the Blackfeet have been coming in closer and closer. All kinds of rumors are going around of Indian war—real, horrible, disastrous war. Damn you, Kaitlin, I know Black Eagle! I know him well. You stay the hell out of the north field and the north woods!"

"But Genevieve—"

"Genevieve is an Indian pony now. There aren't any finer horse thieves in the world than the Blackfeet. If you ever really cared for a living thing around you, she might not have disappeared!"

Kaitlin gasped, stunned. Tears teased her lashes. She'd tried so very hard . . .

"You're the only living thing around me that I don't particularly care much about, Shane MacAuliffe!"

Her words seemed to have been as sharp as a knife, for his eyes flashed and his jaw tightened. "I pulled you out of a New Orleans sewer. Maybe that's where you belong!"

She struck him. And suddenly she was being dragged across the room, and tossed on their bed.

"I've seen the fire in you," he told her. "I've seen you smile, and laugh. By God, it's there. It was there for Daniel Newton."

"Daniel's a gentleman—"

"And a half-assed fool. And he isn't for you. But damn you, Kaitlin, the fire is there. Within you."

"Maybe you haven't the spark to light any fire within me!" she snapped.

Shane's eyes narrowed. Then he spoke softly. Too softly. "Oh, but I do. Oh, but I do!"

She leapt up, suddenly afraid. She had never really been afraid of him before, but she had never, never seen him so angry.

He blocked the door with his body. She couldn't possibly reach it and throw it open.

"Well, let's see, we have agreed. You've courage, my love. And a will of steel. But that won't help you now. Not one bit. Whether I wooed you or won you, Kaitlin, I made you my wife. And you agreed to the terms. And I'll be damned if I'll let you try to cast me out one minute longer. You want a match, Mrs. Mc-Auliffe? I'll light a boxful of them, Mrs. MacAuliffe, and so help me, we will find the fire within you!"

"Don't you dare talk to me so, Shane—" she had begun, lifting her chin and trying to walk on by. But she couldn't do so. His hand caught her arm tightly.

"You're right. Let's not talk."

She was stunned by the sudden ferocity of his kiss, swept away by the passion within it. Indeed, he had the match to light the fire within her, for within seconds, she felt the soaring heat throughout her body. She felt his touch on her flesh, and she seemed to feel it within her blood, too. And she wanted his kiss, wanted his touch, more than she had ever imagined wanting it before.

She heard the rent of fabric, and she thought with a certain amazement that he had actually torn her clothing. And it didn't matter. Not in the least.

But his eyes touched hers, in challenge, in defiance. She cried out, slamming her fists against his chest, but he didn't seem to care. They were falling together, and the softness of the bed was there to catch them. He whispered in her ear, soft. His kiss feathered against her throat.

And the heat began to rise.

His kiss was silk against her naked flesh. His whisper brushed her skin with tiny laps of flame. His hands caressed the length of her, so intimately. She was dimly aware that her fingers moved against his chest, stroked, caressed. She breathed softly against his lips, and they were locked within a frantic kiss once again.

Something was different. Her anger had dissipated, but an intensity remained. She was profoundly aware of his words, his whispers. The things that he said. Intimate things. Each touch became exquisitely keen. He was demanding so much, and yet gave to her so tenderly. Clothing seemed to melt away, and they were entwined as one, and everything that had been sweet before was ever more so now. Tonight, the stars seemed to explode in their room. She reached for the sky, and for a moment, her fingertips brushed it. And the stars burst out upon her with the most extravagant beauty she had ever imagined.

A cry tore at her throat. Just in time she swallowed it down, despairing that she might give so much to a man so determined to spend his nights away from her. She drifted down, down from the startling ecstasy, cloaked for long sweet moments in magic and mist.

Then she swallowed hard, careful not to speak.

Time passed slowly. She felt Shane's tension. Then he rose. And dressed.

"I'm sorry, Kaitlin. No, damn you, I'm not sorry. You're my wife. And I want you to be more than a cook. I'll not be stopping at Nelly Grier's when I've a black-haired beauty at home, even if she has emerald eyes flashing nothing but hatred my way. Black-haired, and black-hearted."

"No!" she cried. "No! It's not me, Shane Mac-Auliffe. You prove time and time again that you prefer the company at Nelly's to that at home—"

"Damn! I prefer a spark of warmth!"

Stark pain streaked through her. This afternoon, she had given to him . . .

She picked up her pillow and threw it at him with a vengeance. "I hate you, Shane! I hate you!"

The glittering passion in his golden eyes was deeper than she had ever seen it. She nearly cringed, certain that he meant to harm her.

But he did not. He turned, and left her. The door closed with a loud slam.

"No, no, that was a lie!" Kaitlin whispered. Too late. "I love you, Shane."

She jumped out of bed, splashed water on her face, and dressed quickly. It had already grown dark outside, but she didn't care. She raced out to the stables.

Chancey was there, working. He must have seen Shane come in and leave.

"Chancey, where's Shane?" she demanded.

"Why, I think he rode off to the north field. Said there was supposed to be some good hunting up that way." She barely heard him as he kept talking. "Course, what that fool man is hunting out in the dark, I don't know."

Kaitlin didn't answer him. She was busy saddling old Henry.

"Kaitlin, what do you think you're doing?" Chancey asked worriedly.

"I have to talk to him."

"Talk to him later."

"No, no, I have to talk to him now. It can't wait!"

Chancey kept calling after her. Kaitlin ignored him as she rode off. She pushed old Henry hard, racing a good twenty minutes into the night. There was a moon out to guide her.

Old Henry was quickly lathered, and despite the tempest in her heart, Kaitlin reined him in after a while. She would reach the north field soon enough. Perhaps she'd need to be careful. Shane might well shoot at her if he were there.

But he wasn't in the north field. Someone else was. She saw the horses before she recognized her danger.

Then she realized that the numerous horses moving in a semicircle were mounted by strange men. Indians.

Her heart began to pound. She stared at them, watching with an awful fascination. They were dressed warmly against the winter in their buckskins. She could dimly see that their faces were painted. She had seen sketches of Blackfoot war parties . . .

And she had just come upon one. A scream rose in her throat. She tried to wrench old Henry around. He snorted, fighting her lead. He hadn't been treated so rudely in years, Kaitlin was certain.

And he wasn't going to take it now. "Henry, damn you!" she cried, slamming her heels against his flanks. And he did begin to run. At a slow lope. "Please, please!" she cried. She felt the cold wind against her face, but not strongly enough.

She looked to her side. The Indians were running her down. There was one to her left, and one to her right. Two of them had already raced their ponies ahead of her.

She was going to die. She was trapped. Within seconds, steel would pierce through her flesh.

But she didn't die. The Indian to her left brought his pony slamming against old Henry. He reached out, able to ride with only the tautness of his thighs keeping him upon his mount. He swept her up from her horse, and onto his own.

And began to race away.

Shane hadn't been anywhere near the north field. He'd ridden Diablo out to stare at the moon, his heart and soul still in a tempest.

I hate you, Shane . . .

She had said those words, said them clearly. But hadn't he given her every reason to do so?

Yet he hadn't believed it. She tried to hide things from him, but he knew her . . . better than she knew herself. And he believed with all his heart that he could please her. He knew exactly where he had taken her, and where they had been together when they made love.

She was wrong about Nelly Grier's. Hell, he couldn't even go there anymore.

Not since she had entered his life. Fulfilling every promise. His home was beautiful. Francesca was the happiest that Shane had ever seen her. They had everything . . .

If only they had one another.

He looked up at the sky and closed his eyes, a slow smile curving his lips. Maybe he should tell her. Just come out and tell her. Maybe it had happened slowly. Maybe it had happened at the very beginning. It didn't matter when. He didn't mean to ever hurt her, he didn't mean to ever force her into anything. He didn't even really care if they ever had a child, not if she didn't want one.

He just loved her, that was all. And he needed her.

Maybe if he just spoke to her, they could call a Christmas truce once again.

He turned Diablo and rode back toward home. At the stables he dismounted, but Chancey came hurrying out from the barn.

"Shane, Kaitlin's still out."

"Out? Where?"

"She come tearing out here right after you left. She said that she had to speak to you right away. She went on out to the north field. And she hasn't come back yet."

He felt as if his heart had jumped up into his throat. He leapt up on Diablo once again and spurred the horse into a gait like the speed of the north wind.

And yet he came to the field too late. There was no one there. He heard the sound of the wind in the trees, and nothing else.

Kaitlin was gone. He dismounted and walked the field. He knelt down.

There was one black eagle feather on the ground.

He cried out his agony, thundered it to the night. It didn't matter. There was no one to hear.

At length he gritted his teeth and rose, his hands clenched at his sides. He couldn't battle Black Eagle alone. Well, he could stage a one-man war against the Indian, but he wouldn't win. They'd kill him, and then they just might kill Kaitlin, too.

Jesu, he had to get Kaitlin back. He had to. She'd come like a Christmas gift, in truce, and she'd turned his life around, and now, he knew, he would have no life without her.

Shane exhaled slowly, then mounted Diablo once again.

There was a chance. There was a chance . . .

Black Eagle didn't celebrate Christmas, but maybe, just maybe, Shane could call a Christmas truce with the Indian, too.

He rode hard back for his house, praying that God would grant both him and Kaitlin the time that he needed.

Please, God, for Christmas . . .

Three . . . four . . . five . . .

Twenty-one . . . twenty-two . . . twenty-three . . .

Kaitlin stared at the last number etched into the skin of the teepee.

It was Christmas Eve.

"Dear God, please, for Christmas. Let him live. I'll never ask for anything again, I promise. Just let me see him again, let me tell him that I do have a gift for him this Christmas. Let me tell him that he's going to have his son. Oh, please, let us leave here together!''

Kaitlin whispered the words out loud. She continued to pray fervently.

Outside the teepee, the night wind howled.

KAITLIN WAS STARTLED BY THE SOUND OF THE BUCKSKIN flap rustling as Black Eagle entered the teepee. In the flickering shadows created by the small fire in the center, he appeared large and foreboding, menacing.

Her heart seemed to stop. He had killed Shane.

''Dear Lord!'' she breathed. The world seemed to be spinning around her. A blackness reached out. She would have welcomed it. Anything other than accepting the fact that Shane might be dead. Her throat was dry, her eyes were filling with tears, blinding her.

''Come, Kaitlin,'' Black Eagle said.

No, she would never follow him anywhere. He could kill her right there, right where she waited.

''Kaitlin!'' This time, a different voice. She brushed at her eyes, and stared toward the entrance. Shane was there. She leapt to her feet and went bounding the few steps toward him.

But Black Eagle stood in her way, dragging her back to his side. ''I've not yet received my Christmas gift,'' Black Eagle told Shane.

Kaitlin stared at her husband, fear running along her

spine. What was Shane up to? What was he trying to do?

Shane's eyes were on hers reassuringly as he spoke to Black Eagle. "That's right. You have not received your gift. Come, and I will bring you to your gift."

Shane left the teepee. Black Eagle set a hand upon Kaitlin's arm, dragging her along.

They came out into the snow-covered day. The sun was already falling. Pinks and oranges flared across the sky in dramatic streaks. The Blackfeet teepees, lined up against the horizon, appeared like a set of near-perfect, A-shaped hills in the soft pastel shadows that were beginning to form.

By the teepee, Black Eagle's people were lined up. Some were warriors, stripped of their paint now, yet standing just as proudly.

And the women were there. Beautiful Yellow Flower who had been the kindest to Kaitlin, heavy-set Cries Like the Wind who had mocked her with the most vengeance. Even the children flocked around, watching Black Eagle and Shane, the curious white man who had come among them before, and came among them now, despite the warnings that he might well be killed.

Diablo waited before the teepee. Black Eagle called out an order, and another horse was brought up. Kaitlin was surprised when Yellow Flower came forward, speaking softly to Black Eagle. She wondered if the chief's temper would flare at such an interruption, but Black Eagle paused, listening to the woman. Black Eagle grunted, then he actually seemed to smile. But he liked Yellow Flower, and Kaitlin was convinced that Yellow Flower was in love with Black Eagle. She didn't understand why the two were not man and wife, but standing there, shivering in the cold and waiting, she didn't really care. All that she could care about was Shane.

He had mounted Diablo, and he waited. Watching her.

So intently. His gold eyes blazed, and she longed so
desperately to run to him. But his gaze warned her, too.
He was still in the middle of negotiations.

"Kait-lin!" Yellow Flower said. Kaitlin spun around
and gasped softly. Yellow Flower had gone for Genevieve. Her little mare stood before her, decked in an
Indian rope bridle and an Indian saddle. Kaitlin stared
at Shane, hesitating.

"Black Eagle has had her brought out for you."

Kaitlin caught hold of a handful of the mare's mane
and swiftly leapt up on the horse. Black Eagle had
mounted his paint, and the three of them were ready.
One of the warriors said something to Black Eagle. Black
Eagle laughed and answered in English.

"This man keeps his word, and his bargains. He will
not injure me. Nor is he a fool. If he were to do so, you
would kill him and his woman. Slowly. You are aware
of this, MacAuliffe, right?"

"Very aware," Shane replied politely. "Shall we
go?"

Black Eagle nodded and Shane urged Diablo forward.
Kaitlin's mare followed at a brisk trot. Black Eagle kept
pace behind them.

In a few moments, the A-line hill of teepees began to
fade behind them as they left the winter village of the
Blackfoot behind. They must have ridden for about
twenty minutes before Shane reined in at last. Kaitlin
couldn't begin to imagine where they were, and the shadows of night were beginning to fall around them. Then
she heard a rustling and strained her eyes toward a group
of trees. There had been some kind of a lean-to built
there. And as she stared at it, a man suddenly appeared.
Her eyes widened in surprise. It was Chancey.

"Shane?" he said cautiously.

"Yes, it's me," Shane said. "And Black Eagle is
with us. He has brought my Christmas present, but I

must now give him his before I am allowed to keep mine.''

Even in the shadows, Kaitlin could see Chancey's broad smile. "Fine, Shane. That's mighty fine.''

Shane dismounted and trudged through the snow toward the lean-to. He disappeared inside it.

Black Eagle waited in silence.

Then Shane reappeared carrying a little black-topped bundle wrapped in doeskin. For a moment, Kaitlin wasn't sure what it was.

Then she gasped as the bundle moved. Shane set it down. The bundle squealed and began to run.

It was a child. A baby really, Kaitlin thought, a little boy of no more than three or four.

Black Eagle answered the squeal with a hoarse, glad shout. He flung a leg over the neck of his pony and leapt gracefully to the ground, then ran to the boy, arms outstretched.

The boy was in his arms. Black Eagle rose and spun around in the shadows, cradling the boy against him.

Kaitlin looked at Shane. She could wait no longer. She ran to him, floundering a bit in the snow, nearly falling, but was then caught up in the strength of his arms.

"Kaitlin . . .''

She heard his whisper. Felt the warmth of it against her cheek. She wound her arms around him, not willing to be parted by the fraction of an inch.

Black Eagle did not come between them again. It was Shane himself who set her aside as the Indian walked up to him, still cradling his son.

"Your Christmas present is yours," Black Eagle said, "and mine . . . is mine. This is a good thing, this exchange of gifts.''

"I think so, too," Shane said softly.

"It is an old custom? Part of your Christianity?''

Shane smiled. "Well, yes. You see, Christ was our god's gift to us. And on the night when he was born, wise men saw a star in the sky to follow, and they did so, bearing gifts for a newborn king. In honor of his birth, we bring gifts to one another."

Kaitlin felt a smile curve her lips as she watched Black Eagle. She had never imagined that such a man could be so tender, so gentle.

But all men, she realized, loved their children. Black Eagle was really no less—or no more—than any other man.

He looked at Kaitlin, then smiled at Shane. "You've given me a very fine gift."

"And you, sir, could have given me none finer," Shane replied.

Black Eagle stretched out a hand. Shane clasped it. Then the Indian turned with his little boy in his arms and mounted back up on his big paint. He glanced back.

"Kaitlin!"

"Yes, Black Eagle?"

"The mare is your Christmas gift."

She smiled. "Thank you. Thank you very much. I don't have anything for you. If—"

He interrupted her with his soft laughter. "Maybe you *have* given me a gift. I am going home now. I am going to tell Yellow Flower that she will be my Christmas gift. I have my son returned to me. His mother is dead a long time now. He will have another."

Black Eagle waved, and kicked his pony. Then he was swallowed into the shadows of Christmas Eve.

"Oh, Shane!" Kaitlin breathed.

Chancey cleared his throat. "I think we'd better be heading back now. Maybe we've got Black Eagle into the Christmas spirit, but I'd hate to count on the sudden conversion of his whole tribe."

"Right, Chancey, we'd better head back." But Shane

was still holding Kaitlin, and Kaitlin was still looking up into his eyes. Neither of them could really care at the moment if they were surrounded by the entire Indian nation. "Chancey, you go on. You ride ahead and tell them all that everything is all right. That Kaitlin and I are coming home."

"I shouldn't be leaving you alone out here," Chancey muttered. "You're like a pair of babes in the woods right now, you are!"

He grumbled more as he drew his buckskin from around the side of the lean-to and mounted up. He was still grumbling when he cast his heels against the horse's side and started off through the snow.

They were alone. Alone in the white wilderness, with the last of the light fading fast, and stars beginning to appear above them, even as the light faded away.

"Oh, Shane . . ." Kaitlin whispered.

He kissed her at last. A kiss fueled with both passion and tenderness, a kiss that robbed the last of her breath away and set her heart to pounding fiercely.

She kissed him in return. With all barriers fallen, with all the warmth and desire and love he could have wished. They stood there, barely aware of the soft pelting of snow that began to fall upon them.

Then Kaitlin finally broke away, barely able to stand, so glad of his arms around her. "Oh, Shane, I do love you! I was trying to find you, trying to tell you—"

"And you found the Indians instead," he said softly. He cradled her fiercely against him. She was reminded of the way that Black Eagle had held his child, and she had never felt more loved, more protected, more cherished.

"Oh, Shane, it's true! You did find me in a New Orleans sewer. And I did come from an awful home, and it was torn to shreds by the war. And I wanted— material things. I never knew how little those things meant until I became so certain that I lost you. And I didn't mean to be so horrible, except that I was afraid. Shane, forgive me, please?''

"Kaitlin!" His arms swept around her again. So fiercely. "Kaitlin, I was horrible to you from the moment we met. But you see, I was fascinated with you then. I think that I was very afraid myself. You see, I risked love once. And I didn't dare believe in anything good.''

"We were all wounded," Kaitlin whispered. "You, me—even Black Eagle. Maybe we've started to heal one another.''

Shane smiled. A broad, tender, crooked smile. "Maybe," he agreed. "Did he—hurt you?"

She shook her head. "I think he meant to. But he saw your ring on my finger, and he refused to touch me because of his respect for you.'' She started to tremble. "Oh, Shane, even the Indians knew you better than I did!''

He laughed. "Not so, Kaitlin, but it doesn't matter. None of it matters anymore. I've got you back. And it's beginning to snow harder. Think we'd best head home.''

She shook her head, her eyes dazzling as they met his. "No. I can't let you go.''

"Then we'll ride Diablo together. I'll tie Genevieve to him so she can follow us home.''

Once they were mounted, Kaitlin leaned her head against his chest, unable to believe that she was in his arms, and that they were on their way home. "How did you manage to come for me? Black Eagle had warned that he would kill even you if you disturbed him.''

Shane's arms tightened around her. "I was nearly insane when I realized that you were gone, and what had happened. I would have ridden straight in for you, except that I knew that I couldn't save you alone, and that there wasn't enough manpower here to make any assault on Black Eagle and the entire tribe. Then I realized that I could make an assault on that fool trapper who had taken Black Eagle's boy, and so I rode on into his camp.''

"Peacefully?"

"Guns blazing," Shane admitted, "but I had to convince him that I meant business. He gave up the boy to me, because I promised him a whole-scale war and an end to his future business trade if he didn't. Of course, I also promised him a bullet through the head. That seemed the most convincing argument."

Kaitlin laughed softly. "Oh, Shane . . . And I thought that I was going to spend Christmas in a teepee, unloved, unwanted!"

"Never, Kaitlin, never," he whispered huskily. "It was a year ago you came into my life. A year ago today, remember? And I told myself that you were a Christmas gift. I just didn't realize then that you were the greatest Christmas gift I was ever going to receive."

"Oh, Shane!" She turned in the saddle, flinging her arms around him, nearly unseating them both. She gave him a sloppy kiss, and he kissed her in return. Somehow managing to keep them balanced in the saddle. In time they parted. Diablo snorted as if he were certain his master and mistress had gone mad.

"All right, Diablo," Shane told him, "we're almost there."

And they were almost there. Francesca was on the front steps despite the cold, waiting. When she saw Kaitlin, she gave a glad cry and came racing down the steps and into the snow.

"You're home, Kaitlin, you're home! You're all that I asked for for Christmas, I prayed for you every night, and now you're here! Oh, Kaitlin!"

She hugged Francesca, hugged her and hugged her. And when she was done, she held on to her still. And Daniel and Mary were there, eager to hug and hold her.

Even the Reverend Samuels was there with Jemimah, all ready to greet her.

She had come home for Christmas. She had truly come home.

There was so much commotion for the longest time. Mary had seen to it that a hot bath filled with sweet rose scent awaited her first in the kitchen. Mary was convinced that she had to feel awfully dirty after her stay with the Indians. The Blackfeet had actually believed far more in bathing than a lot of white folk Kaitlin knew, but since Mary had gone through so much trouble to provide the delightful bath, Kaitlin decided to enlighten them later about the tribe. She smiled. Mary was a good friend. So was Daniel. They were wonderful people.

Just not quite so wonderful as Shane.

When she was bathed and dressed—wearing that beautiful gown Shane had bought for her the year before, the night they had wed—she came back to the parlor. Everyone wanted to speak with her, to be with her. To Kaitlin, it was fine. She sat there in the parlor, before the fire. Mary served her mulled wine, Francesca curled up next to her on the sofa with her head in her lap. There was a big fir tree in the parlor, too. Chancey had dragged it in. "Ain't decorated much, ma'am," he told Kaitlin, "but I was thinking that maybe you and Shane and Francesca might want to get to that tomorrow. None of us ever gave up hope, you know. It was Christmas. And we just wanted you back for Christmas."

Kaitlin gave Chancey a big kiss, and that brought a blush to his cheeks. Then she realized that Shane had been very quiet all night. He was just standing there, leaning against the mantle, watching her.

Then, at last, it was time for everyone to go to bed for the night. They were all staying, the Newtons and their baby in one of the guest rooms, the reverend and Jemimah in another. It would be an early morning, with the lot of them traveling into town for Christmas services.

They'd have carols then, Kaitlin thought. She hugged Francesca close. There'd be carols in the church. And tonight, Santa just might come down the chimney.

Shane had said that he would give her Christmas. He had done just that.

And finally, she was alone with him. He hadn't let her walk up the steps. She assured him she hadn't been through any hardships, but he wouldn't let her walk up the steps anyway.

He carried her, his eyes locked with hers all the way. She wound her arms around his neck, smiling.

"Is Santa coming down the chimney for Francesca?" she asked softly.

"I think that Santa came tonight for Francesca, too," he said, smiling tenderly in return. "But yes. He's brought her a bright new dress and a beautiful doll. I'll have to see that he places it under the tree correctly very soon. He's coming for you, too."

"He came for me already," Kaitlin told him. "He came when I saw your face tonight."

"But there will be a present under the tree for you, too. I—" He paused. "I never gave up hope."

"Oh, Shane, I really won't have anything for you under the tree—" she began. Then she broke off. "Oh, but I do have something for you!"

They had reached their room. Shane still held her, closing the door behind them with his foot. Moonlight streamed into the room.

His eyes blazed down into hers. "I said that you were my Christmas gift. The finest gift that I have ever received. I truly need no other."

"But I have one, my love!" Kaitlin whispered. "I think we're going to have . . . no, I'm positive now. We're going to have a baby. Next year, I think that you'll have your son."

His arms tightened around her. "Kaitlin . . ."

For a moment he was utterly still.

Then he hugged her, set her down, and let out a cry, a joyous cry. It was something like a yell, something like a shout.

And Kaitlin was certain that it woke the entire house.

It did. There was suddenly a banging on their door.

Shane threw it open.

The Reverend Samuels stood there. "Shane, Kaitlin, is something wrong? Is someone injured—"

"No, no, we're fine!" Shane said quickly. "I was just receiving my Christmas gift."

The reverend gasped. Kaitlin giggled, realizing that the reverend had assumed that he was shouting about something indecent.

"Shane MacAuliffe, there's a child in this house—"

"And there's going to be another one! Good night now, all. No, not good night. It's past midnight. It's Christmas. Merry Christmas, everyone. Merry Christmas. Now go to bed!"

He closed the door with a firm snap. He smiled at Kaitlin. "Merry Christmas, my love!"

She smiled, and flew into his arms. "We do have the greatest gifts in the world," she whispered. "Gifts of love."

He held her tenderly, then kissed her lips. "Come, give me mine!" he whispered back.

And with the snow falling softly beyond the window, her home filled with the most wonderful Christmas spirit, Kaitlin curled her arms around him.

And gave him the gift of her love.

SEASON'S GREETINGS
from ...
SHANNON DRAKE

"I love Christmas, and there is no story more wonderful to write than one that deals with the Christmas spirit. At no other time of the year are we reminded just how important love, in its many facets, can be. For my characters, people dealing with the hardships that life has dealt them, love itself becomes the greatest Christmas present one can imagine."

SHANNON DRAKE is the author of eight historical romances, including DAMSEL IN DISTRESS, which Avon Books will publish. She has received numerous awards from Waldenbooks, *Romantic Times* and *Affaire de Coeur*. She also writes under the names "Heather Graham" and "Heather Graham Pozzessere". The mother of five children, she lives in Coral Gables, Florida.

Surrender

Lisa Kleypas

To Patsy Kluck with love

Prologue

December 1875
Boston

"COME ON IN," HALE SAID, THROWING OPEN THE front door with a flourish. He gestured for Jason to precede him into the house.

Jason followed him into the entrance hall, appreciating the house's splendidly dark interior and quietly luxurious atmosphere. He raised his eyebrows and whistled silently.

"I'm glad to see you're properly impressed," Hale remarked with a grin. A dour-faced butler approached them, and Hale greeted him casually. "Hello, Higgins. I've brought a friend from college to stay for the holidays. Jason Moran, a fine fellow. Higgins, take our coats and tell me where my sister Laura—no, don't bother, I hear her singing in the parlor. C'mon, Moran." Hale strode past the staircase toward a room off the hallway. Jason followed obligingly, hearing a thin, girlish voice crooning "Deck the Halls."

A tall Christmas tree laden with ornaments and tiny wax tapers trembled in the center of the room. A slim adolescent girl in a blue velvet dress stood on a chair that was close to toppling over. She clutched an angel with glass wings in her small hand, rising on her toes in an effort to place it atop the tree. Jason started forward, but Hale was already there, snatching the girl by the waist and whirling her off the chair. "Here's my girl!"

"Hale!" she cried, throwing her arms around his neck and peppering his cheek with enthusiastic kisses. "Hale, you're home at last!"

"What were you doing up on that chair?"

"Putting the angel on the tree."

Hale held Laura's fragile body aloft as if she were a rag doll and inspected her thoroughly. "You're prettier than she is. I think we'll put *you* up there instead."

She laughed and handed him the angel. "Here, you do it. And don't break her wings."

Instead of lowering Laura to the floor. Hale transferred her to Jason, who took her in a startled but automatic reaction. Afraid she might be dropped, she gasped with surprise and threw her arms around his neck. For a moment they stared at each other while Hale bounded onto the chair.

Jason found himself looking into a pair of soft green eyes fringed with dark lashes. He could have drowned in those eyes. Regretfully he saw that he was too old for her. He had just turned twenty, while she couldn't have been more than fourteen or fifteen. Her body was as light as a bird's, her breasts and hips not yet developed. But she was an exquisitely feminine creature with long chestnut hair that fell in curls down her back, and skin that looked as soft as rose petals.

"Who are you?" she asked, and Jason set her down with great care. He was strangely reluctant to let go of her.

"Ah, yes," Hale called down, in the midst of fastening. the angel to the prickly sprice branch, "introductions are in order. Miss Laura Prescott, may I present Mr. Jason Moran.''

Jason took her hand, holding it as if he were afraid it might break. ''I am pleased to make your acquaintance, Miss Prescott.''

Laura smiled up at the tall, handsome man. He was making an obvious effort to speak carefully, but he couldn't hide the touch of a lilting brogue in his voice, the kind that housemaids and street peddlers and chimney sweeps had. His clothes were nice, and his black hair was thick and windswept. He was big and lean and healthy-looking, and his black eyes snapped with liveliness. ''Are you from Harvard?'' she asked.

''Yes, I'm in your brother's class.'' Realizing he was still holding her hand, Jason dropped it immediately.

''Moran is an Irish name, isn't it?'' As Laura waited for an answer, she sensed his sudden wariness.

''Yes,'' Hale answered for him in a loud whisper. ''He's Irish through and through.''

Laura's smiled at her brother. ''Does Mother know?'' she whispered back.

''No, I thought we would let her discover it for herself.''

Anticipating her narrow-minded mother's expression when she saw their Irish guest, Laura giggled softly and glanced at Jason. She saw that his black eyes had turned cool and unfathomable. Disconcerted, for she had not meant to give offense, she hastened to soothe him. ''Mr. Moran,'' she said, ''do forgive our teasing.'' She smiled, timidly placing her hand on his arm. ''We always tease our friends.''

For her it was a bold gesture, touching a man even in so impersonal a way. Jason could not know just how untoward it was. All he knew was that she was the most beautiful creature he had ever seen. Even in his ambitious dreams of being wealthy and having a fine home and a well-bred wife, he had not been able to imagine anything like her.

She was an aristocrat by birth, while he would never amount to more than a peasant in the Prescotts' estimation. For someone like him it was the highest honor just to be allowed to sit at their table. No matter how rich or important he became, he would never have a chance of marrying a Boston Brahmin. But he had beaten impossible odds many times before. Silently he vowed that he would do it again. When it came time to marry, Laura Prescott was exactly what he wanted.

It would take time and careful planning. Jason never counted on luck, which had always been in short supply in the Moran family. To hell with luck—all he had ever needed were his own resources. He did not return Laura's smile. In no way would he betray the thought that seared across his brain . . . that someday she was going to be his.

1

November 1880
Boston

THE LAST THING JASON MORAN EXPECTED WHEN HE
opened the door of his library was the sight of his wife
being kissed by another man. Perhaps someone else's
wife would resort to clandestine meetings, but not his.
There were no secrets to Laura . . . or so he had thought.
His black eyes narrowed while the unfamiliar sensation
of jealousy froze the pit of his stomach.

The pair sprang apart as soon as the door opened. The
light Strauss music from the party drifted in, dispelling
any illusion of privacy the two might have had. Laura
raised her hands to her cheeks in surprise, but that did
not conceal the fact that she had been crying.

Jason broke the silence in a mocking voice. "You're
not being an attentive hostess, darling. Some of the guests
have been asking for you."

Laura smoothed her chestnut-brown hair and composed herself with miraculous speed, assuming her usual
emotionless mask. "Don't look so anxious, Perry," she
said to the other man, who had flushed scarlet. "Jason

understands a kiss between friends.'' Her green eyes flickered in her husband's direction. ''Don't you, Jason?''

''Oh, I understand all about . . . friends,'' Jason replied, leaning his shoulder against the doorway. He had never looked as dangerous as he did in that moment, his black eyes as hard and bright as diamonds. ''Perhaps your friend will be kind enough to allow us some privacy, Laura.''

That was all the prompting Perry Whitton needed to make his escape. Mumbling something apologetic, he skittered through the doorway, pulling at his high starched collar as if to relieve the rush of blood to his face.

''Whitton,'' Jason mused, closing the door behind the retreating figure. ''Not the most obvious choice for a romantic liaison, is he?''

Perry Whitton was a shy, middle-aged bachelor, a friend of some of the most influential women in Boston society. He had innumerable female acquaintances, but never showed a romantic interest in any of them. Whitton's looks were pleasant but unthreatening, his manner engaging but not flirtatious. Any husband would feel completely secure in leaving his wife in Whitton's company.

''You know it was not like that,'' Laura said in a low voice.

Perry had been an acquaintance of the Prescotts for years—the kiss had been a gesture of sympathy not passion. As Laura had welcomed him to the party, Perry had seen the strain on her face and the unhappiness beneath her social pleasantries.

''You are as lovely as always,'' Perry had said kindly, ''but I would presume to say that something is troubling you.''

It was indeed. Laura had no intention of confiding in

him about her problems with Jason, but to her horror she realized she was about to cry. She would rather have died than make an emotional scene. Understanding her dilemma, Perry had taken her to a private place. And before she could say a word, he had kissed her.

"Jason, surely you can't think there are romantic feelings between Perry and me," she said in guarded tones.

She quivered with unease as her husband approached her and seized her upper arms. "I own you," he said hoarsely. "Every inch of you." His eyes raked over the satin evening gown she wore. "Your face, your body, your every thought. The fact that I don't choose to partake of your favors does *not* mean I'll allow you to bestow them on any other man. You are mine, and mine alone."

Laura's astonished green eyes met his. "You are hurting me. Jason, you know the kiss meant nothing."

"No, I don't know that." He glanced down at her body in that insulting way again, his cruel gaze seeming to strip off her garments. "You're a beautiful woman, beautiful enough to make even Perry Whitton want you. He may have made the mistake of thinking he could find some warmth in that slender little body. Perhaps he isn't aware that you're as lovely and cold as a marble statue."

Laura flinched and turned her face away. Jason could see a moist patch on her cheek where her tears had not yet dried. He had never seen her cry, not in all the time they had known each other. "What were you crying about?" he demanded, his voice as rough as the blade of a saw.

Laura was silent, staring at him uncomprehendingly. In her family there had never been displays of anger or violence. Hale's boyish antics had provided the only excitement in the Prescotts' placid world. During the last years when her brother had been away at school, her life had been as quiet as a nun's. As Jason glared at her, demanding that she explain herself, she was too over-whelmed to speak.

Cursing savagely, Jason yanked her against him. Her racing heartbeat pounded against his, and her skirts flowed around his feet. His dark head bent, and his mouth crushed hers. She whimpered and tried to pull her head back, but he caught her jaw in his fingers and held her still. His lips were hard and bruising, his kiss infused with raw anger. She gasped and went rigid, enduring the brutal onslaught.

Jason let go of her so swiftly that she stumbled back a few steps. "I can feel how my touch disgusts you," he jeered. "It must be humiliating for the daughter of Cyril Prescott to be fondled by a grocer's son. You were meant to marry a Boston Brahmin, but instead you became the wife of a workingman, a shanty mick. I bought you, paid for you with money so new the ink was barely dry. I know how your friends pity you. God knows you have reason to pity yourself."

Laura's face turned white, the marks of his fingers showing on her jaw. They stared at each other in the brittle silence. When it became clear he was going to say no more, she turned and fled the room as if the devil were at her heels.

Jason dropped his black head and rubbed the back of his neck wearily. He was filled with self-hatred. He had promised himself he would never hurt her, and once again he had broken that vow. He had spent his entire life trying to overcome his heritage and hide his rough edges. Most of all he had devoted himself to making money, for he had realized in his youth that being rich was the only way to compensate for the lack of a proper name and bloodlines.

In the past two months of marriage, Laura had organized his life and provided for his comforts with an efficiency he would never take for granted. Managing the household, entertaining their friends and guests, and accompanying him to social events were things she did with ease. Her taste was flawless, and he didn't question her opinions even when it came to his own clothes. Subtly she influenced him in matters of style and discrimination, and he valued her advice.

Jason knew how other men envied him for his wife, and he took pride in her accomplishments. Laura co-sponsored charitable functions for the benefit of the poor and was a member of the Ladies' Christian Association. Her leisure pursuits were all proper and respectable: attending lectures, going to the theater, and encouraging the arts in Boston. Everyone agreed she was a quiet but charming woman, a model of self-restraint. Not for a minute did Jason regret marrying her. But that did not make her contempt for him any easier to bear.

He remembered the day he had approached Cyril Prescott for Laura's hand in marriage. In spite of their distinguished name, the Prescotts' fortune was dwindling. Such "first families" sometimes found it necessary to sacrifice one of their daughters to the vulgar newly monied class. Marrying Laura had not been as difficult as Jason had expected. It had boiled down to a matter of money, and he had been easily able to meet Cyril Prescott's asking price. "I would not consent to this," Cyril had said, looking both indignant and shamefaced, "if I thought you would prove to be an unworthy husband to my daughter. But you appear to hold her in high regard. And there is obviously no question that you will provide well for her."

"She'll have everything she wants," Jason replied smoothly, concealing his triumph at finally obtaining the woman he had wanted for so many years. Afterward he had proposed to Laura in a businesslike manner, informing her of the decision that had already been made between him and her father. They never had a courtship—

Jason had felt it would be unwise to give her an opportunity to spurn him, which she most certainly would have done. Instead he had maneuvered the situation so that she had no choice but to accept him as her husband. He knew there was no other way he could have had her. She was desired by every eligible man in Boston. Had it not been for him, she would have become the wife of a gentleman with blood as blue as her own.

In time, Jason had thought, she would learn to accept him . . . and then perhaps he could begin to reveal his feelings for her. Unfortunately he had not anticipated how repelled she would be by his touch. She had such obvious disgust for her socially inferior husband that, God help him, he—who had always been so self-contained—couldn't seem to stop himself from losing his temper around her.

Keeping her head down, Laura strode rapidly along the hallway, her only thought being to escape. A short distance away was the large music room, which also doubled as a ballroom. The crowd of guests indulged in light conversation and danced to the buoyant waltz being played by the orchestra. Oblivious to the music and laughter, Laura made her way through the entrance hall to the front door and slipped outside. The November air was damp as it bit through her brocaded satin gown. She shuddered in misery and wrapped her arms around her middle, staring out at the dimly lit street where lacquered broughams and liveried drivers waited for the guests to depart.

Drawing herself into the porch shadows of the fashionable six-story Beacon Street home, Laura wondered what she was going to do. It was obvious that Jason hated her. She could not face him anymore. She was a failure as a wife, as a woman. Tears welled up in her eyes, and she willed herself not to cry. Good Lord, what if someone saw her out here, weeping on the steps of her own home?

Suddenly she heard a cheerful whistle on the street. Anxiously she stared into the darkness. "H-hale?" she cried. "Hale, is that you?"

Her brother's gentle laugh drifted to her. "Hmmm . . . why, yes, I believe it is. Have I crossed the line between fashionably late and too, too late?"

Laura gave a watery chuckle. "As always."

"Ah, you'll forgive me," Hale said, and leaped up the stairs with his customary vigor. "Have you been waiting for me? Damn, you're out here in that thin dress! How long—" He broke off as he took her face in his gloved hands and tilted it up.

Tears spilled from Laura's eyes, and she gripped his wrists tightly. "I'm glad you're here, Hale," she choked out.

"Laura, sweetheart." Alarmed, Hale pulled her head against the front of his wool coat. "My God, what's the matter?"

"I can't tell you."

"Oh, you can and you will. But not here." He ruffled her hair, carelessly disarranging her coiled chignon. "We'll go inside and have a talk."

Laura shook her head. "People . . . people will see—"

"We'll walk around the house and come in through the kitchen." Hale shrugged out of his coat and draped it over her narrow shoulders. "It has something to do with Jason, doesn't it?"

Her throat closed painfully, and she nodded. Without another word Hale put his arm around her waist and guided her down the steps, shielding her from the view of the drivers and passersby. By the time they reached the kitchen, which opened onto the backyard, Laura was shivering violently. The heat and light of the kitchen engulfed her, but they did not take away her numbness.

"Why, Mrs. Moran," she heard the housekeeper's voice exclaim.

Hale favored the older woman with an appealing smile. He had matured into a handsome and solidly built man with green eyes, rich brown hair, and a thick slash of a mustache. His openhearted manner charmed all women. "Mrs. Ramsey, I'm afraid my sister has the vapors," he said. "Could you find a way to inform Mr. Moran— discreetly, mind you—that she has retired for the evening?"

"Certainly, Mr. Prescott."

The vapors, Laura thought wryly. Well, it would work. The excuse was always accepted with quiet understanding. Because of the spoonbill corsets and heavy hairclotb bustles worn under their gowns, women often experienced dizziness and fainting spells. In fact, such episodes were considered proof of a lady's refinement.

"Oh," Hale added as he guided Laura out of the kitchen toward the stairs, "and would you have two toddies brought to the upstairs sitting room, Mrs. Ramsey?"

"Yes, Mr. Prescott."

Laura handed the coat back to Hale, and they began to climb the three flights of stairs to the sitting room. "You probably don't even know what the vapors are," she said with a sniffle.

He laughed. "No, and I really have no desire to find out."

They reached the sitting room. It was Laura's private place. No one intruded, not even Jason, unless she invited them. Like the other rooms in the house, it was comfortable and elegant, with a flowered Persian rug, velvet drapes, plush chairs, tiny polished tables covered with lace and ornaments, and a marble fireplace. Laura had chosen the carefully blended styles of furnishings for the entire house, all matters of taste being left to her discretion. Jason preferred it that way.

"Now," Hale said, sinking to his haunches in front of the fireplace, "tell me everything while I stir up the fire."

Laura gathered up the fringed train of her evening dress and sat in a nearby chair. Morosely she kicked off her damp satin slippers with their two-inch heels and tiny diamond buckles. It pleased Jason for his wife to be dressed in the finest of garments. "I don't know what to tell you," she said. "Jason would be furious if he knew—"

"Tell me everything," Hale repeated patiently, glancing at her over his shoulder. "Remember, I was Jason's closest friend until you married."

"Yes, I remember." Laura's mind turned back to all the holidays Jason had spent with her family. Although he and Hale had been in the same class at Harvard, Jason was two years older. He had never made pretensions about his background. His father had been a grocer, and his mother had peddled a fish cart.

It was highly unusual for someone of Jason's humble beginnings to have climbed as high as he already had. But Jason was intelligent, hardworking, and ruthlessly charming when he wished to be. Something in his voice and the way he moved proclaimed he was a man who knew exactly what he wanted—and what he wanted, he would get. And when he smiled, he was the most handsome man on earth.

"Laura, what's wrong?" Hale asked.

"Everything. It's been wrong since the beginning." She peeled her gloves off and wiped her stinging eyes. "Jason has no idea how overwhelming he is. I don't know how to please him, and when I try I fail miserably. I—I think something is wrong with me. Whenever we try to . . . be intimate, I don't do whatever it is he expects me to do, and—''

"Laura, wait." Hale cleared his throat uncomfortably, his cheekbones tinged with red. "If you're referring to the sort of thing that goes on in the bedroom, I think you had better discuss it with a woman."

Laura thought of her prudish mother and her straight-laced sisters. "Who do you suggest?" she asked.

Hale groaned and clutched his head in his hands, looking down at the flowered carpet. "All right," he said in a muffled voice. "Tell me. But keep in mind that a fellow doesn't like to hear about his sister and . . . that."

She shook her head. "There is nothing to tell you." After a brief pause, she repeated meaningfully, "Nothing."

Hale's astonished green eyes met hers. "Are you trying to tell me . . . my God . . . that you and Jason have never . . . *never*?"

"No," Laura said, embarrassed but strangely relieved to be telling someone.

Hale opened and closed his mouth several times before he could form another word. "Why not?" he finally managed to ask.

She held her head in her hands much as he had a moment before, while her words burst out in a swift torrent. "Jason has approached me a few times, but I—I make him so angry. The last time we argued he accused me of being cold, a-and I suppose I must be, but I can't seem to help myself! I thought that as time passed we might come to some kind of understanding, but things only worsened. He spends his days at his business offices, and he dines at his club, and whenever he is in the house we avoid meeting in the same room! There's not the least bit of trust or friendliness between us. The best we've been able to manage is politeness, but now even that seems to be beyond us."

"I see," Hale said, sounding strange. He stroked his mustache and shook his head.

"And tonight," Laura continued, "I was in the library with Perry Whitton, who kissed me—"

"He *what*?" Hale gave her a disapproving glance.

"Perry and I are friends, nothing more."

"All the same, Laura, you shouldn't have allowed it."

"It happened too quickly for me to say or do anything! And of course Jason walked in and misinterpreted the situation, and said that I must be ashamed of being the wife of a shanty mick . . . and I don't even know what that is!"

"That's what they call an Irishman, one from a peasant family so poor that even the women have to work." Hale sighed heavily. "A mick, a blackleg, a greenhorn. A few of the fellows at Harvard didn't give a damn about his being Irish, but most of them did. Jason was excluded and subtly insulted at almost every turn. After all, his background was the same as that of their servants. You know how they can be." He made a face. "Frankly, I can't blame Jason for being upset if he saw you with Perry Whitton. He is the epitome of all Jason could never be, a gentleman with the right name, the right family, the right upbringing."

Laura nodded in understanding. Boston society was fastidious about every entry in a family's genealogy. Change was regarded with suspicion, and everything depended upon who one's grandfather had happened to be. It was considered vulgar to work hard or make much money. The ideal Bostonian man was genteel, dignified, and intellectual. Someone like Jason, ambitious and driven, a self-made man, was a shock to the more refined Bostonians such as the Whittons.

"Hale," she said fervently, "if I had wanted a man of Perry's ilk, I wouldn't have married Jason. How can

I make him understand that?''

"I don't know." Her brother looked guilty. "It won't be easy to convince him. Your entire family disapproves of his heritage. We all know that Father only consented to the betrothal because of the extraordinary amount of money Jason's made in real estate. And I . . . well, I told Jason at the beginning that I was against the marriage because he's Irish.''

"Y-you couldn't have!" Laura exclaimed, horrified. "Hale, you don't really feel that way!"

"Oh, yes." He nodded stubbornly. "I explained to Jason that I valued him as a friend, but I couldn't approve of him marrying one of my sisters. Especially not you. I knew how difficult it would be for you, never quite belonging in one world or the other. I had known for a long time that Jason wanted to marry someone with a name, someone who could gain him entry into our circles. And—hell, I'll be frank—he comes from crude beginnings, Laura.''

"That doesn't matter to me," Laura said, and cleared her throat awkwardly. "It has never mattered to me that Jason is Irish.''

The maid knocked at the door and brought in their toddies on a small silver tray. Laura took the tray from her and dismissed her with a wan smile of thanks. She gave Hale his drink and sipped slowly on hers, welcoming its bracing effects.

"Well," Hale said, "let's address this business about this 'coldness' of yours. I'll wager some of this is Mother's influence.''

"Hale, I can't blame her for—"

"Don't defend her, sweetheart. She raised all three of her daughters to believe that it is natural for a husband and wife to live as strangers. For years I knew about the ridiculous things she told you and Anne and Sophia, but it wasn't my place to contradict her." He sighed and regarded her sympathetically. "These matters are not complicated, Laura. It's very simple. All you have to do is show Jason that you're willing to accept his attentions, and he will take care of the rest of it. He is an experienced man. Just allow him to . . ." He stopped and began fiddling uneasily with the silk fringe of the brocaded chair. "He wouldn't be cruel to you, Laura, not in that way."

She clasped her hands together tightly. "I wish I could believe that. But I don't know what to think about him anymore. I find myself wondering why I married him."

"Well, why did you?" Hale demanded.

"Father wanted me to, and it was a help to the family."

"Father and the family be damned! You know he wouldn't have forced you to marry Jason. The wedding would never have taken place had you uttered one word of objection."

Laura bit her lip and nodded, ashamed. "Yes, you're right. I . . . the truth is, I was more than willing. I wanted to be a wife to Jason." She drew her legs up and tucked them beneath her. "Jason thinks he doesn't need anything from anyone. But I knew the first moment I met him that he needed someone like me, to help and comfort him, to bring some warmth into his life. I was so certain I could soften him, and bring out another side of him." She laughed shakily. "And instead he seems to be changing me into something I never wanted to be."

It was three hours later when Hale made his way downstairs and discovered that the last of the guests had departed. Sliding his hands in his pockets, he ambled through the ballroom, where the musicians were packing their instruments.

"Was it a success?" Hale inquired of the young lank-haired violinist.

"Quite lively for your kind of crowd," came the cheerful reply.

Hale grinned and wandered past a pair of Irish maids carrying trays of empty glasses. "Pardon, miss," he inquired of one of them, "where might Mr. Moran be? Retired for the evening? No? Ah, drinking in the library. I'm not surprised. Mr. Moran does have a taste for whiskey, doesn't he?"

Jason was sitting in a chair before the fire, holding a bottle of liquor loosely in his hand. His legs were stretched out, his head resting against the brocaded upholstery. His black evening coat had been discarded, while the sleeves of his starched white shirt were rolled up to the elbows. His eyes were half-slitted as he stared into the flames, while the firelight played over his raven hair. He did not move as Hale walked into the room and closed the door.

"*Usquebaugh*," Hale said, using a Gaelic word Jason had once taught him. He gestured casually toward the whisky. "You micks call it the water of life, don't you?"

"Go to hell."

"Very likely." Hale dragged up a heavy chair with his foot and collapsed into it. "First, however, I'm going to have a talk with you."

"If you're half-witted enough to think I'm going to listen—"

"I believe I'll begin with a few observations." Green eyes met black, and they exchanged a long glance, the glance of adversaries who knew each other's secrets. "So far everything has gone according to your plan, hasn't it?" Hale said. "Remember telling me about the plan years ago? Remember what you said?"

Jason arched a black eyebrow. "I said that by the time I was twenty-five I would have graduated from Harvard with honors."

"And established yourself in the Boston business community."

"Yes."

"And married a girl whose name would allow you into the most elite social circles."

"Yes."

Hale smiled ironically. "At the time, although I admired your ambition, I didn't believe you could do it. But you've accomplished all that. You married my own sister. You're being referred to in Boston as 'that damned Irish tycoon,' and by the time you reach thirty, you'll have multiplied your fortune several times over." He leaned forward, losing some of his flippancy as he demanded, "What, then, is the cause for bitterness? Why are you behaving like such a bastard to Laura, when you have everything you ever wanted out of life?"

Jason swished the whisky in the bottle and stared into its swirling contents. He was tempted to confide in Hale, but he could not let go of the grudge between them.

"Don't answer, then," Hale said. "I already know why."

Jason's eyes gleamed dangerously. "You've always known all the answers, haven't you? A Prescott's prerogative."

Hale shrugged.

Jason extended the whisky bottle with a scowl, and Hale took a drink without hesitation. "You've been talking with Laura," Jason said.

"Yes, and she's owned up to a few things I've been suspecting for some time."

"It's a dangerous game, prying into matters that have nothing to do with you."

"Nothing to do with me?" Hale exclaimed, his temper sparking. "Laura is my sister, my *favorite* sister, and you're making her miserable! Of all the girls in Boston you could have married and made miserable, why did it have to be her?''

Jason rested his forearms on his knees, a shock of black hair falling over his forehead. He answered slowly, watching the fire with a brooding gaze. ''There weren't all that many girls to choose from. It had to be someone with a name, and someone with the qualities I wanted in a wife. And most of all it had to be someone whose family was in financial straits and had need of a rich son-in-law.''

''So when it came time to marry, you cast your eyes around and there was my youngest sister—''

''I decided to marry Laura the first Christmas I spent with your family.''

Hale frowned, the ends of his mustache curving downward. ''That long ago?''

''Yes. Laura was only fifteen. When the family sat down to dinner I nearly made some excuse and left. I would rather have faced a firing line than confront that endless row of spoons and forks at each plate. I didn't know which one to pick up first, or how to eat the damned asparagus. And there was your mother, watching every move I made like a hawk. But Laura was slower and more painstaking than everyone else, and I was able to imitate everything she did. Halfway through the meal I realized she knew I was aping her. She was being slow and precise in order to make it easier for me.''

''Hell, *I* never bothered with Mother's blasted rows of forks.''

''You didn't have to,'' Jason said flatly. ''You had nothing to prove.''

''And so you decided to marry Laura because she helped you get through a meal?''

''Because I knew she would be the kind of wife I needed.''

Laura had said much the same thing. Hale set down

the bottle of whisky and stood up, glaring at his former friend. "Ah. A housekeeper. A social companion. A teacher of etiquette. A pretty ornament to impress the hoi polloi. There were other girls you could have married if that was all you wanted. Laura has more to give than that, and she deserves more than to spend the rest of her life trying to make you into a gentleman."

Jason smiled nastily. "You think she's too good for an Irishman?"

"Not at all. I think she's too good for *you*."

Retrieving the whisky bottle, Jason gestured toward the door. "Understood. Now get the hell out of here."

Hale paced around the room in frustration. "I've never seen Laura as high-strung and nervous as she was tonight. You're crushing all the fire and spirit out of her."

Jason stood up to face him. "*Fire* and *spirit*," he repeated sarcastically, thinking of his pale, poised wife, "are not words I would apply to your sister, Hale."

"Oh? Now I'm beginning to understand how little you really know her. She's the most adventurous, free-spirited girl I've ever . . . why, once on a dare she sneaked into Father's room and cut off half his mustache while he was sleeping. She loves swimming and skating and riding. She's a crack shot, a first-rate pianist, an excellent dancer. She's always dreamed of going to Egypt and seeing the pyramids, and traveling up the Nile in a *dahabeah*—"

"A what?"

"*Dahabeah*. One of those long boats."

Jason stared at him with narrowed eyes. "Hale, I don't know who the hell you're talking about, but it isn't my wife."

"It damn well is! And there's something else you should hear—"

"I've heard enough."

"Falling-out or not, I should have talked to you before

the wedding about Laura. This notion you both seem to have—this supposed coldness of hers—''

"Out," Jason said tersely, herding him toward the door.

Hale talked rapidly. "Dammit, Jason, you obviously haven't realized how sheltered she's been. My other two sisters had a devil of a time adjusting to marriage after the way they'd been reared. If Mother were a Catholic, she'd consider the *convent* too permissive for her daughters. Most girls have opportunities to flirt and hold hands with men, enjoy a stolen kiss or two. My sisters had none of that. As you know, Jason, I have a great deal of respect for my mother—but there's no denying that she's a bitter woman. My father has been unfaithful to her, not once but many times. My parents' marriage went sour long before Laura was even born. Laura's been brought up with some mistaken ideas about men and women, and by God, you've probably confirmed every last one of them! All because you seem to expect her to hop into your arms like some barmaid!"

"The lecture is over," Jason snapped, kicking the door open with the side of his foot.

"*Listen*, damn you! Before she married you, Laura had never been alone with a man before, not for a minute. She's not cold, she's an innocent, a complete innocent who doesn't even know how to kiss. She's always been shy around men, especially those with a tendency to be overbearing. And all you do, all you've *ever* done, is frighten and accuse her! How is she supposed to be responsive to you?"

Jason's hands dropped to his sides, and his black eyes fastened onto Hale's agitated face.

"If you treat her with just a little patience or kindness you might be able to make her happy," Hale said in a cutting voice. "I've seen you with women. I've seen you seduce the most hard-hearted of them inside of a quarter hour. But for some reason all your renowned charm seems to vanish when it comes to Laura.'' He tugged his own sleeves down and straightened his coat lapels. ''You've been married for two months, and so far all you've done is build a mountain of misunderstandings. You and I may no longer be friends, Jason, but for Laura's sake and your own, I hope you give some thought to what I've said.'' Turning away, Hale walked to the front hall, snatched up his greatcoat, and left without a backward glance.

Jason stared after him, his brows drawn together in a frown. Slowly he went to the stairs and sat down, raking his hands through his disheveled hair. He thought of his wife in bed, clad in one of her demure white gowns, her long hair braided loosely, her skin flushed with sleep. He had gone in there countless nights to watch her while she slept, being careful never to awaken her. The sight of her never failed to arouse him unbearably.

When Laura was awake, however, her green eyes seemed to say what everyone else did, that Jason was unworthy of her, that Cyril Prescott's daughter should never have married so far beneath her. But . . . what if that expression in her eyes was not disdain? What if it was something else entirely? Was it possible that he had made his own wife afraid of him?

Cursing, Jason thought over the past weeks and counted the scant number of times he had been gentle with Laura—God, no, he had been too busy dwelling on her resentment of him. As much as Jason hated to admit it, Hale had been right about something. There were misunderstandings that had to be cleared away, for both their sakes.

Laura's cup rattled in its saucer as Jason's broad shoulders filled the doorway of the breakfast room. Hastily she set the saucer down and lowered her gaze to the linen tablecloth. The silence was agonizing. Should she say something? Something accusing, something appeasing. Words of forgiveness? . . . reproach? Perhaps—

"Laura."

His voice was quiet and serious. Blankly she looked up at him, her eyes shadowed from a sleepless night.

Jason was struck by how young she looked, silhouetted against the white lace curtains at the window. Her chestnut hair was pulled into a coiled braid at the nape of her neck and tied with velvet ribbons. The pointed basque of her chocolate-brown dress was buttoned high up to her throat, the sleeves long and puffed at the tops. In spite of the strain evident on her delicate features, she was as lovely as always.

Jason could not stop his gaze from flickering to the curve of her breasts molded beneath the tight-fitting bodice, and the flash of white throat above the tiny lace collar. Quickly he looked away before she could read his overwhelming desire. He wanted her desperately. It would have been a simple matter to find release with another woman, but Laura was the only one he wanted. Perhaps, he thought cynically, it was a just punishment for his past sins, being married to a woman who was revolted by his touch.

"Jason," Laura said, gathering up her courage. "After last night, I—"

"No," he interrupted. "Let me speak first."

She fell silent in confusion. There was an expression on Jason's face she had never seen before, earnest and uncomfortable. The way his eyes searched hers caused a wave of heat to rise from her neck to her face.

"I'm sorry for what I said—and did—last night," Jason said in a low voice. "I was angry. I wanted to hurt you."

Unconsciously she raised her fingers to her throat. "You did," she replied softly.

"It will not happen again."

Laura had never been so surprised, not even the day he had proposed to her. She heard herself murmuring something, but the voice did not seem to belong to her. "This is the f-first time you've ever apologized to me."

Jason smiled at that, his eyes alight with self-mockery. "It may be the first time I've ever apologized to anyone. I've always thought of it as a sign of weakness I couldn't afford."

Laura did not know if she was more relieved or astonished by his oddly agreeable manner. "Will you have some breakfast?" she asked, trying to hide her nervousness.

"No." Jason ventured further into the room, lean and handsome in his tailored black coat, gray trousers, and quietly patterned vest. As he came close to her, she rose from her chair and backed away a step or two. He appeared not to notice her involuntary movement. "I have a great deal of business to attend to this morning," he said. "And I'll be home late tonight." A brief hesitation followed before he added, "I thought that tomorrow morning we would leave to spend the rest of the week at your sister's home in Brookline."

"Brookline? But your work—"

"The world won't come to an end if I stop working for a few days."

Laura was astounded. For as long as she had known him, Jason had been obsessed with his work. "We have never accepted Sophia's invitations before," she said. "Why would you want to spend time with my family when you've made it clear—"

"Yes, I know what I've made clear—and what I haven't." He took another step toward her, and she skittered back once more. "Laura," he said gently, capturing her wrist with ease. He held her hand so lightly that she could have pulled away with little effort. "If you would rather not go to Brookline . . .''

"Oh, no, I—I think it would be a fine idea."

His thumb slipped into her palm and lingered in the soft hollow, and she felt the sensation of his caress all the way down to her knees.

"Good," he murmured.

They were standing close enough for her to detect the scent of his cologne. She felt him looking down at her, and in vain she waited for him to release her hand. But he waited patiently as well, making no move to let go. After long seconds dragged by she raised her head.

"You haven't said you'll forgive me," he remarked.

"I—I do."

His thumb still played idly in her palm, and she knew that he could not help but be aware of her agitation. Slowly, easily, his free arm slid around her. Laura endured the closeness for a few seconds before a natural reflex caused her to break free of him with a sound of protest. Horrified, she retreated to the side of the room, certain he would jeer at her. She waited for a rebuke that never came. Instead there was silence.

Jason approached her with the smoothness of a panther, not stopping until she was flattened against the wall and he was just inches away. He rested one forearm over her head, his body looming over hers. For an instant she recalled how it had felt to be crushed against that hard body.

"Laura . . ." His voice was husky. His hand slid to the back of her neck and tilted her face toward him. "In the past two months you've guided me in many things. And in spite of my display last night, you've even managed to teach me a few manners. But now . . ." Before she could move, he brushed his lips across her forehead. "Now there are some things I'd like to teach you."

Nervous chills ran down Laura's spine. She could not deny him. It was a wife's duty to submit to her husband's embrace, no matter how much she dreaded the prospect. "Whatever you wish," she said emotionlessly, her nerves writhing in turmoil.

A smile pulled the corner of his lips at her dutiful answer. "What I wish for is a kiss from my wife."

Laura searched his midnight eyes for mockery, and found an oddly challenging gleam. He expected her to refuse, she thought. She would show him that she was not afraid of him. Only a kiss . . . it was not such a dreadful request.

She held her breath and summoned all her courage, standing on her toes to accomodate the difference in their heights. Gingerly she pressed her lips to his, her palms falling to his shoulders for balance. To her surprise, the closeness was not unpleasant. His mouth was warm against hers, his shoulders hard and steady underneath her hands. He did not crush her in his arms or frighten her as he had so many times before.

Red-faced and trembling, she ended the kiss and sank to her heels, beginning to breathe again. But it appeared Jason was not through with her. His dark head bent, and his lips drifted over her temple, the curve of her cheek, the tiny hollow behind her earlobe. Laura's hands clenched into fists against his shoulders.

He slid his hands over her silky hair, pushing her head back. He took his time with her, noting that although she was not responding to him, she was not rejecting him either. Gently he brushed her lips with his own. She kissed like a child, her mouth innocently closed. Jason realized that the sexual urges so familiar to him were only just awakening in her.

The tip of his tongue traced her lower lip, lingering at the center. Laura jerked away from him in surprise, touching her fingers to the damp surface. Why had he done that? Was it wrong for her to allow it?

Jason's eyes held her in a dark, velvet prison. Carefully

he pulled her back against his body. "It's all right," he murmured, his breath mingling with hers. "It's all right, Laura . . . did I frighten you?"

"No," she said faintly.

He smoothed her hair and kissed her temple, careful to keep every movement slow and gentle. "Would you put your arms around my neck?"

She hesitated and then obeyed, her breasts resting against his chest. The warmth of his hands cupped her jaws, holding her head still, and his lips teased hers with fleeting touches. "Kiss me back," he whispered.

Laura felt light-headed, her fear dissolving in a wave of slow, sensual curiosity. She relaxed in his arms, her lips no longer closed so firmly, accepting the gently playful mouth that moved over hers. The tip of his tongue ventured further and further, probing until she opened her mouth with a gasp. She felt his tongue begin a languid search for hers, stroking deep in a way she had never dreamed of.

Eventually he lifted his mouth, and she realized dazedly that she did not want the kiss to end. She rested her head on his shoulder, soothed by the long, repeated strokes of his hand along her spine. His palms pressed her buttocks and hips forward until there was not an inch of space between their bodies. They were separated by the thick layers of her skirts and petticoats, but even so she could feel the hard ridge of his loins.

Jason held her close between his thighs, allowing her to become accustomed to the feel of a man's body. His lips wandered over her moist forehead, while the uneven gusts of her breath against his neck caused his manhood to swell even more blatantly. He felt her trembling as he fondled the downy nape of her neck. "Afraid?" he asked.

"I . . . I don't know."

"There's nothing to be afraid of." He rubbed his lips

over hers in a roughly teasing caress. When she did not respond, he raised his head and looked at her questioningly.

Her eyes were luminous and turquoise-green, while her kiss-reddened lips were softer and fuller than usual. Wonderingly she lifted her hand to smooth back the hair that had fallen over his forehead.

Suddenly they were interrupted by the opening of the door to the kitchen. It was Phoebe, a housemaid who had been in the Prescott's employ for nearly ten years. Phoebe's round face turned the color of raspberries, and her mouth fell open at the sight of husband and wife clasped together in the breakfast room. "Oh, my. Ex-excuse me," she exclaimed in horror, and disappeared behind the door.

Laura tried to smooth her hair and dress, while her skin burned with embarrassment.

"We are married," Jason reminded her dryly, tightening his arms around her back.

"You should let me go—"

"Not yet. Is it so unpleasant to be held by me?"

"I would not like anyone else t-to break in upon us again." She closed her eyes as she felt him nuzzling her ear.

"If you would prefer some privacy," he said in a soft voice that raised every hair on the back of her neck, "we could go upstairs."

She tried to pull away from him. "I—I have many things to do today if we are to leave for Brookline so soon. I do think you should let me go—"

"Then go, if you're so damned eager to fly out of my arms." He released her with a slight scowl. But his tone was far more gentle than usual, and she felt his gaze caressing her as she turned away. "Laura."

She stopped without looking at him. "Yes?"

"I am not going to force you to do anything," he said

quietly. "I have wanted you for a long time, and I haven't yet forced you."

He was more overwhelming in his gentleness than he had ever been in anger. Laura was astonished by the feelings that swept over her: the desire to walk back to him and press herself against his body, to slide her fingers through his coal-black hair, to feel his mouth on hers again. She left the room quickly, her heart pounding with the knowledge that in less than a few minutes her husband had turned her entire world upside down.

2

A FRESH SNOW HAD COVERED THE GROUND, GIVING THE rebuilt farmhouse a picturesque appearance. As the driver opened the door of the double brougham, a burst of icy air swept away Laura's pleasant lethargy. The drive from Boston with Jason had been surprisingly enjoyable. In response to her questions, he had talked to her about his construction enterprise in the Back Bay, an apartment building of twenty-five flats complete with elevators and steam heating.

"I would like to see it," Laura had remarked, and he regarded her with a skeptical smile.

"I'll take you there when we return."

Laura nodded in assent, while her insides quivered in

delight. Jason had never been so nice to her. She began to think that the next few days might not be as harrowing as she had feared. Since their marriage, they had never spent longer than an afternoon with her family. When any of the Prescotts were near, Jason was quiet and abrupt, his manner challenging. The Prescotts, in turn, were stiff and polite. Laura always felt caught between two opposing forces, and she was miserable when they were all together. But if everyone made an effort to be pleasant, it might pave the way for future gatherings.

Jason stepped out of the carriage and reached up for her, catching her around the waist. Laura pulled her hands from her tiny fur muff and grasped his shoulders. He swung her down without letting her feet touch the portable steps.

"Thank you," she said with a breathless laugh.

His dark eyes studied hers, and he smiled ruefully. "A house full of Prescotts," he said, keeping his hands on her waist. "I feel as if I'm about to brave a lion's den."

"You got on well enough with them before we were married," Laura pointed out.

Suddenly he grinned. "Yes, until I made you a Moran." Still holding her, he looked over her head at the large house, surrounding fields, and wooded copses. Well in the distance was the outline of the Boston State House dome, and the tall buildings near it.

The Prescotts often gathered at Sophia's Brookline home during the winter. The firstborn of Cyril Prescott's children, Sophia was a plain but sociable woman. She had a talent for entertaining, and it was universally agreed that Sophia was one of the most accomplished hostesses in Boston. Her husband, Judge T. Horace Marsh, was a rather stiff-necked blue blood, but Sophia's influence had caused him to soften during the past few years.

Sophia was one of the rare breed of Bostonian women

who liked to dispense with unnecessary formality. In her home the younger people were allowed the free use of first names, a custom which irked the older generations. No one was allowed to remain a stranger in the Marshes' gatherings. They were all cajoled into joining the constant rounds of whist and backgammon, sleigh rides and dancing parties.

Sophia appeared on the landing of the outside steps, her lips curved in a welcoming smile. She was clad in a stylish winter dress of gray cashmere and garnet velvet. "My dears, how wonderful to have you here at last," she said, pressing Jason's hand between hers, then embracing Laura. "Come inside at once. We have a splendid fire, and hot tea for the ladies, and something stronger for the gentlemen. Anne and Howard are here, and so are the Warrens—oh, and Jason, you'll be pleased to learn that Hale arrived not an hour ago." Sophia inclined her head toward them confidentially. "I believe Hale is seriously thinking of courting the Warrens' daughter Prudence. I told him that the two of you might not be averse to chaperoning them on the sleigh ride this afternoon."

Laura and Jason exchanged a questioning glance, and Jason replied while holding his wife's gaze. "Of course I'll chaperon Hale," he said, a little too nicely. Laura suppressed a laugh, pitying her brother.

Jason guided her into the house with his arm at her back, pulling her to the side as the servants moved past them to carry their trunks upstairs. Slowly Jason untied the laces of Laura's velvet-trimmed mantle. She was unable to look at him as she felt his fingers at her throat.

Jason handed the garment to the waiting arms of a maid, and glanced over Laura's head to his sister-in-law. "I wouldn't mind a glass of the 'something stronger' you mentioned, Sophia."

"I suggest you join Hale and the other men in the parlor," Sophia replied. "They are congregated around a bowl of hot punch, discussing whatever it is men discuss amongst themselves.'' She slipped an arm around Laura's shoulders and smiled. ''We sisters must confer with Cook about the dinner preparations.''

Jason's black eyes glinted with amusement. ''Certainly,'' he said, and although his voice was bland, it was obvious he knew they were planning to gossip.

Together Sophia and Laura watched his broad-shouldered form as he left, then they wandered toward the kitchen. ''Now, out with it,'' Sophia said. ''How did you manage to drag Jason here?''

''It was his decision,'' Laura replied. ''No one is more surprised than I.''

''Hale confided to me that he had a talk with Jason, but he would not reveal what was said between them.''

Laura frowned darkly. ''I will not have Hale interfering in my marriage, no matter how well-intentioned he is. I will speak to him about it.''

''Oh, don't be cross with him! You know how Hale adores you. He cannot bear to see you unhappy.'' Sophia peered at her younger sister. ''*Are* you unhappy? Jason is not being unkind to you, is he?''

''Not at all.'' Laura folded her arms in a stubborn gesture.

''Hmmm. The two of you look well enough. And Jason is as wickedly handsome as ever. If it were not for his regrettable background, he would have been the prize catch of Boston.'' With studied casualness, Sophia added, ''But of course there will always be those who say you must be pitied for marrying a shanty-born Irishman. No one would blame you for feeling ashamed.''

''Why should I be ashamed of a man who has lifted himself from poverty to prosperity? Jason has had to fight for everything he's ever had. Nothing has been given to him. Nothing has been easy for him. He is a man of intelligence and strength. I'm *not* ashamed of him, yet for some reason Jason finds that as difficult to believe as everyone else!''

There was a gleam of satisfaction in Sophia's eyes. ''Then you must persist until you do convince him. It is a woman's duty to make the best of her lot, Laura. And there are *certain things* a wife owes to her husband.''

Laura turned red up to her hairline at Sophia's delicate emphasis on 'certain things.' ''Hale told you everything, didn't he?'' she asked, feeling betrayed.

''I won't deny it.''

''I should have known I couldn't trust him to keep my confidence.''

''Hale felt you would benefit from the advice of an older sister,'' Sophia said implacably. ''You and Anne and I were not given an adequate education in how to be good wives. We learned all of the practical things and none of the truly necessary things. We never learned about trust and affection, and most of all loyalty. Father's philandering embittered Mother years ago. She never wished for her daughters to risk the danger of loving a man and perhaps being hurt by him.''

Laura regarded her speculatively. ''I wouldn't have expected such frankness from you, Sophia.''

''I have discovered many things in the past few years. I have learned to love my Horace, and not to withhold myself from him.'' She raised her eyebrows slightly. ''I suspect that Jason has not been the shining example of a devoted husband. But a good wife could make him into a good husband. *If* he's as intelligent as you claim. And the best revenge, my dear, against those who would mock or pity you for your common red-blooded husband, is simply to be happy.''

What seemed to be at least a dozen children ran and cavorted around the four sleighs lined up in front of the house. Some of them were Sophia's offspring, others belonged to the Warrens, and the remainder were distant Prescott cousins. Laura stopped at the top of the circular steps with Prudence Warren, a vivacious and friendly girl she had met once or twice before.

"How lovely the sleighs are," Prudence exclaimed, and Laura agreed. Each vehicle with its shiny black runners was pulled by two horses with festive tassels and bells affixed to their harnesses. A driver in a top hat sat at the front of each sleigh. Laughing young men and women were piling into the sleighs and covering themselves with wool and fur blankets, while others were helping the children clamber aboard.

"Now I can believe Christmas is only three weeks away," Prudence said.

Laura looked at her with a faint smile. "Are you and my brother planning to exchange gifts?" she could not resist asking.

"That depends on Hale," Prudence said airily. "If he gives me something proper and acceptable—candy or a book are all Mama will allow—then I shall give him something in return."

The two of them watched as Hale stomped toward the last sleigh with two giggling children under his arms, loudly demanding that someone relieve him of his burden. Jason walked around to him, reached for the children one at a time, and settled them into the vehicle. The little boy reached for the ends of Hale's mustache and refused to let go, causing Jason to laugh. The scene reminded Laura of the days when her husband and brother had been close friends, and she smiled wistfully. It was good to see them being civil to each other. She could not help but hope that they might someday regain their closeness.

"Your husband is quite charming," Prudence said, following her gaze. "And good with the children."

He was, Laura saw with a touch of surprise. Expertly Jason separated a pair of quarreling siblings, rescued a tot who was wandering close to the horses' hooves, and carried a little boy on his back from one sleigh to another. While Jason organized the group and conferred with the drivers, Hale bounded up the circular steps to Laura and Prudence.

"Laura, sweetheart," he said cheerfully, grasping her small gloved hands.

Remembering the way he had confided her private affairs to her sister, Laura pulled her hands from his and gave him a frosty glare. "I've had a revealing talk with Sophia," she said.

He looked sheepish, but didn't bother to pretend he didn't understand. "I'm sorry."

"I didn't give you permission to tell anyone about Jason and me."

"Sophia hit upon it with some damned clever guesses, and hang it, I couldn't lie to her."

"You could have said nothing," Laura said coolly.

"But with Sophia that's the same as admitting everything! Sweetheart, don't get all ruffled, there's a—"

"I have a right to be ruffled, you traitor." Laura folded her arms over her chest and turned away.

Swearing under his breath, Hale regarded her guiltily and then offered his arm to Prudence.

"Hale, whatever is—" Prudence began, but he interrupted her with a scowl.

"Don't ask, Pru. With three sisters, a fellow's always in one stew or another." He walked Prudence down the steps, while Jason passed by them on the way up.

Jason raised an eyebrow as he looked from Hale's face to Laura's. He smiled at the sight of his wife dressed in a smart sleighing costume of black satin and brocade, and a lynx-trimmed mantle. A tiny black bonnet trimmed with red ribbons and ostrich plumes was perched on her head. Every hair was in place, every ribbon and pleat perfectly arranged. Jason wanted to scoop her up and kiss her right there on the steps.

Laura's glare faded immediately as she saw him. He was especially handsome today, his black hair smoothly brushed, his wool overcoat tailored to his broad-shouldered form. "I was coming to find you," he said, sliding his hands over her ribs, his thumbs resting just underneath her breasts.

She held onto his arms, her green eyes shyly meeting his. "It is quite a large sleighing party," she said.

"Yes, and we're the only married couple of the group. I hope we can keep all of them in order."

"I have no doubt of it." She used her mittened hand to whisk away the snow that clung to his shoulder. "A horde of Prescotts should provide no difficulty for you."

Jason tilted his head and regarded her with a slow, quizzical smile that made her heart turn over. "We'll see if your faith is justified." He kept his arm around her as he helped her down the steps. "We're riding in the last sleigh to keep all the others in sight."

He lifted her into the sleigh and strode to the front of the line of vehicles, where the first driver awaited the signal to go. Slowly the sleighs began to move. Laura sat opposite Hale and Prudence, while Sophia's four children were bundled between them. The youngest, a seven-year-old girl named Millicent, crept into Laura's lap and huddled under the woolen robe.

Jason came to join them, climbing into the empty space beside Laura. Together they arranged the blankets, the child, and their tangled legs, until Laura began to laugh. Finally she was tucked securely against Jason's side, her leg wedged against his muscled thigh, her head near his shoulder. Disregarding Hale and Prudence's interested gazes, she leaned against him.

Millicent sat up in Laura's lap, asking questions about the horses, the trees, and anything else that struck her fancy. Jason answered her patiently, reaching out to tug one of the little girl's long brown curls. The deep murmur of his voice was at once soothing and exciting to Laura, flavored with the hint of a brogue that would never quite disappear. She listened to him and watched the sparkling scenery around them, the frozen ponds and snow-laden birch and pine that lined the sleighs' path.

The group in the lead sleigh began singing, and gradually the tune was picked up by the entire line of vehicles. Laura joined in with the others, smiling at Hale's enthusiastic rendition.

> *Over the river and through the wood,*
> *To grandfather's house we go;*
> *The horse knows the way to carry the sleigh,*
> *Through the white and drifted snow . . .*

Observing Hale and Prudence together, Laura decided her brother was truly smitten with her. She glanced at Jason to see if he had noticed Hale's unusual behavior. Jason read her thoughts exactly. He bent his head and whispered to her. "I expect your father would approve of a match between the Prescotts and the Warrens."

"Not entirely," she whispered back. "The Warrens are rich in respectability but poor in common sense. Their family fortune has shrunk to almost nothing. And Father has always wished for Hale to marry a girl with an impressive dowry."

"Hale could try working." They were both aware that Hale's position at a Boston bank was little more than a sham, designed to protect the Prescotts' interests. The genteel occupation was common among young men of Hale's position in society. It would have been slightly vulgar for him to be seen actively working to accumulate wealth, as if he were one of the immigrant nouveaus.

"A Prescott?" she asked doubtfully.

Jason grinned. "Not easy to imagine, I'll admit."

Hale interrupted them indignantly. "Here now, what are you two whispering about? I feel my ears burning!"

Before Laura could reply, the line of sleighs came to a stop. Jason half-rose from the seat and stared far ahead of them, using a gloved hand to shield his eyes from the glare of the snow. "Looks like a tree limb blocking the path," he said, jumping down. "I'll be back in a moment."

"I'll lend a hand," Hale said, and leapt after him.

Laura and Prudence were left with the curious, excited children. Wilfred, Sophia's small and bespectacled ten-year-old son, gazed at the inviting drifts of snow. "Aunt Laura, can I get out? Just for a minute?"

"I don't think that would be a good idea," she said cautiously. "I'm certain we'll be under way at any moment."

"Just for a minute," Wilfred wheedled, and Millicent took up the plea.

"Aunt Laura, can I go with him? Please, Aunt Laura—"

"I don't think—" Laura began, and Wilfred interrupted.

"Why, the others are all getting out!" the boy said hotly. "And they're . . . why, they're throwing snow b—"

Prudence shrieked as a soft white clump of snow flew past her ear. Suddenly the air was filled with happy shrieks and pelting snowballs. Wilfred leapt out of the sleigh and scampered to a nearby tree, scooping up a handful of fluffy snow on the way.

Laura set Millicent aside and stumbled after the boy. "Wilfred! Children, all of you behave! There is no—" She ducked with a gasp as a snowball came flying toward her and landed on the ground behind her. "Who threw that?" she demanded, trying to sound authoritative. The scene was chaos, men and women ducking and throwing, children screaming with delight.

Laura burst into laughter, running as fast as she was able to the protection of her own tree. Leaning against it, she tore off her mittens and began packing her own snowball. She felt like a little girl again, free and uninhibited.

Jason made his way back to the last sleigh, keeping his head low. The vehicle was empty. He looked around quickly, wondering where the hell his wife had gone. It was certain that she was not participating in this free-for-all—she was probably hiding somewhere until it was over.

"Look here, Moran!" Hale's voice came from far ahead of him, and Jason turned quickly enough to evade a hurtling snowball. Jason returned the fire, hitting Hale squarely in the chest. Hale clutched the white splotch of snow on his coat and keeled over clownishly, causing a multitude of children to yelp happily and fall on top of him.

Jason chuckled and began to stride toward the squirming pile of youngsters. Suddenly he felt a solid *thump* between his shoulder blades. Spinning around in surprise, he saw the flap of a black cloak from behind a tree. His eyebrows drew together. Laura? No, his timid, docile wife would not have dared. Another snowball hurtled toward him, and he avoided it deftly, his eyes narrowed in curiosity. He saw a pair of discarded mittens on the ground. "Laura?" he said, perplexed.

His wife peeked at him from behind the tree, the plume on her hat dancing. Her eyes sparkled with merriment, but there was also an alert quality in her expression. It was clear that she had no idea if he would lose his temper or not.

With an effort Jason cleared the astonishment from his face. He felt a smile twitching at his mouth. "So you want to play . . ." He reached down to scoop up a handful of snow and began to stalk her.

Understanding what he intended, Laura shrieked and
fled, gasping with laughter. "No, Jason! Remember, I'm
your wife!"

Her skirts slowed her down, but she darted among the
trees, venturing deeper into the woods. Hastily she flung
clumps of snow behind her. She felt a small *thwack* on
her posterior. His aim was deadly. "I surrender!" she
called out, her voice quivering with laughter. "Jason, I
surrender *wholeheartedly*!"

But Jason was nowhere to be seen. "Where are you?"
she called, turning in circles. "I admit defeat!" She
packed a snowball together as quickly as possible, in
case he refused to be a gracious victor. "Jason?" There
was a crunch of ice behind her. Whirling around, she
saw Jason just before he pounced on her. She gave a
short scream and tried to hit him with the snow, only to
send them both falling to the plush white-blanketed
ground.

Jason twisted to cushion the fall with his own body,
then rolled over, pressing Laura into the snow. His husky
laughter mingled with her giggles, and he raised himself
on his elbows to stare into her face. "Surrendering
wholeheartedly," he said, "means laying down your
weapons."

"I didn't have a white flag to wave."

"Your aim is good," he said.

"You make a large target."

He grinned and picked up a large fistful of snow,
brandishing it threateningly.

"I've already surrendered!" she squeaked, covering
her face with her wet hands.

He dropped the snow and pulled her hands away, keeping hold of her wrists.

Her smile faded as she stared at his dark face and felt
the weight of him between her thighs. He stopped smiling

at the same instant, his gaze falling to her lips. She remembered the way he had kissed her in the breakfast room—the hot, wet interior of his mouth, the urgent hardness of his body. He was going to kiss her again . . .

"Has the tree limb been taken care of?" she asked.

"Yes. We should be leaving soon." Jason drank in the sight of her flushed cheeks, her half-closed eyes, the crystal-white puffs of her breath in the air. He wanted to take her right here, in the cold and the snow, wanted to sink into her slim, exquisite body and feel her mouth open and sweet underneath his.

He loosened his gloves finger by finger and pulled them off. With one fingertip he stroked a damp tendril of hair off her forehead. "Are you cold?" he murmured.

She shook her head blindly. The cloak kept her insulated from the dampness of the snow, and the length of her body pressed to his felt as if it was glowing with heat. His fingertips moved over the sides of her face like points of fire, trailing to her jaw and tilting her chin up. His breath was like steam against her skin.

She lifted her icy-wet fingers to his face, timidly exploring the line of his cheekbones, the tips of his slanting eyebrows. His head angled over hers, and his lips nudged hers in a velvet-soft kiss. With a small sound of pleasure, she slid her arms around his neck, and then the glittering white world around them seemed to fade away. He brushed another savoring kiss over her mouth, and then another, until her lips parted and she unconsciously pulled at his neck to bring his mouth harder against hers.

He gave it to her as strongly as she wanted it, allowing his hunger to dictate the movements of his lips, his tongue. Her slim fingers combed through his midnight-black hair and kneaded the back of his neck. Deliberately he tightened his knees on her thighs, and she arched into his body with astonishing fervor. The fact that she was responding to him at last made him as shaky as a boy with his first woman. The frightening truth was that he needed her as he had never needed anyone. She was his, and she alone could take away the loneliness and nameless hunger he had felt ever since he could remember. She was his, and he wanted her to acknowledge it with her body and her heart.

"Laura," he said, burying his mouth in her neck. "Laura—"

Hale's drawling voice was a shock to both of them. "You two are the most disgraceful pair of chaperones I've ever seen."

Laura started at the intrusion. Her eyes flew open and she tried to struggle wildly to a sitting position. The skirts and petticoats tangled around her legs, weighting her down.

"Easy—it's only Hale," Jason said, filling his lungs with a deep breath of cold air.

"Don't let him tease," she whispered, clutching the front of his coat. "Not about this."

"No," Jason said soothingly. "I'll kill him if he tries." He stood up and reached down for her. She took his hands and allowed him to pull her upright. Then she was utterly still, her crimson face averted as he reached around her to brush the snow from her cloak.

Hale regarded them both with a self-satisfied smile. His mustache twitched like a cat's whiskers. "A nice respectable married couple," he continued mischeviously, "should be doing their utmost to preserve order and propriety, and instead I find you here rolling in the snow like some—"

"Enough, Hale," Jason said curtly.

He looked surprised. "Why, Laura, you aren't *embarrassed*, are you? I'm your brother, and besides—"

"Hale," Jason said in a voice of warning, and even Laura felt her spine tingle at the sound of it.

Hale sobered immediately. "The others are climbing

back into the sleighs. I came to find you before your absence became widely noticed.''

Jason regarded him sardonically. ''Thanks.''

''No thanks necessary,'' Hale said, and gestured for them to accompany him. ''I'll go back with you.''

''No.'' Jason shook his head, pulling Laura's unresisting form closer to his. ''Go on ahead. We'll be there soon.''

''Don't take long.'' Hale looked at Jason over Laura's head, gave him a brilliant smile, and raised his hand in the gesture of a victorious prizefighter.

Jason scowled at him and pointed threateningly toward the sleighs. Hale left with all due haste.

Laura, who had missed the exchange, wedged her arms against Jason's chest to keep from being too close to him. She couldn't think when she was near him. He straightened her hat and pulled out the broken red plume, handing it to her apologetically. She accepted the bedraggled feather and looked at Jason with dismay.

''I've never seen such a blush,'' he said huskily, and hugged her to him.

Her arms crept around his back. ''Shouldn't I blush?'' she asked, her voice muffled in the front of his coat.

''Not with me.'' He kissed her forehead, and she shivered at the masculine scrape of his jaw.

Laura could not fathom the reason for his sudden tenderness. Perhaps he had decided to play some sort of game with her. ''Jason,'' she said bravely, ''things cannot change between us, not in the course of a few days.''

''Yes, they can.'' His thumb stroked the side of her neck, lingering at her pulse. ''For the past two months I've let my pride stand in the way of what I really wanted. That's going to change. We know as little about each other as we did on our wedding day. And that''—he kissed the side of her throat—''is damn well going to change.''

Laura was silent and troubled, wanting suddenly to cry. It was all happening too fast. How could she give herself to him when she knew all too well that he could turn cruel in one capricious moment?

Jason read her expression and experienced the taste of bitter regret. She was so young, and he had hurt her in ways he had not understood until now. "I won't hurt you, Laura," he said quietly. "Not anymore. And I'll have your trust no matter what it takes."

The evening was filled with games, amusing stories, and music at the piano. After dinner the guests gathered in the parlor, which originally had been two smaller rooms which Sophia had converted into one large one. Laura sat with Sophia and a group of married women while they laughed and discussed the latest happenings in Boston. The unmarried girls had formed their own group a short distance away, while the men congregated around the fireplace or puffed on cigars in Judge Marsh's smoking room down the hall.

Laura could not keep her eyes from her husband. As usual, Jason was dominating the group in his own charismatic way. What he lacked in sophistication he made up for with the spark of irreverence that was quintessentially Irish. Jason never seemed to be bored except when confronted by a particularly starchy Bostonian, and then he was capable of saying or doing something just outrageous enough to make everyone laugh. Because he made no pretenses about his background, no one guessed at his sensitivity about it. He was fully aware that there were many who enjoyed the appearance of friendship with him, but few who would have tolerated the idea of him marrying into their families.

Toward the end of the evening Laura noticed that Jason had become quieter than usual, his gaze frequently diverted toward her. She could feel him staring at her, and when she looked back there was an intent gleam in his eyes that made her flustered. She nervously declined when Sophia pushed her to play the piano, but her older sister was insistent.

"Do play something for us, Laura. Something lively."

"I can't. I'm sadly out of practice," Laura said.

"But why? You used to play all the time before . . ." Sophia stopped, but Laura knew she had been about to say *before you married Jason.*

Laura stiffened as she felt Jason's hand at her back. "Play something," he said quietly.

She felt a spark of indignation at what sounded very much like an order. She knew that Jason liked to show off his accomplished wife—he wanted her to play for the same reason he dressed her in fine clothes and jewels. Well, if he was determined to put her on display, he could share the limelight!

She turned her head to regard him challengingly. "If you turn the pages for me."

His dark gaze did not waver from hers. "All right."

"Splendid," Sophia exclaimed, rifling through pieces of music to find what she wanted. "It's a pity you cannot play, Jason, otherwise I would choose something you could do together. I suspect you never had the patience for lessons, hmmm?"

He smiled. He did not point out that pianos and music lessons had not been a great concern for a family that had scratched and clawed for every penny. "Page-turning is one of my more underappreciated talents," he said, guiding his wife to the piano bench and helping her sit. He arranged the music in front of her. "Now, Laura," he said silkily, and she knew he was enjoying her annoyance, "when it is time for me to turn, just nod your head."

She glared at him discreetly. "I'd rather kick your leg."

One corner of his mouth lifted in a half-smile. "You're full of surprises today," he said. "I'm beginning to wonder if my Irish temper hasn't rubbed off on you."

She began to enjoy being pert with him. "My temper is entirely my own."

"I didn't know Bostonians had tempers."

"They do," she said crisply. "The slow-burning kind."

"Better to let out their anger at once and have done with it."

"I doubt you'd enjoy having a wife who gave vent to explosions of temper whenever she felt inclined."

"You're wrong," Jason said, resting his weight on one leg and draping his forearm on the piano. A lock of black hair fell over his forehead as he stared down at her. "I'd enjoy having her very much."

Laura's cheeks turned apple-red. She touched her fingers to the keys and tried desperately to remember how to play. There was no possibility of getting through the piece without making countless blunders. Not when he was near—not when he was in the same *room* with her.

But somehow her hands moved, recalling the sprightly melody with ease, and she did not falter. His lean fingers turned the pages at just the right pace. And all the time she was so terribly aware of him. When he leaned close enough that his shoulder brushed hers, she felt an unfamiliar ache in her breasts.

She finished the piece with a short sigh of relief and graciously accepted compliments from Sophia and the others. Jason helped her up, his hand strong at her elbow, and someone else took her place at the piano.

"Well done," he said.

"Thank you." Laura wished he would take his hand from her arm. She could not help remembering what had happened earlier today, the weight of his body pressing hers into the snow, his demanding mouth teaching her things she had been innocent of.

"Why don't you play for me at home?" he asked.

"Because I don't wish to," she said bluntly.

He scowled, drawing her to the side, away from the others' observation. "Why the hell not?"

"Jason, your language—"

"Tell me why not."

Recklessly she cast aside her fear of his temper and told him. "Because I would not like having to perform at your command, whenever you wish to be entertained, or whenever we have guests you wish me to play for like some. . . . some trained monkey!"

"Dammit, Laura," he said softly, "I won't be blamed for depriving you of something you enjoy. If you don't feel like playing when I want you to, tell me to go to hell."

In spite of their quiet tones, the tension between them was perfectly apparent. Laura sensed the glances being directed their way, and she straightened her spine until it resembled a fireplace poker. "I won't be drawn into public arguments with you," she whispered sharply. "That may be done where you come from, but it's not done in Boston society!"

"It's done all the time in the North End," Jason said, relaxing a little, sliding his hands into his pockets. "And my grandparents thrived on it in County Wexford. Perhaps we should give it a try once in a while."

She looked scandalized. "Jason, the very idea—"

"I'll buy you an iron skillet to threaten me with. That will lend us a touch of authenticity."

In the midst of her anger Laura felt a smile tugging at her lips. "I do not want a skillet. And I do not want to play for you."

Jason looked at her with those disturbing black eyes, and although they were in a room filled with people, she felt as if they were alone.

As the hour grew late the guests became drowsy. They
began to retire, the ladies gliding to their rooms, where
maids waited to assist with the removal of bustles, petticoats, and corsets, and the brushing-out of intricate
coiffures. Laura walked upstairs with Sophia while Jason
remained with the men, who lingered over cigars, bran-
dies, and unfinished conversations.

"Things seem to be going rather well," Sophia remarked as they neared Laura's room.

"You're referring to the guests?" Laura asked cautiously.

"Two in particular," came the airy reply. Sophia
stopped and pressed her cheek to Laura's. "Good night,
dear."

"Good night," Laura replied ruefully, and went to
her room, where a small, cheerful fire was burning in
the grate. The bedroom was decorated in bright floral
chintz patterns of coral and green, the windows draped
with cream lace curtains. A light netted canopy hung
over the old high-post bedstead. But what most attracted
her eye was the masculine trunk in the corner of the
room, opened to reveal her husband's possessions.

She and Jason would be sharing the room. Laura remained still, while inside she felt a flurry of panic. Foolishly she had not considered the possibility until this
moment. Of course they would be expected to share a
bed . . . there were so many guests, and Sophia barely
had enough rooms for all of them.

"Missus Moran?" The maid's quiet voice broke
through her scattered thoughts. "Would ye like me to
help wi' yer dress now, or—"

"Yes, do," Laura said, still staring at the trunk. She
hardly felt the tugs at the hard-to-reach fastenings that
trailed down the back of her gown.

Jason would want to stay the night with her. From the
way he had been behaving lately, she had no doubt of

that. But he had claimed he would not force her. If she pleaded with him to keep his distance, what would he do? Certainly he would be angry, but she did not think he would hurt her.

But *would* she ask him to leave? A mixture of fear and excitement nearly made her dizzy. What if she let it happen? What had Hale said . . . these matters were simple . . . just show Jason she was willing to accept his attentions.

Am I willing? she thought to herself. She could find no clear answer. It was up to Jason. If he approached her in a kind manner, if she could just let herself believe that he would not mock or hurt her, she would be willing.

She dressed in a white nightrail embellished with hundreds of tiny ruffles and tucks, the long sleeves and bodice ornamented with frothy lace. The white cambric wrapper she wore over the nightrail was even more elaborate, bordered with three deep lace ruffles at the hem and more lace from the wrists to the elbows.

Deciding to attend to her hair without assistance, Laura dismissed the maid with a smile of thanks. She sat at the walnut-veneered dressing table and stared into the small tilted looking glass. One by one she pulled the pins from her hair until the tangled chestnut waves fell down her back. Brushing it would take a long time, and the task was soothing in its monotony.

Laura was nearly finished with her hair when she heard a rap on the door, and her husband entered without waiting for permission. Their eyes met in the looking glass, his very dark, hers wide and green. Slowly she set the brush down. Still watching her, Jason pulled off his green-and-black-patterned waistcoat and narrow black necktie, and tossed them onto a chair.

The silence was heavy between them, the tension deepening until Laura could not bear it. With an incoherent murmur, she jerked up from the chair and strode rapidly to the door. She didn't know where she was headed, she only knew that she could not stay there alone with him another moment.

Jason caught her easily, his arm wrapping around her waist. He pulled her quaking form against his. "No, don't," he whispered against her ear, his hand sliding under her hair. His palm stroked up and down her narrow back.

"Not now. Please, not tonight," she managed to say.

"It all started with that damned wedding night," he murmured, fondling the back of her neck. "It was all my fault."

"No." She swallowed and shifted against him, and his hold tightened. "I behaved like a child," she ventured. "I—I turned you away."

"I didn't understand why, not at the time."

"I was . . . you were . . ." She flushed, overwhelmed by the memory . . .

Their wedding day had been long and nerve-wracking and tiresome, and by the time they had retired for the night Laura was exhausted. Jason had been emotionless and matter-of-fact throughout the wedding and reception, and she wondered if he had any feelings for her at all. After allowing her time to change into her nightgown, he appeared in her room with his shoulders squared as if for an unpleasant duty. Since that was precisely what her mother had informed her was soon to follow—an unpleasant duty—Laura regarded her husband with a mixture of reluctance and alarm.

Jason had never looked as tall and overpoweringly large as he did in that moment. In order to hide her fear, she kept silent and looked away from him, her heart thumping violently as she heard the sound of his breathing. He slid one hand behind her head and the other around her rigid back. His warm, hard mouth pressed against hers for a long time, and she squeezed her eyes

shut, her body frozen with confusion. She knew that
something was wrong, felt that he wanted something
from her that she was not able to give. His hand moved
over her back and then to her breast. It was when he
touched her there that she pushed him away in a quick,
nervous movement. ''Don't,'' she said without thinking.

His eyes narrowed in anger, as if he had been expecting
the rejection. ''You'll have to get used to the idea of
being my wife,'' he said, and reached for her again.

This time his mouth was hurtful, and his hand roamed
over her body with insulting boldness. She tolerated it
for as long as she could before jerking away with a tearful
plea. ''Don't touch me, I can't bear it!''

He looked as though she had slapped him. She covered
her face with her hands, her whole body shaking. It was
with relief and horror that she had heard him walk out
of the room and slam the door . . .

The episode had been repeated a few times since then,
until Jason had not approached her anymore. Until tonight.

''You were so strong,'' Laura whispered, ''and you
wanted so much. Things I didn't understand . . . things I
still don't understand. I know now that you didn't intend
to frighten me, but you did. There was such a look in
your eyes . . .'' She took a trembling breath.

It was fortunate she did not look up, for the same
expression was in Jason's eyes right then, a hot glow of
hunger.

''I didn't realize how innocent you were,'' he said,
raising his hand to her head, stroking her flowing hair.
''The mistake was mine. I was too damned impatient for
you. When you stiffened and pulled away from me, I
thought it was disgust you were feeling, not fear.''

''Disgust?'' she echoed in bewilderment.

''Because you knew I was so far beneath you. Because
you'd been forced into marriage with someone whose

ancestors were nothing but peasants in the poorest country in Europe. I knew what everyone had been telling you, that I was not fit to touch—''

''No!'' Impulsively she covered his mouth with her fingers. ''I was not forced into marrying you,'' she said in astonishment. ''Did you think I had no choice?''

His blank look was her answer.

''Oh, Jason, my father gave me every opportunity to refuse your proposal! Didn't you know that?'' She smiled tremulously as she saw the shock on his face. Had he been so accustomed to prejudice from others that he had expected it of his own wife? ''No wonder you made those remarks about buying me! But I was more than willing to marry you. The decision was mine to make.''

Jason pulled Laura's hand away from his lips. ''You don't have to say that.''

''I'm not lying, Jason. It's the truth.''

He shook his head stubbornly. ''I made the bargain with your father before I proposed to you.''

''And you thought he would have made such a bargain without my consent? You thought I was merely a pawn with no say of my own?''

He scowled at her. ''Yes.''

''You were wrong,'' she said with a touch of impatience. ''I *wanted* to marry you. For heaven's sake, I've wanted to be your wife since I was fifteen years old!''

Suddenly Laura realized what she had said, and she covered her mouth with her hand. The bald declaration seemed to echo in the small room. *Don't let him ask why*, she thought frantically, *please don't let him ask why*.

Mercifully he didn't.

But he stared at her strangely, his black eyes seeming to read her most private thoughts. Blindly she lowered her head, and was confronted with the broad, shirt-covered expanse of his chest. He spoke softly, his mouth against her hair. "I want to set aside the past, Laura. I want to share a bed with you tonight." The tip of his finger traced the delicate edge of her ear, causing her to shiver. "Most of all, I want you to trust me to be gentle with you."

She had imagined and dreaded this moment for so long. Jason had never been this way with her before, so tender and careful. The choice of surrender was suddenly made easy. Tears sprang to her eyes. "I don't know what to do," she faltered.

"I'll show you."

3

DEFTLY HIS FINGERS MOVED AMONG THE BUTTONS AND bows of Laura's wrapper until the garment slipped from her shoulders. Jason pushed the white cambric down her arms and over her wrists. She stood before him in her nightgown, her soft body unconstricted by stays and laces. He settled his hands on the natural curve of her waist, his senses enthralled by the scent and nearness of her.

Little by little he sank his hands into her loose hair until he was cradling her scalp. He bent his head and covered her mouth with his. Laura shivered at the masculine brandy-taste of him. The tip of his tongue coaxed her lips to part, and he kissed her as if he would never have enough, his hands easing her head back. Swaying dizzily, she reached for his waist to keep her knees from buckling. He wrapped his arms around her until her breasts flattened against his hard chest and her thighs were leaning into his. Her mouth twisted wildly, her tongue seeking his, her slim body molded to him like a second skin.

They broke the kiss at the same time, gasping roughly. Laura took advantage of his loosened arms and stepped back, clasping her hands to the center of her chest. Her heart thundered in a way she thought he must be able to hear. She glanced from Jason's flushed face to the thrusting outline at the front of his trousers. Hastily she looked away, but not before he had seen.

"Curious? Here, come closer." He drew her forward, tender and predatory. "Don't be afraid."

"No, Jason, I don't—" She stumbled against him, and he caught one of her hands, bringing it to his groin.

Heat radiated through the cloth of his trousers, seeming to scorch her hand. She blushed and tried to pull away. He covered her hand with his own and kept it pressed against his rigid flesh.

"Have you ever seen what a man looks like?" he murmured among the wisps of hair at her temple.

She turned her hot face into his shoulder, shaking her head.

"Never spied on Hale and his friends taking a swim, or—"

"No, never." She gave a choked laugh, still hiding her face.

A teasing note entered his voice. "You were a proper little girl." Slowly he let go of her hand. Her fingers remained against him for a scant second, then withdrew to the safer territory of his waist.

"My mother made certain that all of her daughters were proper."

"She wanted to keep you sheltered from men," he said without asking.

"Well, she . . . has never had a good opinion of them."

"Because of your father."

"Yes." Laura stared at him curiously. "Hale must have told you about that."

"Why don't you tell me?"

"My father is a good man, a kind one. But . . . there have always been other women. Sometimes his involvements are merely flirtations. Sometimes they are more than that." She shrugged helplessly. "He has always been discreet, but Mother has known for years. She says it's to be expected that a man will be faithful to a wife for only so long. She says that most husbands will stray because . . ." Abruptly Laura fell silent.

"Go on."

"I don't think—"

"Tell me."

She obeyed reluctantly. "Because they are creatures of a bestial nature." Her green eyes met his. "Mother also said that you were probably more bestial than most."

Jason grinned, knowing that of all the people who had disapproved of their marriage, Wilhemina had objected the most. "Her opinion of my character has never been a secret." He became serious, lifting her chin with his fingers. "Do you believe what she said about unfaithful husbands?"

Her gaze skidded away from his. "I don't know."

His voice was very quiet. "Do you think I've been unfaithful to you?"

Startled, she looked up at him. Her mouth went dry. "Things have not been right between us," she managed to whisper. "You've had cause to be."

There was a flash of something vibrant, perhaps anger, in his eyes. But his hand was still gentle on her chin. "By now you should know me well enough to be certain of a few things," he said, his gaze boring into hers. "I never lie. When I make a promise, I keep it." Laura wanted to shrink away, but she was mesmerized by his intensity. "I took you as my wife because I wanted you and no one else. I made a vow to forsake all others. It's been hell going to bed alone, knowing you were just a few doors away. More than once I thought about going to you and taking what was already mine."

"Why didn't you?" she whispered faintly.

"Pride. That and the desire for you to open your arms to me willingly." His smile had a self-mocking quality that made her uneasy. "And so I've waited. And since the day we were married I've been planning my revenge for all the times I couldn't have you."

Laura turned pale at his quiet tone. "What . . . what kind of revenge?"

He drew closer, his hard-planed face serious, his mouth nearly touching hers. "I'm going to give you such pleasure that you'll weep for each and every night we could have had together." He picked her up and carried her to the bed.

The firelight spread its wavering glow throughout the room as Jason lowered Laura to the mattress and stripped back the covers. Ferociously he tore off his shirt and bent over her, his hands framing her face as he kissed her. Instinctively she adjusted her mouth to his, answering the sweep of his tongue with delicate touches of her own.

Curiously she touched the hair on his chest, trailing her fingers through the thick, springy mass. She found a thin line of silken hair arrowing down to the waist of his trousers, and she rubbed the back of her knuckle across it in a questioning touch. To her surprise, she felt

Jason's breathing turn ragged.

He growled low in his throat and sought the peak of her breast through the bodice of her nightgown. Finding the hardening tip with his mouth, he nibbled gently. Laura gave a startled cry and twisted away from him, holding her hand to her breast.

"Did I hurt you?" he asked huskily.

Her cheeks pinkened, and she shook her head.

He pulled her protective hand away, replacing it with his own, his thumb circling the throbbing nipple. As he caressed her, he stared into her eyes, watching the green depths soften with pleasure. "You're so beautiful, Laura . . . I want to see the rest of you."

She didn't make a sound while he untied the bodice and took hold of the hem to draw it up her legs. She pressed her knees together modestly, feeling the cool air sweep over her legs . . . hips . . . waist . . . chest. Casting the garment aside, Jason gathered her slender body against his. When he pulled his head back to look at her, there was an absorbed expression on his face that she had never seen before. For him, too, time was suspended, and the outside world had disappeared. His kiss was relentless, flavored with desperation as he sought to make her understand how much he wanted her. Laura clasped her arms around his neck and sank her fingers into his black hair.

With a muffled groan, Jason let go of her just long enough to shed the last of his clothes. He pulled her to the mattress with him and slid his hands over her body with incredible gentleness. Her gaze wandered over him, and for a moment she couldn't breathe as she saw his naked, fully aroused body, primitive and golden in the firelight. Pinning her between his muscled arms, he lowered his head to her breasts. He covered the point of her nipple, his tongue gliding wetly across the aching bud. "Do you like it when I kiss you here?" he murmured.

"Yes . . . oh, yes . . ."

His mouth swept over her breasts, and he used only the lightest touches of his teeth and tongue. Wonderingly he stroked the length of her neck, the vulnerable hollow between her breasts, the downy smoothness of her stomach. Laura explored his body with the same sensitive lightness, bashfully touching the hair under his arms, the lines of his ribs, the lean surface of his flanks.

His palm ventured over her knees, his fingers tracing the line between her thighs. Her legs were still clenched together, resisting as he insinuated his hand between them. "Laura," he muttered, and she understood what he wanted. She felt the power and urgency contained in his body, the turgid length of him burning against her hip. "Laura, open to me."

She closed her eyes tightly and parted her knees enough to allow the gliding pressure of his hand. Jason kissed her breasts, her throat, whispering that she was safe, that he would take care of her. His lips brushed against hers, coaxing them apart, and his tongue reached for hers in skillful enticement that sent every hint of fear spinning out of reach.

His fingertips trailed over her stomach and dipped into the hollow of her navel. He paused at the triangle of soft chestnut hair at the top of her thighs, playing lightly through the curling strands. She began to breathe hard as his fingers slid deeper between her legs, stroking and withdrawing. Biting her lips, she tried to hold back a moan.

In spite of the desire that raged within him, Jason smiled triumphantly at the dazed, almost unwilling pleasure on Laura's face. He had brought that look to her eyes. He was the only man who would ever know her intimately. Watching her closely, he slid his teasing fingers inside her. She groaned with pleasure, her hands climbing up his back.

Although her caresses were unskilled, they stirred Jason to violent readiness. Wanting her too much to wait any longer, he pushed her thighs wider and lowered his body between them. He felt her tense, and he cupped her head in his hands, his lips brushing against hers. "Sweet darling . . . easy now, *mo stoir*. It will hurt, but only for tonight." He positioned himself and pressed forward, gritting his teeth with the effort to be careful.

Laura clung to him, moaning his name as he sheathed himself within her. There was pain, a white-hot burning that caused tears to spring to her eyes. She writhed and tried to push him away, but he rode her movements easily. His lips drifted through the tear tracks on her face. "Easy," he whispered. "*Gradh mo chroidhe* . . . you belong to me now."

She began to relax as he cradled her in his arms, the hard force of him buried inside her. His mouth moved to her breasts, pulling gently on her aching nipples. Her heartbeat roared in her ears, and her lips parted as she breathed his name. He slid deeper within her, his hands beginning a slow sojourn over her body. The steady thrust of his hips brought pain, but she felt an urge to push up against him, and the sensation was intensely sweet.

His body surged into hers, pulled back until he had almost withdrawn completely, then surged forward again. Laura gasped as she felt the inner tension increase. Her muscles tightened, and she gripped his upper arms until her fingers were numb. Half-frightened by the unfamiliar sensations, she tried to draw back from them, but it was too late. A burst of pleasure filled her body, causing her to strain against him with an incoherent sob. Jason smothered her cries with his mouth and pressed deep within her until her shuddering ceased and she was satiated and quiet beneath him. Only then did he release his own desire, thrusting one last time and groaning with violent satisfaction.

Laura was too exhausted to move or speak. Jason rolled to his side and pulled her with him. It took the last of her strength to lift her arm around his waist. For a long time they lay with their bodies entangled and their breath mingling.

Jason was the first to speak. "You'll never occupy a bed without me again, Laura Moran," he said lazily. His fingers brushed away the tendrils of hair that clung to her forehead and cheeks.

A shy smile stole over her face. "Jason?" she asked, shivering as he cupped her breast in his warm hand.

"Mmmm?"

"What did those words mean?"

"Which words?"

"The Gaelic words you were saying . . . before. It sounded something like . . ." She paused and wrinkled her brow thoughtfully. "*Masthore*. And then you said something like *grammacree*."

Jason was frowning. "Did I say that to you?"

"Yes." She looked at him expectantly. "What does it mean?" To her amazement, she saw a flush of color that went across his cheekbones and the bridge of his nose. "Jason?"

"It means nothing," he muttered. "Just . . . words of affection."

"But what *exactly*—"

He kissed her, and as he had intended, the question flew from her mind. "You're the most beautiful woman I've ever known," he said against her lips as his hands wandered from her breasts to her thighs. "I'm going to give you everything you've ever dreamed of."

She laughed unsteadily, for Jason had never said anything of the kind to her before. All at once he seemed younger, the usual harshness of his face softening in the darkness, his smile almost boyish. "There's nothing I want," she told him.

"A golden carriage, drawn by horses with diamond bridles," he mused, rolling to his back and swinging her above him.

Laura crossed her arms modestly over her breasts. Her long hair hung in a curtain around her. "That isn't necessary."

"Ruby rings for your toes . . . a castle with silver towers, a ship with moonlight sails to carry you across the sea—"

"Yes," she said. "I'll take the ship."

"Where would you like to go?"

"Everywhere."

Jason laced his fingers behind her neck. "Would ordinary sails do? We'll travel anywhere you wish—perhaps spend a few months in Europe. Or the Orient." He raised his brows suggestively. "Or the Mediterranean."

Laura stared at him in wonder. "Jason, you're not teasing, are you?"

"I'm being serious. We never took a wedding trip."

"You said you couldn't afford to leave your work."

"I can afford it now," he said dryly. "Where would you like to go?"

"Cairo," she said with dawning excitement. "I've always wanted to see the pyramids."

"And make an excursion up the Nile?"

She blinked in surprise. "How did you . . ." She frowned suspiciously. "Is there anything Hale *hasn't* told you?"

Jason chuckled. "No. But that's the last of your brother's meddling. And you have my promise for a trip in the spring."

A sweet smile curved her lips. "Thank you, Jason."

He stared at her as if spellbound. "You can thank me another way."

"How?"

He took hold of her wrists and pulled them away from

her body, his gaze lingering appreciatively on her round breasts before moving back to her face. "Lean down and kiss me."

She complied without hesitation, flattening her hands on his shoulders, lightly touching her lips to his. Beneath her she felt his body respond, desire flowing hot in his loins. Her eyes widened, and she tried to move away. He rolled to his side and slid his thigh between hers.

"Again?" she asked breathlessly.

"Again." His lips drifted over her neck in a moist, searing path. He murmured sweet beguilements in her ear, teased and fondled her until she was gasping and reaching for him hungrily. Laughing softly at her impatience, Jason slowed the pace even more, touching her as if she were as fragile as an orchid, as if more than the tenderest brush of his fingers would bruise her. He drove her past eagerness, past all reason, until all she could do was wait helplessly for him to release her from the silken prison. At last he slid into her, and she purred in exquisite relief, her green eyes half-closing.

Jason shuddered as he felt her arms closing around his back, her hips tilting to cradle his. He had never expected to find such fulfillment. All the bitterness, all the unspoken longings that had haunted him for so long, were quenched in the sweetness of her body.

The urgent rhythm of her hips pulled him into a flowing tide of pleasure, and he fought to keep his movements slow and easy. Laura muffled her moans of ecstasy against his shoulder, and Jason felt the shattering sensations sweep through him as well. He buried his face in the river of her hair, wrapped her in the shelter of his arms, held her tightly in the moments of darkness and bliss.

"Laura, dear. Laura." Sophia's voice called her from sleep.

She groaned, her face half-buried in the goose-down pillow. She squinted at her older sister, who stood by the bed. Sophia wore a velvet gown with an elegant knee scarf, a sash tied around the lower length of the skirt to gather it in at the knees. The curtains at the windows were tied back, letting in the white winter sunshine.

"What time is it?" Laura asked in a sleep-roughened voice.

"Eight o'clock, dear. I thought it best to wake you rather than allow you to sleep until a scandalous hour and become the subject of embarrassing speculation."

Laura began to sit up, then gathered the sheet to her breasts with a gasp as she realized she was naked. She blushed, throwing a cautious glance at her sister. Sophia seemed unperturbed.

"Is Jason downstairs?" Laura asked timidly.

"No, the men breakfasted early and went to hunt fowl," Sophia said.

"They went *hunting*?" Laura frowned in a befuddled way.

"The charm of the sport escapes me. I doubt they'll find a single thing to shoot. But after observing Horace's habits for years, I've come to the conclusion that men simply like to carry their guns through the woods, drink from their hunting flasks, and exchange ribald stories."

Laura tried to smile, but a quick, anxious frown followed. "How did Jason look at breakfast?" she asked.

"No different than usual, I suppose." Sophia's clear brown eyes rested on her steadily. "How should he have looked?"

"I don't know," Laura murmured, sitting up in bed. She winced, feeling battered and sore in every part of her body.

"I'll tell the maid to draw a hot bath for you," Sophia said considerately. "And I'll send up some cambric tea."

"Thank you." Laura continued to clutch the sheet

closely, her fists winding and twisting in the soft linen. Sophia left, and Laura stared at the closed door, struggling with a mixture of emotions. "Oh, Jason," she whispered, distressed at the prospect of seeing him this morning. In the light of day, the recollection of her behavior was mortifying—she had been shameless, foolish, and he was probably laughing secretly at her. No, she couldn't face him now, not to save her own life!

But there was no possibility of avoiding him. Sighing miserably, she crawled out of bed. She was refreshed by a hot bath that soothed her aches and pains. After much deliberation, she decided to wear a dress of shimmering olive-green faille that brightened her eyes to emerald. The maid came to assist her with the tightening of her corset laces, and spent a long time fastening the tiny loops and buttons on the back of her dress. The skirt was pulled tightly over her figure in front and gathered behind in a modest bustle topped by a huge bow. Painstakingly Laura twisted and re-twisted her hair into a perfect coiled chignon and anchored the chestnut mass with a gold comb.

Finally there was nothing left to do. She squared her shoulders and walked downstairs. She was relieved to discover that the men had not yet returned. Some women were attending to their needlework in the parlor, while others lingered in the breakfast room. The food was being kept in crested silver warming dishes, and Laura inspected the array with a smile.

Sophia knew how to serve the proper Bostonian breakfast, the heavy old-fashioned kind. The sideboards fairly groaned under the weight of fruit, oatmeal, preserves and molasses, waffles, biscuits, toasted bread, eggs, cheese, and custard. There was a variety of meats, including chicken with cream gravy, ham, and smoked fish. An empty plate held a few crumbs of what had once been an apple pie. As far as New Englanders were concerned, there was never an inappropriate time of day to serve apple pie.

"Everything will be cleared away soon," Sophia told her. "Come, have something to eat."

A plate was thrust in her hands, and Laura smiled, picking up a tidbit here and there. But she was too nervous to eat, and in spite of her sister's entreaties, she barely touched the food.

"More tea?" Sophia asked, hovering about her with maternal concern. "Chocolate?"

"No, thank you," Laura replied absently. She stood up. "I think I'll find something to read. Or perhaps I'll try my hand at the piano again. I have missed playing— I'd forgotten how soothing it is. I'll close the door so as not to disturb anyone."

"Yes, do whatever you like," Sophia said, regarding her with a touch of worry. "Laura, you don't seem quite yourself this morning."

"Don't I?" She felt her cheeks turn pink. "I'm perfectly well."

Sophia lowered her voice to a whisper. "Just set my fears to rest and I'll ask nothing else: Jason treated you kindly, didn't he?"

"Yes, he was kind," Laura whispered back. She leaned closer as if to impart a highly personal secret, and Sophia tilted her head obligingly. "I am going to the piano now."

Smiling wryly, Sophia waved her away.

Laura seated herself at the small rosewood piano with a sigh, her fingers running over the ivory keys as if waiting for inspiration to strike. Then they settled in a pattern she remembered from long ago, a melody that was melancholy and sweet. It suited her mood perfectly. She fumbled a few times, her touch uncertain from lack of practice. As she played, concentrating on the music, she sensed the parlor door opening. Her fingers slowed, then stilled. All she could hear was carpet-muffled foot-steps, but she knew who the intruder was.

A pair of strong hands slid over her shoulders, up the sides of her neck, back down. The palms were warm, the fingertips cool. A low, vibrant voice sent a thrill down her spine. "Don't stop."

She pulled her hands from the keys and turned to face Jason as he sat on the small bench beside her. He had never looked so fresh and vital, his hair attractively tou-sled and his skin ruddy from the icy breezes outside.

For a moment they stared at each other, measuring, asking silent questions. Laura dropped her gaze, and it happened to fall on the muscled thigh pressed close to her own. She remembered that thigh wedged between hers, and embarrassment rushed over her.

"You left me this morning," she heard herself say.

Jason leaned over her downbent head, unable to resist nuzzling the nape of her neck. "I didn't want to wake you. You were sleeping so deeply."

She shivered at the heat of his breath and tried to stand up, only to have him catch her firmly around the waist and pull her back down. Automatically she braced her arms against his chest. "Look at me," he said quietly, "and tell me why you're skittish today."

Laura's fingers plucked nervously at his black-and-tan brocaded vest. "You know why."

"Yes, I know why."

She heard the trace of amusement in his tone. Her eyes flew to his, and she saw that the midnight depths were warm with laughter. Immediately she was horror-stricken. Oh, he was laughing at her, he was jeering at the way she had behaved last night, his chaste wife who had moaned and clung to him so wantonly.

"Let go of me," she said, pushing at him in earnest. "I know what you think, and I won't—"

"Do you?" His arms tightened until she was pinned

against his chest, and he smiled at her small scarlet face. "I think you're adorable." He dropped a kiss on her forehead while she struggled helplessly. "I think you need to be reminded of a few things." His mouth joined hers, pressing her lips apart. She could not keep from responding any more than she could stop her heart from beating. As her lips clung to his, he let her hands slip free, and her arms wrapped around his neck. Their tongues touched, circled, slid together languorously.

Gradually Jason released her mouth, and she gave a protesting moan. "I think," he said huskily, "you need to be taken back to bed."

Laura's eyes widened with alarm. "You would not embarrass me in front of the others that way."

He kissed her hungrily. "They'll understand."

"They will not! They're Bostonians."

"I think I'll carry you upstairs. Right now." He made a move as if to lift her, and she clutched at his shoulders.

"Jason, no, you can't . . ." Her voice trailed off as she saw that he was only teasing her. Her frown of worry dissolved into a scowl.

"Laura," he murmured with a smile, "do you need proof of how much I want you?" He drew her hand to his loins, and she caught her breath at the feel of him, hard and urgent, more than ready to take her. "I never thought it was possible to want a woman so much," he said against her ear. "And if it weren't for your blessed modesty, I *would* take you upstairs . . . or right here . . . anywhere . . ." He sought her lips, his mouth soft and coaxing, setting fire to every nerve.

"Jason," she whispered, leaning against him, "you would tell me if I displeased you last night, wouldn't you?"

"*Displeased* me . . ." he repeated in astonishment. "Laura, no one has ever pleased me *more*. Where did you come by such an idiotic notion?" Suddenly his dark eyes were stern. "If that's what you're fretting about, we really are going upstairs."

This time he was clearly *not* teasing. Alarmed, Laura tried to appease him. "No, I believe you, Jason, I do—"

"Convince me," he challenged, and choked off her words with a sultry kiss. She twisted to fit him more closely, her fingers sliding between his vest and shirt. The pounding of his heart was as wild as her own. She was lost in a wave of sweet madness, not caring what happened next, dimly aware that she would not object if Jason pulled her to the floor and took her right there.

They were interrupted by the harsh clanging of a tin drum and a shrill, metallic blast. The sounds seemed to pierce Laura's eardrums and sent a shock through her body. Jason let go of her with a muffled curse and nearly fell off the piano bench. Together they stared at the intruders.

A pair of giggling imps stood before them. It was Sophia's children, Wilfred and Millicent, holding tin instruments and banging them loudly.

"Lovely children," Jason remarked pleasantly, reaching up to rub the back of his neck, where every hair was standing up straight.

"You were kissing Aunt Laura!" Millicent cried in glee.

"So I was," Jason agreed.

Wilfred pushed up his glasses and squinted at them. "Uncle Hale said to come play for you."

Jason looked at Laura with a rueful grin. "Excuse me. I have two little elves to catch."

"What will you do when you catch them?" she asked in pretend worry.

He smiled darkly. "Bury them outside in the nearest snowdrift."

Wilfred and Millicent screamed in delighted terror and

scampered from the room as Jason chased them.

"Don't forget Hale," Laura called after him, and laughed.

In the days that followed Laura was unable to let go of the feeling that she was in a delightful dream that would end with cruel suddenness. Each morning she awakened with a sense of worry that dissolved only when she saw Jason's smile. It was miraculous to her that the husband she had come to dread was now the person she wanted to be with every minute.

Now that she was no longer afraid of his biting sarcasm being turned on her, she talked freely with him. He was an entertaining companion, sometimes thoughtful and quiet, sometimes roughly playful. He was a considerate lover, always sensitive to her pleasure, but with an earthiness that she found exciting.

To Laura's surprise, Jason seemed to relish the discovery that she was not the delicate, reserved creature he had thought her. One morning he swept her away from the others and took her on a ramble through the woods, teasing and flirting as if she were a maiden he was bent on seducing. Saucily she ducked away when he would have kissed her.

"No," she said, picking up her skirts and making her way to a fallen tree trunk. "I know what you intend, and I will **not** be taken advantage of in the snow."

He followed readily. "I could make you forget the cold."

"I don't think so." Primly she stepped over the tree trunk, and gave a little shriek as he made a grab for her.

"I never back down from a challenge," he said.

Swiftly she picked up a long birch stick and turned to face him, touching it to his chest as if it were a sword. "So this is the reason you brought me out here," she accused, "for an unseemly frolic in the middle of the woods."

"Exactly." With deliberate slowness he took the stick and broke it in half, tossing it aside. "And I'm going to have my way with you."

Backing up step by step, Laura considered the possibility of compromise. "One kiss," she offered.

He continued to stalk her. "You'll have to do better than that."

Her eyes sparkled with laughter, and she held out her arms to keep him at bay. "I will not bargain with you, Jason."

They eyed each other assessingly, each waiting for the other to make the first move. Suddenly Laura darted to the side, and found herself snatched up in a pair of strong arms. She laughed exuberantly while he lifted her by the waist as if she weighed nothing at all. Slowly he let her slide down until their faces were even, her feet still dangling above the ground. Without thinking, she twined her arms around his neck and fastened her mouth to his in a kiss so direct and natural that Jason staggered slightly, his senses electrified. He had to put her down before he sent them both tumbling in a heap. Spellbound, he stared at the woman in his arms and thought of what an arrogant fool he'd been. He'd assumed he knew her so well when he didn't know her at all.

"Jason," she asked wistfully, "do we really have to go back home tomorrow?"

"We can't stay here forever."

She sighed and nodded, wondering how long the truce between them would last once they were back in all-too-familiar territory.

It was with reluctance that they finally left the Marshes' Brookline home the next day and returned to their own Beacon Street address. Sophia had been able to guess at Laura's remaining worries and gave Laura an uncharacteristically long hug good-bye. ''Everything will be all right,'' Sophia whispered, patting her on the back. ''After seeing Jason with you the past few days, I've come to realize that there is no difficulty of yours that time will not solve.''

Laura smiled and nodded, but she knew that in this matter Sophia wasn't right. Time meant very little. Two whole months of marriage had not accomplished for her and Jason what the past four days had. And there were problems that still faced them, problems that could not be resolved no matter how much time went by. She had to find some way of prying past Jason's deepest reserve, the barrier that kept them from reaching an intimacy beyond the physical pleasure they shared.

As he had promised, Jason took her to the site of his most recent building. It was the first time she had actually seen one of his projects under construction. Before now she been wary of showing too much interest in his business concerns. Now she inundated him with questions.

''What sort of people will be renting the apartments?'' she asked. ''Small families? Young men?''

''And young women, on a cooperative basis.''

''Young women without chaperones?''

He laughed at her faintly censorious tone. ''Yes, self-reliant women with their own careers, sharing an apartment together. Is that too radical a proposition for a Prescott to approve of?''

''Yes,'' she said. ''But I suppose the Prescotts cannot hold back progress.''

He grinned and drew her arm tighter through his. ''We'll make a liberal of you yet.''

As Jason walked her around the property, Laura was impressed, even a little awed, by the size of the undertaking. The air was thick with the noise of the steam shovel, the crew of men spreading gravel and swearing, the dust everywhere. Part of the property included a former rubbish dump, which was being covered with clean gravel.

The slight train of Laura's skirt dragged through the patches of muddy ground, and she paused every now and then to tug at it impatiently. She was outfitted in the most practical garments she owned, a wool and grosgrain walking dress of a deep plum color, a matching cape, and sealskin boots with double soles. The heavy draperies and tightly molded skirt prevented her from moving with Jason's ease, and he was forced to cut his strides to match hers.

Jason slowed their pace even more as they were approached by a thin, ragged figure from the street. Laura's eyes darkened with pity as she looked at the elderly man, who wore tattered clothes that were hardly adequate protection against the cold. His gray beard was thin and yellowed, his skin veined, and he reeked of gin. He spoke in a heavy Irish brogue that Laura could barely decipher.

"Here now, sir, d'ye have a coin t' spare for an ould man? The wind is sthrong an' could today."

Laura looked up at Jason, whose expression was unreadable. "Indeed it is," he said. He reached into his pocket and pulled out some coins, placing them in the outstretched hand.

The old man peered at him with watery eyes that suddenly brightened with interest. "Sure now, yer frae the ould sod."

Jason's slight accent became more pronounced than usual. "My grandfather left County Wexford during the first potato rot."

"Aye, ye have th' look o' Wexford, eyes an' hair black as coal. Meself, I come frae Cork." The man nodded in thanks, gesturing with the coins clutched tight in his bony fist. "God bless ye, sir, an' yer bonny wife."

Laura glanced back at him as they moved on; he was

scurrying furtively across the street, hands tucked underneath his arms. "Poor man," she said. "I hope he buys something to eat."

"He'll spend it on drink," Jason said flatly.

"How can you be certain?"

For a moment she thought he wasn't going to reply. "He can get whisky cheaper than bread," he finally said.

"Then why did you give the money to him if you knew . . ." Laura frowned and stared at the ground, feeling the tension in his arm, knowing that something had struck a raw nerve.

Jason felt a powerful urge to tell her what he was thinking, but his habit of privacy concerning his past warned him against saying anything. He opened and closed his mouth several times, feeling heat creep up from his collar as he fought an inner battle. There was no reason to confess anything to her, no need for her to know. And if Laura understood what his childhood had really been like, she would feel contempt for him. She would feel the same disgust that he felt whenever he remembered it. God knew why now of all times he felt driven to tell her what he had once vowed never to speak of.

Jason stopped walking and turned his gaze to the steam shovel as it bit into the hard ground.

"What is it?" she asked gently. "What did he remind you of?"

He spoke as if the words were being dragged out of him. "I knew men like that when I was young. Men driven from their home by poverty and disease, and most of all hunger. They didn't care where they went, so long as they escaped from Ireland. Often they landed in Boston with no money, no work, no relatives. They . . ." He stopped and took a short breath before continuing. "They used to beg for a warm place in my family's room at night, when the winter was bitter."

"Your family's room? Don't you mean your house?"

He didn't look at her. "We lived in one room of a basement. No plumbing or windows. No light except when the door to the sidewalk above was opened. Filth kept draining in from the street. It was little more than a gutter."

Laura was silent with amazement. That could not be true, she thought. He could not have come from that kind of poverty. She had known the Morans had not been a family of great means, but Jason was talking as if they had been slum-dwellers!

"But your father was a grocer, wasn't he?" she asked awkwardly. "He had enough money to send you to school."

"That was later, when his business began to succeed. Even then he had to trade his soul for the money. He managed to convince some local merchants and politicians that I would be a worthwhile investment." Jason's mouth twisted. "For the first several years my father ran his grocery in our cellar room. Until I was nine or ten, I remember eating nothing but scraps and foodstuffs gone bad, the worst of whatever he couldn't sell."

"But your education . . . How . . . ?"

"My father was one of the few who allowed—no, pushed—his sons into the free public schools. He couldn't read. He wanted at least one of us to be able to."

"Did you want to?"

"At first I didn't care. I was an uneducated brute who wanted nothing except food and what little comfort I could find. And there is an attitude in the North End, that a man isn't meant to rise above the life he's born to. The Irish are fatalistic about such things. I thought the only way to get something I wanted was to steal it." Jason smiled grimly. "When I couldn't find coal or wood to scavenge, the family had to stay in bed all day to keep warm. God knows I saw no use in learning to read.''

''What made you decide to try?''

He answered distantly, as if he were only half-aware of her presence. The memories were never far from his mind—they were what drove him—but until now he had never allowed himself to speak of them. ''I saw men laboring on the wharves until their backs were ruined. And the hostlers and stablers living in worse conditions than the horses they cared for. All the Irish laborers and domestics who will work for any wage—they call them 'green hands.' There was nothing I wouldn't have done to escape it.'' Jason looked at her then, his black eyes unnervingly intense. ''I worked all the time. On the docks, in saloons, anywhere there was a coin to be made. In school I studied hard, made the highest marks. I never lost at anything—baseball, footraces, public debates. Every man of means I crossed paths with became a mentor. But the admission into the Boston Latin School was nothing short of a miracle. I'll owe favors for that from now until kingdom come. That was when everything changed, when I finally knew what it was I really wanted.''

Laura did not ask what that was, for she was afraid of the answer. She suspected that what Jason really wanted was what he could never have, to assume a place in the most powerful circles of Boston society that would never be allowed to an Irishman. Such positions had been decided generations ago, and no intruders were admitted into the sacred circles. No matter how much money or power Jason acquired, he would always be considered an outsider.

''And then Boston Latin led to college,'' she prompted quietly.

''When it came time for that, some Irish businessmen helped to foot the bill. I eventually repaid their investments many times over.''

"Your family must be very proud of you," she said, and was puzzled when he didn't answer.

While she was still trying to absorb all of what he had told her, Jason took her by the shoulders, his gaze hunting for pity or revulsion. She felt neither, only a desire to comfort him. She thought of what he must have been like as a boy, hungry and too poor to hope or even to dream.

"Oh, Jason," she said softly. "I didn't suspect you had such desperate odds against you. You should have told me before."

She saw that whatever he had been expecting from her, it had not been that. His face was utterly still. She touched his lean cheek with her gloved hand.

"You should be repelled, knowing where I came from," he muttered.

Laura shook her head. "I admire you for it. I admire you for what you've made of yourself."

He gave no reply, staring at her in an almost calculating way, as if he wanted to believe her but could not. Her hand fell to her side, and she gave him an uncertain smile.

They were interrupted by the approach of the construction foreman, who had seen them from a distance. Eagerly he greeted them and conferred with Jason on some details of the project. Laura watched them, struck by how quickly the bitterness and memories on Jason's face had vanished, replaced by his usual calm authority. It dismayed her to see how easily he hid his feelings. She was afraid she would never fully understand him.

After bidding the foreman good-bye, they walked to the double barouche and Jason muttered to the driver that they were going home. Laura clambered into the velvet-lined carriage, arranging the mass of her bustle, petticoats, and heavily draped skirts in order to sit comfortably. Jason sat beside her, closed the door, and pulled the morocco blinds at the window shut. Obligingly he leaned over to help tug a fold of her skirt out from beneath her. The carriage started with a small jolt.

"Jason," she said in a low voice.

"Yes?"

"I hope you don't regret telling me about your past." Hesitantly she reached out to stroke his chest. "I know there is much more you've left unsaid. Someday I hope you will trust me enough to tell me the rest."

His hand closed in a fist over hers. Surprised, she darted a look at him, wondering if she had somehow made him angry. There was a dark blaze in his eyes—but it was not anger. He wrapped his other hand around the back of her neck. His thick black lashes lowered, and he looked at her with a narrowed gaze.

"Laura, why did you marry me?" he asked roughly.

She was startled, and turned a shade or two paler. Clumsily she tried to dodge the question by making light of it. "I believe this is called fishing for a compliment, Mr. Moran." She smiled, but he did not respond. His silence forced her to continue. "Why did I want to marry you . . . well, there were many reasons, I suppose. I . . . I knew you would be a good provider, and you were Hale's friend, and during those four years you spent Christmas with us, I became acquainted with you, and . . ." Her gaze dropped away. She tried to pry herself free, but she was held fast against one hundred and eighty pounds of obstinate male, and they both knew she would not be freed until she gave him what he wanted.

"The truth," he muttered.

"I can't tell you something I don't know."

"Try."

Helplessly she tugged at her trapped hand. "Why is it necessary?"

"Because I thought I'd forced you into marrying me. A few days ago you told me that you married me of your own free will. I have to know why."

"I don't *know* why." Laura gasped as he twisted and dragged her across his lap. She was bound in a cocoon of skirts and stays, her head forced up by the pressure of his arm. "Jason, please, I don't know what you want—"

"The hell you don't."

"Let me go, you bully!"

He ignored her demand. "Then we'll take another tack. If you had a choice, then tell me why you didn't marry someone from your own social rank. There were young men with good names and adequate means—you could have had any of them."

"Oh, a prime selection," she agreed, glaring at him. "Hordes of blue-blooded snobs reared to do nothing except preserve the money their grandfathers made. I could have married some dignified Brahmin who would insist on eating oatmeal every morning of his life, and tucking an umbrella under his arm even when it wasn't raining, and complaining until he was an old man about not being accepted into the Porcellian club at Harvard!"

"Why didn't you?"

"Jason, stop this!" She writhed until her strength was exhausted.

"You told me you wanted to marry me since you were fifteen," he said ruthlessly. "Why?"

She trembled with distress, her eyes glittering with sudden tears.

"No, don't cry," he said, his voice gentling. "Laura, I've told you things I've never confessed to anyone. It can't be any more difficult for you than it was for me."

His handsome face was so close to hers, and there was something pagan in the blackness of his eyes. Laura drew the tip of her tongue over her dry lips and swallowed. Her blood was rushing so fast it made her light-headed. "The first time I met you," she managed to say, "Hale had brought you home for the Christmas holidays. You kept watching me during that awful dinner . . . remember?''

He nodded slightly.

''You looked like a wolf in a cage,'' she said. ''The room seemed too small for you. You didn't belong there, but I could see how badly you wanted to, how determined you were. And I knew I could help you.''

''Dammit, you didn't marry me to be helpful!''

Futilely she tried to free her arms. ''We'll be arriving home soon—''

''I won't let you go until I have the answer. Was it that you liked the idea of marrying a social inferior? So you could always have the whip hand?''

''No,'' she gasped.

''The money? You wanted to be the wife of a rich man, no matter how vulgar his bloodlines.''

''Jason, you . . . you louse!'' She struggled furiously. Had she been able to slap his face, she would have.

''Why did you marry me?''

''Because I was a fool, and I thought you needed me, and I—'' She was so upset she was shaking, and she was terrified to realize she was on the verge of blurting out the truth.

''Why did you marry me?'' came the relentless demand.

Her eyes stung sharply. ''Jason, don't make me—''

''*Why?*''

''Because I love you,'' she choked, finally goaded into defeat. ''I've loved you from the first moment I saw you. That was the only reason . . . the only one.''

4

A TREMOR WENT THROUGH JASON'S BODY, AND HE pressed his lips to her forehead. He had never wanted anyone to love him before. There had never been room in his life for anything or anyone who would distract him from his ambition. Until his engagement, there had been affairs, but never without the mutual understanding that they were temporary. Laura was the only woman he had wanted for always.

"You're cruel," she sobbed, wondering what she had just done. It had been the mistake of her life to admit her feelings so soon. She should have waited, should have held her ground. "You're a bully, and selfish, and—"

"Yes, and a louse," he murmured, brushing her tears away. He kissed her wet eyelids. "Don't cry, *mo stoir*, don't."

Desperate to soothe her, he kissed her with all the gentleness he was capable of. He reached down and pulled her arms around his neck, while his tongue flickered in her mouth. His muscled arm was hard against her back. Slowly her tears ceased, and her trembling fingers slid into his hair.

At this sign of her response, Jason finished the kiss

with an infinitely soft stroke of his tongue and took his mouth from hers. He had to stop now, or he wouldn't be able to control himself. But her slim body molded to his, and her breasts shifted against his chest. He tried to move her off his lap. "We'll be home soon," he said gruffly, more to himself than to her. "We'll be home and then—"

Her red lips pressed against his, sweetly luring him away from sanity. Greedily Jason angled his mouth over hers, his tongue thrusting savagely. She writhed in response to the painful throb between her legs and returned his passion with equal force. His hand searched frantically through the mass of her skirts for her legs, her thighs, unable to reach any part of her through the tightly binding garments.

The carriage stopped, and Jason tensed with a muffled curse. Laura gasped incoherently, her fingers clenching into his coat. It took several seconds for her to understand that they were home. She looked at Jason, her gaze unfocused. Her hair was falling around her shoulders, pins dropping right and left, her hat dislodged, and her clothes disheveled.

Clumsily she raised her hands to her hair, flushing with mortification. She thought of the way the maids would giggle at the story of the cool, composed Mrs. Moran walking in with her clothes askew and her hair looking like a bird's nest.

The driver began to open the carriage door from the outside, and Jason caught at it easily. With a brief word to the driver, he pulled the door shut. Turning to Laura, he watched her twist handfuls of hair and jab pins in her chignon. "Can I help?"

"You have helped quite enough," she said in agitation. "How like you this is! When you want something you must have it regardless of time or place, and all other considerations be damned."

"When it comes to you," he said, "yes."

She glanced at him then, and found a caressing warmth in his eyes that caused her hands to falter. Painstakingly she rearranged her clothes, repositioned her hat, and gave him a nod when she was ready to leave the carriage.

After he walked her up the steps and into entrance hall, Laura stopped in the middle of the polished parquet floor. Quickly the housekeeper came to take her cape and Jason's coat. "Mrs. Ramsey," Laura murmured to the housekeeper, "I'll be down soon to discuss the plans for dinner. First I must change from my walking dress."

"Yes, Mrs. Moran. I shall send one of the maids to help you—"

"That won't be necessary," Jason interrupted matter-of-factly, taking Laura's elbow.

The housekeeper's face wore a mixture of speculation and delighted horror. Clearly she wondered what might take place upstairs. It was still broad daylight outside—an unthinkable time for a husband to lay with his wife. "Yes, sir," she said, and headed for the kitchen.

Laura tried to pull her elbow from his. "Jason, I don't know what you intend, but—"

"Don't you?" He guided her up the stairs without the slightest appearance of hurry.

"This can wait until evening," she whispered. "I know you must have many things to attend to—"

"Yes, important things."

As soon as they reached her room, he yanked her inside and closed the door with his foot. His mouth covered hers impatiently, his breath a scalding rush against her cheek. He pulled off her hat and worked at her hair, scattering pins until the long chestnut locks fell down to her waist.

"Jason, I need time to think about all that has happened—"

"You can think about everything to your heart's desire. Later.'' His hands moved restlessly from her breasts to her hips. ''Did you mean what you said in the carriage?''

''About your being a bully?'' She tilted her head back as his lips found the sensitive hollow beneath her ear. ''Yes, I meant every word.''

''About loving me.''

It would be useless to deny it now. Laura swallowed and forced herself to meet his dark eyes. Jason looked almost stern, his mouth set with a firmness that made her want to cover it with enticing kisses. ''Yes,'' she said huskily, ''I meant that too.''

Without another word he turned her around and unfastened the back of her dress. In his haste, his fingers were less agile than usual. The heavy dress collapsed along with masses of petticoats. Laura heaved a sigh of relief as her corset laces were untied and the contraption of stays and silk was tossed to the other side of the room. She heard the sound of cloth ripping and felt her torn cambric drawers slip to the floor.

Shivering, she leaned back against him, her head dropping on his shoulder. His palm rubbed in a circle over her abdomen. ''Tell me again,'' he said against the perfumed softness of her neck.

''I love you . . . Jason . . .''

He turned her in his arms and hungrily sought her mouth with his, while he pulled the hem of her chemise up to her waist. Laura responded lovingly, her lips parting, her body arching to his. But as she felt the demanding pressure of his arousal against the inside of her thigh, she pulled away from him.

''No, we can't,'' she said. ''I must get dressed and go downstairs. Mrs. Ramsey will be waiting—''

''Mrs. Ramsey be damned. Take off the chemise.''

''I shouldn't,'' she said weakly.

''Don't you want to?'' He approached her slowly, and

she backed away until her shoulders bumped against the wall. She was mesmerized by the darkness of his eyes. When he stared at her like that, she could refuse him nothing. Unsteadily she grasped the hem of the chemise and pulled it over her head.

Jason reached for her, his hands sliding over her back and buttocks. She wrapped her arms around his neck, every nerve kindling with the intense passion he aroused. Murmuring to her hoarsely, he lifted her against the wall, the muscles in his arms bulging. Her eyes widened, and she gasped in surprise as she felt him enter her in a hard, deep thrust. Obeying his whispered commands, she wrapped her silk-stockinged legs around his hips.

"You're so beautiful," he rasped, kissing her chin, her cheeks, her parted lips. "So sweet . . . Laura . . ."

Rhythmically he withdrew and thrust into her warm body, staring at her flushed face. Laura whimpered and tightened her legs, her heels digging into his muscled buttocks. She clung to him, her hands grasping frantically at his sweat-slick shoulders. Suddenly the exquisite tension coiled inside, tightening painfully. Gasping, she buried her face against his neck and felt herself burning slowly, slowly, her body consumed in a blaze of pleasure. Jason gritted his teeth as he strove to prolong the moment, but he was soon overtaken by his own release.

After a long time, Laura became aware that her toes were touching the floor. She was wrapped tightly in his arms. Hazily she thought that she had never felt so safe, so protected. She pressed her lips to his shoulder. "I've always loved you," she whispered, stroking the dark hair at the nape of his neck. "Even when you were cruel to me, even when you looked at me as though you hated me."

"I wanted to hate you."

"And did you?"

"Almost," he admitted gruffly. "When I saw you

with Perry Whitton. I couldn't stand the sight of another man's hands on you.'' He smiled ruefully. "I'd never felt jealousy before, and suddenly it was twisting at my guts. I wanted to strangle you only a little less than I did Whitton.''

"There was no need to be jealous," she murmured, still stroking his hair. "I've never wanted anyone but you.''

Laura hummed carols as she hung gilded eggshells on the Christmas tree, which was small enough that she could reach all but the top branches. It was a week before Christmas, and she had been busy for days with holiday baking and decorating the house. The scent of evergreens filled the parlor, bringing to mind many childhood memories. Since she had not had time to make more than a few simple ornaments, her mother and Sophia had each given her a few to begin her own collection, including the angel with glass wings that she had loved since childhood. Painstakingly she and one of the maids had strung cranberries to fill the empty spaces, and their fingers were reddened and sore after hours of work. The rest of the room was decorated with garlands of holly, wreaths of gilded lemon leaves, pinecone clusters, and gold velvet ribbons.

Idly Laura wondered how Jason's family would spend Christmas. They would probably gather relatives and friends at their home, sharing memories, talking and feasting together. Laura wished that she dared ask Jason about the Morans, and why they had not sent any invitations or cards. She had only seen a few of her in-laws once. Since Jason's father, Charles, had passed away a few years before, his mother Kate had attended the wedding with some of her children, two of her daughters and one of her young sons. They had not come to the reception afterward. The Morans had been nicely, if plainly dressed, and they'd seemed to be quietly awed by their surroundings. "Brogues you could have cut with a knife," her mother had said disdainfully.

In the past year Laura had exchanged short letters with Jason's mother Kate, but that was the limit of their interaction. She knew from those notes that Jason visited his family infrequently, always during his workday. He never invited Laura or mentioned the visits to her afterward—it was as if his family didn't exist, as if she and they occupied separate worlds that only Jason could traverse.

Deep in thought, Laura tapped her forefinger against her lips. She wished she could pay Kate Moran a visit. There were many questions about Jason that Kate could answer if she cared to. Laura wanted to know more about her husband, more about the past he found so difficult to talk about. Of course, if she asked for Jason's permission to visit the Morans, he would not allow it. And if she went without his knowledge, there was the chance that he would find out.

"I don't care," she muttered. "I have every right to see them." She squared her small jaw. "I *will* see them." Filled with a mixture of determination and guilt—for she disliked the idea of doing something behind Jason's back—she considered the best time to do it. Tomorrow morning, she decided, after Jason left for work.

The Moran home was located in a solidly middle-class section of Charlestown. The two- and three-family houses had once been inhabited by the well-to-do but were now occupied by the overflow of immigrants from the adjoining neighborhood. The street was well-kept, completely unlike the strings of crowded flats and garbage-filled passageways of the South End slum districts.

Laura emerged from the carriage and looked up and down the cobblestone street with interest. It was a dry, brisk day. Lines of work clothes, colored blue, gray, and brown, flapped in the breeze. The air was filled with the scent of stewing meat and vegetables. A young couple walked by her, their arms linked, their heads swathed in knitted caps and scarves. They threw her a few discreet glances but did not slow their pace. A few children interrupted their game of stickball to stand and stare at her and the elegant carriage.

After telling the driver to wait in front of the house, Laura went to the door unescorted. There was no brass knocker. She hesitated, then lifted her hand to rap on the scarred paneled wood.

A boy's voice came from behind her. "Yer knockin' at *my* house!"

Laura turned and was confronted by a small boy of eight or nine. A smile crossed her lips. He was a Moran, no question of it. He had black hair and dark eyes, fair skin, and ruddy cheeks that had not yet lost their childish roundness. His belligerent chin and aggressive nose pointed up at her.

"Donal?" she guessed, knowing that was the name of one of Jason's two brothers.

"Robbie," the boy corrected indignantly. "An who might ye be?"

"I'm Laura Moran." When that elicited no sign of recognition, she added, "Your brother Jason's wife."

"Ooohhh." Robbie regarded her wisely. "Ma says yer a foine lady. What d'ye want?"

"I would like to see your mother."

He grasped the door handle in both hands, tugged it open, and held it for her. "Ma!" he barked into the house, and gestured for Laura to go inside. "Ma, 'tis Jason's wife!"

He urged Laura to accompany him down a long, narrow hallway lined with garments hanging on hooks. The hall led to the kitchen, where she could see the side of the cast-iron stove. There was a graniteware pot on top of the stove, and the air smelled of stewing apples. "Er . . . Robbie, perhaps I should not come in unannounced," she said.

He was puzzled by the strange word. "Unan . . ."

"Perhaps you should tell your mother that I'm here."

"Sure now, I'm tellin' 'er," he interrupted, and called shrilly toward the kitchen. "Ma, 'tis Jason's wife!"

"Who is it, ye say?" came a woman's voice, and Robbie took hold of Laura's arm, triumphantly dragging her past the stove to the wooden table in the center of the kitchen.

Kate Moran, a sturdy, pleasant-faced woman in her mid forties, regarded Laura with round blue eyes. A wooden rolling pin dropped from her hands onto the piecrust in front of her. "God save us," she exclaimed. "Jason's wife!"

"I apologize for the unexpected intrusion," Laura began, but her voice was lost in the bustle that suddenly filled the room. Jason's sisters, both attractive girls in their teens, rushed in to see the visitor.

" 'Tis Jason?" Kate asked anxiously, her flour-coated hands pressed to her heavy bosom. "Och, somethin' has happened to me firstbarn, me precious boy—"

"No, no," Laura said, "Jason is fine. Perfectly fine. I've just come for . . ." She paused, conscious of the many curious gazes on her. "I've just come for a visit," she said lamely. "But I can see that you're busy. Perhaps some other time would be better?"

There was a moment of stillness. Kate recovered quickly, her worry replaced by curiosity. " 'Tis plaised we are that ye are here. P'raps a cup o' tea—Maggie, fetch the teapot, an' Polly, show the lady to the parlor—"

"I wouldn't mind staying in the kitchen," Laura ventured. She was conscious of the family's dumbfounded gazes as she eased herself into one of the wooden chairs at the table. The room was warm and cheerful, and she preferred its informal atmosphere.

Kate shrugged helplessly. " 'Tis here ye'll stay, then." She shooed the children from the room and gave Laura a measuring glance. "An' now tell me what yer about, me dear. To be sure, Jason knows nothin' of yer visit."

"No, he does not," Laura admitted, unconsciously resting her elbows on the flour-dusted oilcloth that covered the table. She hesitated before adding, "I've come to talk to you in the hopes that you would be able to explain some things about his past to me. Jason isn't an easy man to understand."

Kate gave a short laugh. "Nay, there's no understandin' that contrary, prideful boy, nor his fine notions. A hard head like his pa's."

Laura was barely aware of time passing as she sat in the kitchen with Jason's mother. The tea grew cold in their cups while the conversation lengthened. Kate's mood relaxed from careful politeness to amiability. It was clear that she liked to talk, and in Laura she found an encouraging listener. She brought out an old photograph of Charlie Moran so that Laura could see the resemblance between father and son. " 'Twas tuck the first day Charlie opened the store on Causeway," Kate said, beaming with pride.

"He was very handsome," Laura replied, struck by the similarity to her husband—except that Charlie Moran's face had been weathered and harshly lined by years of poverty and backbreaking labor. There was the hint of a smile in his eyes, however, and a vulnerable quality that was very different from Jason's dark, cynical gaze.

"I nivver showed this to Jason," Kate commented.

"Why not? I think he would like to see it."

"Nay, not after the way they left off."

"There was a falling-out?"

Kate nodded vigorously. "It started wi' that fancy school, that taught him that uppish talk an' them high-tone words. Och, the boys tuck it on themselves to tease. An' his pa told him not to spake so high-an-mighty."

Laura thought of how isolated Jason must have been, caught between two worlds. "But his father must have been proud of him," she said. "It was remarkable for an Irish boy to attend Boston Latin, and then college—"

"Aye, Charlie near to burst his buttons." Kate paused. "But he fretted over it too, he did."

"Why?"

"Charlie said 'twas too much schoolin' by far. An' he was right, it tuck me Jason away fer good."

"Took him away?"

"Aye, 'twas plain as day. Jason would have none o' the girls in the neighborhood, foine girls though they were. He would have none o' his father's store, an' none o' his family. The local lads pressed him to take a position at the *Pilot*—'tis an Irish paper, dear. He could've gathered a followin' that would've led him to the state legislature. But Jason said he wanted nothin' but to mind his own affairs." Kate shook her head. "Ashamed he was to be Irish, an' to be the son o' Charlie Moran. 'Twas that they argued over the day before me poor Charlie died. Two stubborn divvils."

"He passed away during Jason's first year of school, didn't he?" Laura asked.

Kate nodded. "When Jason made his money, he thought to buy me a grand house an' send his brothers an' sisters to school. I told him I'd not give up me home. Donal looks after the store, an' the girls hope to marry wi' good Irish lads—the rest o' me brood cares not a whit for schoolin'. Cut from a diff'runt cloth, Jason was."

"But he needs his family," Laura said. "He does, although he may not realize how much."

Kate was about to reply when Robbie's high-pitched voice called down the hallway. "Ma! 'Tis Jason!"

Laura froze, staring in surprise at the kitchen doorway as her husband's broad-shouldered form appeared. Her heart thumped unpleasantly as she saw the ominous glint in his eyes. "Jason," she said feebly. She stood up and attempted a placating smile. "How did you know . . . ?"

His voice was cool. "I came home early. Mrs. Ramsey told me where you were."

Katie regarded her son placidly. "We've been havin' a nice visit, yer Laura an' me."

His expression didn't change, but he bent and kissed Kate's forehead. "Hello, Ma."

Laura winced as Jason took hold of her arm in a grip that was just short of being painful. "It's time to go home," he said softly, and she realized with a sinking heart that he was angrier than she had feared he would be.

After allowing her barely enough time to bid the Morans farewell, Jason rode back with her in the carriage. The tense silence between them sawed at Laura's nerves until they were shredded. "I wanted to tell you, Jason," she said hesitantly, "but I knew you wouldn't have allowed me to go."

He laughed shortly. "I hope you found the Morans entertaining."

"I—I didn't go to be entertained."

"I don't care why the hell you went. But it's damn well going to be the last time you set foot in Charlestown."

"For heaven's sake, it does no harm to anyone if I choose to see your family! I don't understand why you're taking on so."

"You don't have to understand, although you could

if you cared to look beyond the end of your nose. And wipe that wounded look off your face, or I—'' He clamped his teeth together, biting off his next words. His face was dark with fury.

"Why won't you let me have anything to do with your family? Why can't we include them in our lives?"

"Damn you!" he exploded. "My life with you has nothing to do with them! I don't want reminders—by God, I won't have you combing through my past for your own amusement! You don't belong in my family any more than I belong in yours. From now on you'll stay away from them." His lips curled in an ugly sneer. "And if you even think of defying me in this, I'll make you sorry in ways your soft little imagination couldn't begin to conceive."

Laura shrank back from his vicious tone, her green eyes alarmed. "Jason, don't threaten me—"

"Do you understand what I've just told you?"

"Jason, please—"

"Do you understand?"

"Yes," she said, hurt and intimidated. "I'll do as you say."

It was rare that Jason drank to excess, but that evening he closeted himself in the library with his whisky and stayed until well after Laura had retired to bed. He did not come to her room, and she tossed and turned restlessly, missing his warmth and his large, strong body to snuggle against. The next morning she awoke with dark-circled eyes and a sense of injustice. He was trying to punish her, she thought with annoyance. She would show him that she wasn't in the least affected by his withdrawal.

Sitting across the breakfast table from him, she saw with satisfaction that he was suffering from a fierce headache and his eyes were bloodshot. His temper was foul, but he was quiet, and he seemed to find it difficult to look at her. Slowly she realized that his anger was neither petty nor temporary, and that it had less to do with her than with the pain of old wounds. She thought about bringing up the matter of their argument—no, it might be better to keep her silence.

A few days passed, and it was time for them to attend the large Christmas Eve party that Sophia and Judge Marsh were giving. Laura had never felt less like laughing and pretending to be cheerful, but she was determined not to give her friends and family any reason to think she was having troubles with her husband. It took three hours and the help of both maids to dress and arrange her hair.

Her dress was made of deep rose satin, fitted so tightly to her body that there was not a quarter-inch of room to spare. It was embroidered from the square-cut bodice to the hem with thousands of crimson beads sewn in a flowered pattern. A ruffled satin train was draped from the small of her waist down to the floor, flowing gently out from her body as she walked. The sleeves were tight and banded at the wrists with more beads. Ruby combs glittered in the mass of braids and shining curls gathered at the back of her head.

Jason was waiting for her downstairs, his face expressionless. He was attired in flawless black and white, looking polished and astonishingly handsome. Something flickered in his eyes as he glanced over her, and when his gaze reached her face, she was aware of the feminine flutter of her senses.

An endless line of carriages blocked the street where the Marsh home blazed with light. Women in velvet mantles and furs were escorted to the entrance by men in greatcoats and tall hats. Groups of carolers strolled from house to house, filling the night with music. Hot rum punch garnished with raisins and fruit slices lent its spicy aroma to the air, as did the pine wreaths and bayberry candles in every room.

Hale besieged them as soon as they entered the house, cheerfully kissing Laura and urging Jason to join him for a drink with some of the friends they had gone to college with. Dutifully Laura greeted her mother, who looked as stiffly displeased as usual. Wilhemina Prescott glanced at her youngest daughter assessingly. "And how is the situation between you and . . . that man?"

"You are referring to my husband, Mother?" Laura asked, and forced a bright smile to her face. "Splendid."

"I have been informed otherwise. You and he engaged in some kind of quarrel at the party you gave last month."

"It has been resolved, Mother."

Wilhemina frowned. "It is shockingly ill-bred to air one's grievances in public, Laura. I hope you are not taking on the coarse, vulgar habits that his sort of people indulge in—"

"Laura!" Sophia's light voice interrupted. "Dear, you must come and see how the children decorated the tree . . . absolutely charming . . . excuse us, Mother."

"Thank you," Laura said feelingly, trailing after her sister.

"She's in fine form tonight," Sophia muttered. "Father's not with her. She claims he is indisposed. My guess is they have had a row over his most recent fancy-friend."

Laura stayed at Sophia's side for much of the party, while the crowd grew lively with the dancing, music, and potent punch. Her gaze moved around the sea of familiar faces. She caught a glimpse of her husband as he talked with the people gathered around him. It was not difficult to pick Jason out from the crowd—his dark, vivid looks made everyone around him seem colorless in comparison. His manner was livelier and more intense than the cool crispness of the people around him.

Laura smiled slightly. It didn't matter to her if Jason was ever truly accepted by the Boston elite or not. She was glad of the differences between him and the rest of them, glad of his earthy vitality and even his exasperating pride. Impishly she decided to go to him to find some way of enticing him to a private corner. Surely he wouldn't mind a stolen kiss or two.

She made her way through the entrance hall, artfully sweeping up the folds of her train to keep it from being trampled by wayward feet. Hale and one of his friends walked past her to the front door, holding a third young man up by the shoulders. The man was obviously the worse for drink, and they were taking him outside to sober him up in the cold air. Such situations were always handled with dispatch, before the ladies could be offended by the sight of a gentleman in his cups. "Good evening, Mrs. Moran," Hale said wryly, grinning at her. "Step aside for Samuel Pierce Lindon, unfortunate victim of hot rum punch."

"Shall I fetch coffee from the kitchen?" she asked sympathetically.

Hale opened his mouth to answer, but he was interrupted by Samuel, whose head wobbled in Laura's direction. "Moran?" he slurred. "You're the sisshter . . . that one who m-married a m-m-mick."

"Yes, I'm that one," Laura said dryly, knowing that the boy would never have dreamed of saying such a thing were he sober.

Drunkenly Samuel lurched out of Hale's grasp and pinned Laura against the front door. "You're standin' under the mishletoe."

"I'm afraid you are mistaken," Laura muttered, shoving her elbows hard into his midriff. He wound his arms tightly around her and refused to let go.

"Here now!" Hale grunted in annoyance, trying to pry Samuel away. "Let go of my sister, half-wit. Sorry,

Laura . . . he's too foxed to know what he's doing—''

"You drather have a gennleman than a *mick* in your bed, wouldn' you?'' Samuel asked, his liquor-pungent breath wafting in Laura's face. "I'll show you what you're missing . . . One li'l kiss, thas all . . . you green-horn wives don' usually mind sharing your fav—''

Suddenly Samuel was lifted and spun around as if by a tornado. Laura fell back against the door, aghast as she saw a brief scuffle between Samuel and her husband. Jason's face was white with rage, his black eyes blazing. Feebly Lindon swung and missed. A woman screamed while others swayed in ladylike faints. Jason drew back his fist and dropped the young man with one hard blow. He would have beaten him to a pulp had Hale not pounced on him and held him from behind. The crowd swarmed into the entrance hall, chattering excitedly.

"Easy, Moran,'' Hale hissed, struggling to keep hold of Jason. "No need to wipe the floor with him. He didn't hurt Laura—I was here.''

Jason went still, struggling to control his temper. He shrugged off Hale's restraining arms and strode to his wife, taking her by the shoulders. He looked over her worriedly. "Laura—''

"Jason, I'm all right,'' she said shakily. "There was no need to make a scene. He's just a drunken boy. He didn't mean to—''

Her mother's icy voice cut through the hubbub. "How dare you,'' Wilhemina exclaimed, glaring at Jason. "How dare you turn a society gathering into a dockyard brawl! It may be common among the Irish to behave in such a manner, but it is not the way of decent people!'' Her tall, thin body stiffened imperiously. "Your expensive clothes and pretend manners cannot conceal what you are, an ill-bred peasant—''

Laura interrupted, unable to stand any more. "Shut up, Mother.''

Wilhemina's jaw dropped in astonishment. None of her children had ever dared to speak to her so rudely.

Hale snickered, throwing Laura a glance of surprised approval.

Sophia stepped forward and shook her finger at Samuel, who had managed to sit up and was holding his head bemusedly. "Young man, I do not appreciate having my guests accosted in my own home." She turned to her brother. "Please take your friend outside, Hale."

"Yes, ma'am," he replied dutifully.

"Sophia," Laura said in a low voice, slipping her arm through Jason's, "I believe we will be going home now."

Sophia looked from Jason's stony expression to Laura's distressed one. "I understand, dear."

Hale stopped them before they reached the door, clapping Jason on the back. "I . . . er, would like to apologize for Lindon. He'll be devilish sorry for all of this when he sobers up." He extended a hand and Jason shook it briefly, both of them exchanging rueful glances.

Laura was silent during the carriage ride home, wanting to let both their tempers settle. She was angry and upset by Jason's behavior. It had not been necessary for him to make such a scene! Samuel had been obnoxious but hardly dangerous. The problem could have been solved with a few brief words, and Jason knew it. He also knew that if two gentlemen ever found it necessary to come to blows, it was never done in the presence of ladies.

As soon as Jason escorted Laura into the house, Mrs. Ramsey appeared to welcome them. Laura waved the housekeeper away, and Mrs. Ramsey promptly disappeared, having read from their faces that all was not well. Jason turned and began to head toward the stairs.

"Jason, wait," Laura said, catching hold of his arm. "We must talk about what happened."

He shook off her hand. "There's nothing to talk about."

"Isn't there? You must admit that you overreacted."

"I don't call it an overreaction to stop some drunken fool from pawing my wife."

"There was no need to deal with him so harshly. He wasn't aware of what he was doing—"

"The hell he wasn't! Do you think he would have insulted you had you been someone else's wife? A Boston Brahmin's wife?" He sneered at her lack of response. "No. Because he and his peers are accustomed to giving the Irish housemaids a slap and tickle, or visiting the North End shanties for prostitutes, and in their eyes the fact that you're married to an Irishman makes you—"

"Jason, don't," she cried, throwing her arms around his neck and hugging herself to his rigid body. "Must you blame everything on the fact that you're Irish?" She pressed a beseeching kiss on the side of his neck. "Let's talk about this sensibly." She gave him another kiss, this time underneath his ear. "Come sit with me by the fire."

For a moment she thought he was going to refuse her, but then he agreed with a muffled curse and followed her into the parlor. While Laura drew up an overstuffed ottoman and seated herself, Jason stirred the coals in the grate. He threw on a handful of pine knots and a birch log, dusted off his hands, and sat on the floor, propping one knee up. The blaze of firelight played over his rumpled black hair and hard-edged face, turning his skin to copper.

Laura took a deep breath and groped for the right words to say. "Jason . . . that Lindon boy's remarks didn't upset me as much as your reaction did." She stared into the fire, picking at her beaded dress in agitation. "I'm afraid that you may have more in common with my mother and her prejudices than you think," she said. He gave her a

forbidding stare, but she continued doggedly. "Deep
down you seem to believe as she does, that a Brahmin
should never have married an Irishman. You think the
two worlds should be kept separate. But you can never
erase your past . . . your family . . . your heritage. You
can't turn your back and pretend they don't exist."

Jason was silent, motionless. Laura sighed with frustration, thinking that she may as well have been talking
to a brick wall. "Oh, why must you be so stubborn?"
After considering him for a moment, she stood up and
went to the Christmas tree in the distant corner. "I have
something for you," she said, picking up a small package
wrapped in colored paper. "I'd rather give it to you now
than wait until the morning."

"Laura, I'm not in the mood for this."

"Please," she entreated, bringing the gift to him.
"Please, I want you to." Heedless of her fine dress, she
knelt on the floor next to him and dropped the flat package
into his lap.

He regarded it stonily. "I suppose this has some bearing on the conversation."

"Yes, I think so."

Slowly Jason ripped one side of the paper and pulled
out a small photograph in a frame. He went still, his
head bent over the sepia-toned albumen print. Laura had
chosen a simple silver frame ornamented with a garnet
in each corner.

The picture was of Charlie Moran in the doorway of
his grocery store. It was a shock to Jason—he had not
seen his father's face since the day before Charlie had
died. He felt as if he'd received a hard blow to the chest.
"Where did you get this?" he asked after a long time.

"Your mother showed it to me. I asked her if I could
give it to you. She said you'd never seen it."

"No." He stared at the weathered face in the photograph, shaken by the memories it provoked.

Laura watched him with an almost maternal tenderness as he studied the faded image.

"Big, hard-drinking, blustering, hot-tempered Irishman," Jason said. "We could never talk without arguing. The last time I saw him was the worst. We nearly came to blows."

"Why?"

"He accused me of being ashamed of him and the family. I told him he was right. I . . ." Jason looked away from the picture, his jaw tensing. ". . . said things I never should have said. I wanted no part of his plans for me. God knows I was never meant to champion Irish causes, or go into ward politics, or take over his store—" He broke off abruptly. "It doesn't matter now."

"He died the next day, didn't he?" Laura asked.

Jason smiled bitterly. "That night, actually. It was quick, unexpected. Ma sent for me, but he was dead before I reached the house."

"You must have been devastated."

"I was angry because of all I'd said to him." Jason was too wrapped up in the memory to guard his words. "Because he'd gone before I could take any of it back."

"What would you have told him?" she whispered.

"I . . ." He swallowed hard and narrowed his eyes against the sudden glitter of tears. "Dammit." Roughly he rubbed his sleeve over his face, disgusted with his lack of control. "Hell, I don't know."

"Jason, you must forgive yourself," she said softly. "There is no one to blame. It wasn't your fault that you wanted a life different from his. It wasn't your fault that he died."

"I never . . ." Jason was surprised at how the memory could hurt after all these years. "I never made peace with him. He died thinking I hated him."

Finally she understood the burden of guilt he had carried for so long. She couldn't stop herself from reaching out to him. She curved her arm around his neck and laid her palm against his damp cheek. "No, Jason," she whispered. "That isn't true. He knew you loved him. And he was proud of you. Ask Kate and she'll tell you how much." She saw his fingers tighten on the silver frame, and she put her hands over his.

Jason stared at the photograph while the grief and guilt that had weighed on him for years began to ease. It would take time to let go completely, but he knew that Laura was right. The fault was not his—there was no one to blame.

Laura studied the picture along with him. "I want us to keep this on the mantel," she murmured, "for everyone to see. I want it to remind you of the past, and remind you that there is no shame in what he was and what you are."

"Perhaps not to you," he conceded gruffly, "but—"

"It doesn't matter what shallow-minded people think. I fell in love with you because of the man you are. And when we have children, I intend for them to know your family as well as mine. They're going to be proud of their Irish heritage." She smiled unsteadily. "And if you think I can't match your stubbornness, Jason Moran, then you have a thing or two to learn."

He was quiet, his brooding gaze fastened on the photograph, and then he set it aside. "Then we'll keep this damned thing wherever you want it," he muttered. "Hang it on the front door if you like."

A smile of pure gladness broke out over her face, and she knew then that everything would be all right. "Perhaps I will."

Jason pulled Laura into his arms, crushing her to his chest until she could hardly breathe. "I love you," he said hoarsely, burying his face against her hair. "I've always loved you."

"You had a fine way of showing it," she murmured,

nuzzling underneath his jaw. "Impatient, sarcastic—"

"Sassy little devil." He let out a long sigh. "I thought if you knew how I felt you'd throw it back in my face. It was safer to let you and everyone else think I wanted you merely as an ornament, a trophy—"

"While I pretended that I married you out of a sense of duty to my family." She laughed softly. "We should have been honest with each other from the beginning."

He rubbed his cheek against her hair, holding her as if he would never let her go. He had never felt such peace. All his life had been directed toward this moment, this woman. The silence was unbroken by anything except the crackle of the fire. Its golden light glinted off the ornaments on the Christmas tree, the glass wings of the angel, the beads on Laura's satin dress.

Laura was suffused with a glow of happiness. She had always loved Christmas, but now more than ever because it was on this night that their marriage was finally beginning, and no greater gift could be given to her. How many holidays he had spent with the Prescotts, always an outsider. But she and Jason would spend a lifetime together and have their own family. And they would make every Christmas as magical as this one. She held him tightly.

"*Mo stoir*," he whispered, and dragged his mouth from her chin to the valley between her breasts.

Laura recognized the words he had said before. "Tell me what it means," she said, her eyes half-closing as his hand slipped inside her bodice.

"My treasure."

She caressed the back of his neck. "And the other thing you call me—"

"*Gradh mo chroidhe* . . . love of my heart."

She smiled in pleasure. "Is that what I am?"

"That's what you've always been," he said, and lowered his mouth to hers.

MERRY CHRISTMAS
from ...
LISA KLEYPAS

After graduating from Wellesley College, LISA KLEY-
PAS sold her first historical romance novel at the age of
twenty-one and decided to make writing her full-time
career. She has had four novels published and has been
featured in magazines such as *People* and *McCall's*. In
1987 she was given the *Romantic Times'* award for New
Historical Regency Author and in 1989 was awarded
Affaire de Coeur's Golden Unicorn for Best Time Travel
Romance. Lisa is a former Miss Massachusetts and com-
peted in the 1985 Miss America pageant. She is currently
a resident of Texas and is hard at work on her next novel.

A Creole
Christmas

Diane Wicker Davis

1

AT SIXTEEN AND A HALF, COCO COLOMB WAS CON-vinced that love would come to her like Louisiana lightning striking a rooftop in the heart of New Orleans' French Quarter. It would come with a flash of white light, a crash and a boom, and the blinding revelation that she had met her life's mate. It would also—she knew beyond any doubt—change her so irrevocably that even her aunt, Tante Tata, would see that she was no longer a child.

But when would it come? She was of marriageable age and impatient for fate to single her out. Of course, *everyone* knew that fate could be hurried along. She only needed to pray to Saint Nicholas on the first Friday of the month, perform every act of the spell perfectly, and the one she was to marry would be revealed to her. Papa might consider this year of 1880 too modern for such superstition, but Tante Tata—who was so old she knew everything!—had sworn that Cousine Azema had tried it, and she had met her Armand the very next morning!

Coco had spent the last week in a fever of anticipation, and this momentous Friday, in a fog of apprehension. If

it didn't work, she'd have to wait another whole month—
and a month was forever!

Night had long cloaked the French Quarter when Papa
knocked the ashes from his pipe and said, "To bed, my
angels."

Coco shot from her chair with trembling haste and
unalloyed relief, kissed Papa, Maman, and Tante Tata,
sketched a hasty curtsy, mumbled a hastier good night,
and fled along the gallery and up the stairs to the bedchamber she shared with her sisters. Usually laggards to
bed, tonight they followed hot at her heels, as if aware
that something unusual was afoot. Papa always said that
his daughters were as close as the shucks on an ear of
corn—and, unfortunately, no shuck could keep a secret
from another.

Coco dove headfirst into the massive Seignouret armoire in search of her *chemise de nuit*, the voluminous
nightgown whose every dainty tuck, delicate stitch of
embroidery, and gentle fold of lace had been sewn by
Tante Tata's talented fingers. Grasping it, she began to
back out, only to find that her sisters had trapped her.

"What are you up to, Coco?" asked Céré, button-
nosed and plump.

"Do tell us," commanded Mémé, sloe-eyed and thin.

In the cedar-lined depths of the armoire, Coco sighed
irritably. Her sisters were as pesky, as persistent, as
inescapable as mosquitoes. "Only if you promise—"

"We promise!" they chorused, hauling her out by the
hips, as unceremoniously as the sacks of flour Jubilee,
the cook, wrestled out of the storeroom—an act hardly
designed to place her in the mood of piety she needed
to cast a reverent spell.

Reining in a surge of temper, Coco presented them
with her back. Only when their fingers began flying down
the myriad buttons marching the length of her spine did

she deign to glance over her shoulder. "Today is Friday," she whispered portentously.

"So?" queried Cécé.

"The first Friday of the month," she added with unconcealed impatience. Sometimes they could be so thickwitted!

"So?" prodded Mémé.

Coco tossed her *chemise de nuit* onto the canopied tester bed and slipped the Havana-brown bodice of her dress down over her flannel petticoats. "*So* . . . it is the night we can pray to Saint Nicholas."

"*Non!*" cried Cécé. "Papa says that is the greatest foolishness!"

"But—but—" Mémé stuttered in her hurry. "Tante Tata says that Cousine Azema—"

"Exactly!" Coco crowed triumphantly, tearing at the ribbons tying her petticoats around her waist. She hurried to the lavabo, the marble-topped washstand with its elegant bowl and pitcher imported from France, as anything worth having was.

Plucking the pins from her lustrous sable hair, she looked in the mirror and saw Cécé and Mémé staring at one another, their eyes dancing with devilment.

After her prayer to Saint Nicholas Coco would be required to go to sleep without talking or laughing or moving. Her sisters obviously saw this as an invitation—very likely, a duty!—to force her to do one or all three. But she had planned this for too long to be thwarted now. Let them do their worst. It was a point of honor and pride to lay as one dead.

Barely suppressing their laughter, Cécé and Mémé leaped for the armoire to drag out their nightgowns. A few flurried minutes later, they stood by, haphazardly braiding their hip-length hair, their faces alive with mischief, while Coco flung back the coverlets and approached the foot of the bed in some trepidation.

"Today, the first Friday of October, I place my foot on the footboard and pray the great Saint Nicholas to make me meet the one I am to marry," she intoned melodramatically. Drawing a deep breath, she vaulted onto the bed without touching the floor and stretched out on the right side with her hand over her heart, the very picture, she was sure, of reverence and piety.

That picture was quickly disturbed by the whisper of Cécé's steps and the rustle of her gown beside the bed. "Coco is the baby," she said with a naughty trill of laughter.

Mémé took a running jump, landing atop the feather-stuffed mattress with a thump that warned there would be no smooth sinking into blissful sleep and hopeful dreams. "We can't possibly allow her to marry before us!"

Sometimes they could be so *childish*! A long silence ensued, during which Coco grew increasingly worried. What were they up to? She dared not open her eyes to see.

Something began tickling her nose. Something that felt suspiciously like a feather. She squeezed her eyes more tightly shut and stretched her nostrils, praying fervently that the itch would go away, that they would weary of their games.

"Cécé, what do you think Coco's beau will look like?" murmured Mémé.

"He'll have a red nose like Nonc P'tit."

"And a big belly like Cousin Armand."

"And he'll smell like—"

Bay rum, Coco thought, determinedly ignoring them. Nothing smelled better than a freshly shaved man splashed with bay rum. And he'd be tall and lean, with curly black hair—

The itch moved down to her upper lip, drifting from side to side, rousing an unbearable urge to sneeze. She drew a deep breath, concentrating on remaining perfectly still. No matter what they did, she would not talk or laugh or move. They wouldn't get the best of her!

Mémé shifted around on the bed. Cécé leaned closer. It was so quiet Coco wanted desperately to peep through the screen of her lashes. But that would be cheating and everything had to be done perfectly.

What were they planning?

"Her feet!" cried Mémé gleefully.

Her ticklish feet! That was the problem with being as close as the shucks on an ear of corn. Every shuck knew its neighbor's fatal weakness.

The covers were thrown back, and cool air washed over Coco. She stiffened, her toes curling under, her feet straining down to the mattress. Anything else, she might have withstood . . .

Cécé caught one, Mémé the other, and they laughed fiendishly as their fingers danced up and down the soles of Coco's feet. She bit her lip and clenched her teeth and willed herself to be as stiff as the whalebone in her corset.

But . . . but . . . a giggle, hysterical, angry, defeated, began to burble in the back of her throat, forcing its way past her clenched teeth, pushing through her pinched lips.

"I heard it!" cried Cécé, dropping her foot and flopping down beside Coco.

"Me, too!" exulted Mémé, scrambling up to the pillows and plunging down with a giggle.

They tumbled around on the bed like the new pups cavorting in the heat of the kitchen stove, swearing that the spell was broken. But Coco lay still, her hand over her heart. It had only been one little sound. Tomorrow, the next day at the latest, she would meet the one she was to wed.

But the next day came and the next and the next, and Coco met no young man whose presence struck her like a bolt of lightning, drying her mouth to cotton, making her heart beat faster. She dragged herself from bed at dawn every morning to accompany Tante Tata to the French market—just in case he, too, might be an early riser. She walked with Maman to the tiny shop on Royal Street where the very best green coffee beans and chicory were to be found—but no young blade strolling along the banquette caught her eye. By the end of the month she was so desperate, she accompanied Maman and Tante Tata, Papa and her elder brother Pierre to the St. Louis cemetery, where the Creoles gathered to clean the "City of the Dead" in preparation for All Saints' Day. She pulled the weeds that sprang up around the family mausoleum, even hefting a brush to help whitewash its walls—and all the while she kept an eye out for a tall, lean man with curly black hair.

He was nowhere to be found.

Apparently it took only a tiny chirrup of a giggle to break the spell—and for that she would "thank" Cécé and Mémé, as soon as she could think of a suitable revenge. Tante Tata was always warning Coco that her inability to forgive would someday come back to haunt her, but the delicious satisfaction of retaliation was worth any risk. And half the pleasure came from lingering over the plans for it.

The Creole worship of *la famille* extended beyond the living to the dead. November 1st, All Saints' Day, was dedicated to the ancestors whose lives made the present possible. All over the French Quarter mamas climbed into the *mansarde* beneath the roof to find the *immortelles*—wreaths of shiny jet beads—wrapped in newspaper and used from one year to the next. On the morning of that special day they hung the *immortelle* on a hook on the door of the family mausoleum—just as Maman was doing now. She stepped out of the bower of white chrysanthemums and red cockscombs, looking to Tante Tata, who bowed her head to begin the *dizaine*, a decade of the Rosary.

Coco stood at the rear of her gathered family, her rosary beads in one hand, a black-bordered handkerchief in the other. She should have been praying for the souls of her ancestors; she was, instead, sneaking a peak at the families gathered before the mausoleums lining the narrow shell roadway. Since all of the Creoles in the city were related to one another, the faces were familiar ones. There was Nonc P'tit with his red nose. And Cousine Zaza Fortier, who had a running feud with Tante Tata over which of them made the best pralines. *Le Jour de l'An*—New Year's Day—was always a trial and a tribulation with the two of them thrusting platters of pralines on sundry relatives and demanding a judgment as to whose was best. The unfortunate who judged incorrectly, or worse, refused to judge at all, found himself no longer on speaking terms with one or both of them.

Coco herself had solved this dilemma in a thoroughly unscrupulous manner, which bothered her conscience not a bit. She took Tante Tata off to the side, assuring her that hers were the creamiest, the most delicate and delicious pralines made in any kitchen in the French Quarter. However, Coco further explained, she hesitated to hurt Cousine Zaza's feelings. After all, she was growing so feeble (Cousine Zaza could outwalk a sugar-mill mule) and her advanced years (two years more than Tante Tata's) were telling on her. Would there be any objection if Coco told Cousine Zaza that hers were the best pralines? Of course, Tante Tata would know that it was said merely out of kindness, for no one could match *her* pralines! Assured that no offense would be taken, Coco had then spirited Cousine Zaza off to the side to repeat this faradiddle in reverse.

Coco could see no wrong in a solution which left

everyone happy—and her with a supply of pralines that lasted well into spring! Smiling in anticipation of the tins she would receive on New Year's Day, Coco's wandering gaze lit on the supremely masculine figure standing to the left of Cousine Zaza.

Though his posture was royally erect, he was of average height and brawny as a bull, his neck thick, his shoulders massive, and his hands huge. He had an air of stolidity, the calm poise of a man who knew his own worth. His spread feet were planted so firmly he seemed to be rooted in the earth, at one with it and with himself. As Coco watched, he slowly removed his homburg, leaving his thick, rich brown hair to the mercy of the playful wind.

Her mouth dried to cotton. Her heart lurched and began to race. Unfortunately, the accelerating beat did not come from a bolt of love striking from the blue, but from an utterly earthly fury.

So! she thought waspishly. Court Fortier was back from his Grand Tour. Well, she was no longer a girl suffering the throes of first love for her older brother's friend. She was a woman now. Sixteen and a half. Why, she'd made her debut at the French Opera House, where she had occupied a box with her parents, which announced to Creole New Orleans that she was no longer a child. *Throngs* of young men had stopped between acts to chat and request her father's permission to call on her. *They* had not smiled at her with superior indulgence. *They* had not told her she was an adorable child while she was stammering out a declaration of undying love. *They* had not patted her on the head and offered her a *dragée*. As if a sugar-coated almond could soothe a broken heart! Not that it had remained broken for long.

If Court Fortier expected to find her still worshiping at his feet . . .

Coco, plotting the many ways she could effect his humiliation, bowed her head demurely.

Harcourt "Court" Fortier breathed deep of the humid Louisiana air. He'd spent the last two years in France and Italy, England and the Alps, but he'd seen nothing to equal the sights, the sounds, the smells of home. It was good to be back, to sit by the kitchen fire with Tante Zaza fussing over him and his mother kneading the crusty, delicious bread whose match he had found nowhere on his travels. Just as he had found no women to match the beauties of New Orleans—and one beauty in particular.

His gaze wandered from Tante Zaza's flat pie of a black hat to the Colomb family. Coco stood at the rear with her head bowed and her demeanor so demure and unassuming it summoned a sparkle to his dark brown eyes. Court's mouth, wide and mobile with a touch of sensuality in the full lower lip, spread slowly in a grin. The Coco he remembered was always at her most demure when her delightfully fertile brain was hatching a scheme.

She was the very picture of innocence in her *demi-deuil*, the half-mourning colors of black and white. And the prevalent fashion of the hourglass figure and the slim, straight skirt suited her so admirably that Court's gaze grew as warm as his blood. Standing so still with her head bowed over her rosary and the wind whipping tendrils of lustrous, sable hair around her small, exquisite face, she looked as cool and serene as a magnolia blossom. But he knew she had only to move and that deceptive illusion would vanish, for Coco Colomb was all iridescent light and quicksilver movement and mercuric mood, as sassy and lively as he was cautious and phlegmatic.

He'd waited a long time for her to grow up. He had

adored her as the baby he'd carted around on his hip. He had laughed at her childish pranks, admiring the fool-hardy courage that sent her into the boughs of the court-yard oak—from whence he'd rescued her, not because she was afraid but because her Tante Tata had fallen into hysterics. He had patiently endured Coco's first awkward attempts at flirtation, never smiling when her fluttering fan thwacked the tip of her nose or when she stumbled over the hem of her skirt while trying to bat her eyelashes and walk at the same time. He had thought he had the patience to endure the wait for her, but at fourteen she had suddenly developed lush, ripe curves and, with them, a startling awareness of herself as a woman. The problem was that she was not yet a woman while he was very much a man. When she had cornered him in the courtyard on a moonlit night, confessing her love in passionate, if stuttering, prose, he had realized he was on ground as treacherous as a Louisiana swamp. Within days he had fled New Orleans—and temptation—for the old tradition of the Grand Tour. Home now, he was ready to lay claim to Coco Colomb without further delay.

The *dizaine* completed, Tante Zaza crossed herself and turned to Court, her broad face crinkling in a smile. "I should like to speak to Cousine Tata," she said.

Which was a ploy as transparent as the black veil hanging from the brim of her hat. Speaking to her cousin was the last thing she wished to do. However, she would suffer even that torture if it would allow her to nudge him in Coco's direction—something she had been trying to do for years with his willing participation. Since her plan fell in neatly with his own, Court refrained from teasing her and offered his arm.

"And how was *la belle France*?" asked his old friend, Pierre Colomb, before pausing to introduce his shy wife, Marie.

Court tipped his hat and found himself besieged by Cécé and Mémé, who had always, even when he was a boy, looked upon him as *un vieux garcon*, an old bachelor of the agreeable and trustworthy variety. Fortunately, he did not have that effect on Coco, who hung back with her small chin lifted and a challenge shining in her ebony eyes.

"Court," cried Cécé impulsively, "is it true that all of the French mademoiselles wear a tournure?"

He stoically removed his admiring gaze from Coco. "A tournure?"

"A bustle!" she said eagerly. "Madame Deslattes, our modiste, says—"

"Cécé!" burst out Papa Colomb, his face flushing red. "A lady does not discuss the intricacies of her toilette with a gentleman—even one as close to us all as Court!"

"Really, Cécé," murmured Coco with a mischievous moue of distaste. "You will have Court thinking we have sunk to the level of savages."

"Hardly." He suppressed a smile as he bowed deeply before her. "So, Coco, you are all grown up."

"So, Court, you are back," she said, her expression as cool as the granite slabs of the mausoleum.

He studied the haughty tilt of her head, the challenge still glittering in the black eyes that gazed directly into his. Had her cheeks not burned with bright spots of color, he would have thought she had forgotten both her former attachment to him and its uncomfortable end. Obviously, she remembered it as clearly as he did. Even now he could see her tender mouth trembling and her eyes welling with unshed tears. He could see the *dragée* clutched in her small hand and hear the threat she had flung at him: "I'll never forgive you for this, Court Fortier!"

Because her unquenchable pride was one of the things he loved about her, he would be patient—for a while.

But should she wish to linger over the revenge she would surely want to take, Coco Colomb would quickly learn that he, a man of twenty-five, was no boy to be toyed with.

IN THE FOYER OF THE FRENCH OPERA HOUSE *LA CRÉME des Créoles* were on parade. It was the opening of the season in the temple of the lyric arts, and everyone who was anyone was there to see and be seen. Court Fortier, elegant in tie and tails and top hat, paused to watch Coco hold court for a bevy of beardless boys.

She was, in his eyes, the personification of all that any Creole hoped his woman would be. Her black eyes were large and lustrous, her sable hair thick and curling, and her skin was as smooth and white as the delicate camellias that were budding in the courtyards of the city. Though she lacked the languishing air that was so dangerous to a man's heart, she had a vivacity, a charm, a gaiety that was even more perilous. He longed to join her, to see her eyes turn up to his, to see a smile meant for him alone, but he would not become only one of her many admirers. He had his pride, too.

Smiling, he turned for the stairs. During the intermission, he would join her in the Colomb family box. Perhaps then she would have a moment he could claim for his own.

* * *

Coco loved the opera, not for its music and drama but for its sensational setting and intoxicating aura of sophistication. She had that rarest of maladies, a tin ear, and a singing voice that made a squeaky cricket sound like a classically trained soprano. Though she was, musically speaking, the despair of her *maman*, her lack of appreciation for a flawlessly rendered aria did not detract one jot from her love of *l'opéra*.

She adored the simmering excitement of the crowds, the ladies in *grande toilette*, and the grandeur of the Opera House itself. With its perfectly proportioned auditorium and gracefully curved balconies, its gilding and decorations in crimson, white, and gold, it was a setting worthy of a queen—and she felt like a queen when she sat in the private box overlooking the proscenium.

But the very best part was the intermission, when the box filled with dashing young men engaging in discreet flirtation. Looking forward to those handsome and virile visitors, Coco clapped heartily and shouted a "Bravo!" while the heavy plush curtains slowly sank to the stage floor.

"A little less enthusiasm would be more seemly, Coco."

"*Oui*, Papa," she said breathlessly, turning an eager gaze to the curtains at the back of the box. Who of the latest crop of beaux would be the first to enter? The Breaux brothers with their laughing eyes and ready smiles? Gaspard Trouard with the devil in his grin? Tante Tata said he had a heart like an artichoke—a leaf for everyone—but he was, nevertheless, a favorite with Coco. There was a hint of danger about Gaspard, so unlike Court, who was as safe as Papa or her brother Pierre. If only Court delayed his arrival, he would find her surrounded by admirers. That, she thought triumphantly, should prove she was a child no longer. Not that she cared what he thought, she told herself hastily. She was long over her infatuation with him.

She smoothed her white mull skirt, tugged at the duchesse lace spilling over her hands, and pinched her cheeks—

"Do not fidget, Coco," warned Tante Tata. "A lady is known by her calm demeanor."

But how could she sustain a calm demeanor when she was giddy with the anticipation of giving Court the setdown he so richly deserved!

A gloved hand swept the curtains back and the Breaux brothers entered, nodding to Tante Tata, then Maman, speaking to Papa, then drifting as one toward the Colomb daughters. Within minutes the box was filled with laughing gallants. Coco smiled upon Gaspard Trouard as if her thoughts were for him alone, even as her gaze strayed to the curtain of their box, which was being lifted once more.

Court arrived, pausing for a moment while his gaze shifted from one young man to the next. In spite of his thick and brawny physique, he was the essence of elegance with his black tail coat fitting snugly over his broad shoulders and his white shirtfront gleaming in contrast to his swarthy complexion. At once earthy and worldly, he was a man's man and a woman's delight.

Coco's beaux paled into callow youths by comparison. The Breaux brothers were the merest boys, their cheeks as fresh and smooth as her own, while Court's showed the bluish cast of a man's heavy beard. And Gaspard Trouard, far from being dangerous, was simply a rebellious youth with a fondness for treading the outer edges of acceptable behavior. With a flash of insight, Coco realized that Gaspard would be devastated should he slip into a social solecism, while Court would never do so unconsciously, though he might make a deliberate choice with a be-damned-to-society attitude. It was the difference between a man who knew who he was and a boy who was still searching for himself.

She longed to smile at Court, to beckon him to her, to hear him speak in his deep gravelly voice of all he had seen on his travels. But pride was the evil twin of those yearnings, overshadowing them, choking them back. Her chin lifted with the hint of a mutinous jut, and the smile she longed to bestow on him she gave to Florian Breaux instead.

That young man started visibly, his own smile spreading across a face that had never looked quite so young and vulnerable to Coco. She suffered a twinge of guilt which she ruthlessly suppressed. In the battle to show Court what he had so casually thrown away every weapon must be used to the fullest.

Court exchanged greetings with Tante Tata, almost as if he were a suitor required to pass first muster with the old aunt, who in every household was the authority on family trees and the first obstacle to courtship. He spoke to Maman and Papa, lingered a moment with Cécé and Mémé, and finally arrived at Coco's side.

"*Bonjour*, mademoiselle." A dimple winked in his cheek, softening the hard, square line of his jaw and sending a little spurt of warmth through Coco's veins. The dimple, she remembered, showed only when he was at his most amused. A chilling draft of discomfort vanquished the warmth. How dare he be *amused* by her!

"*Bonjour*, Monsieur Fortier." She plied her lace fan with the skill that had been perfected before the mirrored doors of her armoire. It had been more than a year since she had thwacked the tip of her nose, but now breast-heaving indignation and overconfidence combined to betray her—she thwacked the tip of her chin.

A twinkle of laughter starring his dark eyes, he chided gently, "So formal, Coco."

Her back grew as rigid as the ebony cane he held in

his huge, gloved hand. Ignoring the mortified flaming of her cheeks, she tossed her artfully arranged curls and affected a wide-eyed look of ingenuous candor. "Ah, monsieur, I would not dare to presume on our old acquaintance."

"Would you not, *ma petite chatte*?"

Her eyes met his, glittering with anger. First he made her feel as green as the alligator pears Tante Tata grew in a corner of the courtyard! Then he called her his little cat! "I should have thought, monsieur," she began in frigid accents, "that you would prefer to spend your valuable time with someone more worthy of that . . . honor. Someone like . . . like . . ." Her gaze strayed to the adjacent box, to the young woman sitting alone at the rail. "Someone like Mademoiselle Dupree."

Having reached the advanced age of twenty-five, the mademoiselle had, euphemistically speaking, "tossed her corset on the armoire." She was sweet-natured and kind, but her painful timidity combined with the lack of a dowry had frightened off even the boldest of suitors. Now she had nothing to look forward to but the life of an old aunt, cherished by her brother's children but lonely all the same.

Coco regretted her outburst even before she saw the twinkle vanish from Court's eyes, to be replaced by a dark expression of disappointment. She inwardly writhed with shame and chagrin, but pride throttled the apology that rushed to her lips. She wanted to look away, but her gaze was locked with his, mutely beseeching him to forgive her. But there was neither forgiveness nor understanding in the swarthy face that smoothed into a bland mask.

"Perhaps you are right," he said mildly. "Mademoiselle Dupree is refreshingly free of the games that pass for discourse between men and women. *Mille pardons* for my intrusion, mademoiselle."

Games! Had he slapped her face, Coco could not have been more humiliated or infuriated. Once again he had made her feel inept and infantile. While she seethed with frustration, it seemed she could hear the echo of Tante Tata's favorite proverb: *Each one knows what boils in his own pot*. And boiling in Coco's pot was the unavoidable knowledge that she had been not only infantile but malicious.

Within moments Court appeared in the adjacent box, bowing to Mademoiselle Dupree, sitting in the chair at her side. While Coco watched, her face as crimson as the curtains rising on the proscenium, the mademoiselle's shyness evaporated and a gentle peal of laughter drifted into the dusk of the lowering gaslight.

The *saison de visites* began with the opening of the French Opera's season in November. Coco planned to enjoy it to the fullest, since this would be her first full season to be accorded the privileges of an adult. But the excitement she expected to feel had fallen prey to chronic distress. She could not forget Court's disappointment with her; she could not accept her own disappointment with herself. Mademoiselle Dupree might remain ignorant of her unkind cut, but Coco herself could not forget it. As the day for the Colombs' first "at home" of the season approached, she grew increasingly determined to make amends. Her own thoughts dwelling incessantly on the pleasures of courtship and the hopes of marriage, she decided that the only appropriate amends would be to find a beau for the mademoiselle.

Coco mentally ticked off her list of bachelor uncles and cousins, returning repeatedly to Nonc P'tit Robichaux. Seeming quite ancient to her, he was only ten years older than the mademoiselle. With his sugar plantation on Bayou Lafourche, he had no need of the dowry a wife might bring. And he was so kind and

thoughtful everyone quickly forgot that he was as plain
as rice pudding. The only problem she could foresee was
that Nonc P'tit was as bashful as the mademoiselle was
shy.

"Maman, could we ask Mademoiselle Dupree to dinner after our at home?"

Coco's mother, up to her elbows in bread dough,
paused to blow away the stray curl that persisted in dangling before her eyes. "The mademoiselle? But of
course, *chérie*." She paused to caress her daughter's
cheek with a floor-dusted knuckle. "How thoughtful you
are to think of her. She moves in society far too little."

Coco refrained from squirming beneath this unde-
served praise, which made her feel even worse than before. Should Maman learn the reason for this
thoughtfulness, she would be bitterly disillusioned with
her youngest.

"And Nonc P'tit?" she asked.

Maman studied her daughter's face, a smile gathering
in her eyes. "Why, Coco, you are matchmaking!"

"You've always said that Nonc P'tit needs a good
woman," she said defensively.

"And I very much approve of the mademoiselle, as I
approve of your new concern for others. It makes me
feel quite old to see you growing up so fast."

Which Coco thought was a very odd thing to say since
Maman, while not as ancient as Tante Tata, was very
old indeed.

Tuesday was the Colomb family's at home. Coco spent
a miserable day dressed in her best, sitting arrow-straight,
pouring coffee into dainty demitasses and blackberry
wine into thimble glasses, offering squares of *massepain*
and Tante Tata's pralines to the aunts and cousins, neighbors and friends who arrived to pay their respects.
Throughout the long day, she suffered a frenzy of anxiety

over the plan she had wrought. What if Nonc P'tit and the mademoiselle did not like each other. What if neither could summon the courage to speak to the other. What if . . . what if . . . swirled in her head like harbingers of disaster.

In the dark of evening, the round of visits was begun again, this time by the men. Uncles and cousins, neighbors and friends, they arrived in the company parlor, where Papa had joined his wife and daughters. Coco, her nerves stretched as taut as the strings of the Pleyel piano, longed to snatch up Jubilee's broom and send them all flying.

When the last of the visitors filed out, Coco breathed a sigh of relief and a prayer of thanksgiving. At least Court had not been among their number. She could not have stood his disappointment in her *or* his disconcerting presence. And she certainly did not want him to know about the plot she had hatched to make her unspoken apology to the mademoiselle, for he would surely assume it was done for his benefit.

Papa was notoriously impatient for dinner to begin, at whatever hour it was served. But when it was delayed, as tonight, until nine o'clock, his normally sunny disposition became bearish. The women of the house, Coco in the lead, fled to the kitchen, leaving Papa and Nonc P'tit to wait in the parlor.

Jubilee was carving the ham and Maman was hefting the tureen of gumbo when the old iron knocker on the porte cochere gate began clapping so timidly that only Coco heard it. But then she had been listening for it with a mix of dread and anticipation.

"I'll get it!" she cried, racing out into the courtyard with her skirts lifted high. Her feet flew across the blue-gray flagstones paving the carriageway, until she arrived at the thick wooden door, breathless and flustered. "Welcome, Mademoiselle Dupree. We are so glad you could join us.''

"*M-merci*," the woman said softly, clutching at her grosgrain reticule.

Coco pulled the door closed and turned to lead her toward the courtyard. "It's a lovely night, isn't it?"

"Lovely," murmured the mademoiselle unencouragingly.

Coco searched for a topic of conversation, a sensation of doom settling around her. "I—I saw you at the opening of the opera. The . . . the costumes were quite wonderful, weren't they?"

"Wonderful," came a quiet echo.

Coco rolled her eyes to the star-spangled heaven and prayed fervently: *Mary, Mother of God, help me!* Behind her, the old iron knocker clanged firmly, once, twice, thrice. She swiveled around, startled. She was expecting no one else.

"I'll only be a moment." Leaving the mademoiselle, Coco hurried back to the gate and pulled it open smoothly on its well-oiled hinges. A man stood on the banquette, his hat in his hand, the cool night breeze ruffling his dark hair. "Court!" she burst out, lowering her voice to hiss, "What are *you* doing here?"

"I was invited," he said, his voice deep and unamused.

"Invited!"

"By Tante Tata."

"Tante Tata! Why?" asked Coco, nearly keening with frustration. How awkward the evening had suddenly become.

"I presume because she, unlike you, enjoys my company."

"If you gave me the respect you give to her, *I* might enjoy your company, too!"

"Respect, Coco," he began on a professorial note,

"is not given, it is earned."

In spite of the painful implication that she was beneath contempt, Coco threw back her shoulders and glared up at him. "At least I know exactly where I stand. How fortunate that I would not spend a picayune to better your opinion of me!"

His face, lit by the gas lantern flickering on the wall, transformed from coolly aloof to scowling in an instant. "*Nom de Dieu*, Coco! How long do you intend to punish me for doing the only honorable thing I could do?"

"I—I have no idea what you are talking about," she lied vehemently.

"And I am not such a fool as to believe that! Do you think I have forgotten the little incident with Gaspard Trouard? You were eight when he broke your doll. You were eleven when you finally got your revenge by stealing his set of Napoleonic soldiers and tossing them into the river. It took you three years, during which time you neither forgot nor forgave."

That incident had earned her a spanking she would not soon forget. A spanking which had not dimmed the pleasure she had felt as every tin soldier *kerplopped* into the muddy Mississippi. She should be finding the same glorious elation with her every verbal thrust at Court, but in no corner of her heart could she discover a glimmer of satisfaction. Instead she felt like a spinning top wobbling out of control. At every turn there was confusion and disorientation.

She yanked open the gate, jerkily waving her hand. "Well, come in," she ordered ungraciously. "We can't stand here all night. Papa does not like to be kept waiting for his meal."

Court Fortier was so furious and frustrated he wanted to turn on his heel and stalk away with a Be-damned-to-you-Coco! He had expected her to exact a price for the humiliation he had dealt her two years ago. He had planned to pay that price because the prize was worth it. But now he'd begun to wonder. Had she matured at all in the last two years, she would see that he'd had no choice.

He did, however, blame himself for handling her very poorly. Experience with his sisters should have taught him that a girl trembling on the brink of womanhood believed with all of her heart that she had already arrived. Calling her a child was an unforgivable blow that was sure to lead to consequences as dire as the ones he was now suffering.

Stepping over the portal into the carriageway, he told himself that his patience would be rewarded—and a moment later it was.

"Mademoiselle Dupree, I'm sorry we kept you waiting so long," said Coco, her voice strained. "You of course know Monsieur Fortier."

Court cast Coco a measuring glance. So this was why she had been so unhappy to see him. Married to her determination to exact retribution for every slight was an equal determination to make reparations when she gave offense, either wittingly or unwittingly. And always it was done so casually or secretively that only those closest to her realized what was happening. It was one of the things he most admired about her, a reminder that the prize was, indeed, worth the price.

He bowed over the mademoiselle's hand, leaving Coco to note that he had not bowed over hers. Apparently she was unworthy of such attention. Where once she would have swelled up with wrath, now she was beset by sadness and uncertainty. Why couldn't she smile at him as simply and agreeably as Mademoiselle Dupree? Why couldn't they be friends again? She missed the days when she had taken her joys and sorrows to him, knowing that he would never make light of them.

Uncomfortable with her melancholy mood, Coco

struggled to recapture her old and bolstering rage. He had humiliated her! Called her a child! When she most needed his understanding, he had failed her! The thoughts blossomed with emphatic exclamation points—unaccompanied by her former indignation. Its place had been filled by fleeting memories of her youth; memories that lingered over the many times Court had not failed her. He had been her staunchest ally, her friend and confidant. He'd saved her from a spanking when Papa found her smoking his pipe. He'd hefted her onto his broad shoulders to watch the Mardi Gras parades. He'd held her in his lap and let her cry herself out when her M'mère Robichaux died, and only he had had time for a little girl grieving for her grandmother.

What had he said? *How long do you intend to punish me for doing the only honorable thing I could do?* It seemed to Coco, listlessly trailing behind Court and the mademoiselle, that somehow she was the one being punished.

As if that were not bad enough, her attempt at matchmaking fell as flat as her first attempt at French bread.

On being introduced to the mademoiselle, the florid red of Nonc P'tit's nose began to spread to his cheeks, up to his hairline, down to his collar, until even the tips of his ears were crimson. On being introduced to Nonc P'tit, Mademoiselle Dupree slowly lost every ounce of color, until even her lips were white.

Each remained in those surely uncomfortable states through the long dinner and into dessert. They exchanged neither a glance nor a word, sitting side by side and staring desperately ahead, as if, Coco thought, they feared they might be struck dead should they acknowledge the other's existence. The mademoiselle responded to every question with whispered monosyllables, while Nonc P'tit was bereft of all speech. Whether he meant yea or nay, he bobbed his head like a woodpecker hammering the trunk of a tree.

As the interminable evening progressed, Coco vacillated from disbelief to horror, from compassion to impatience. She longed to kick Nonc P'tit under the table, to beg him to tell the tales of talking alligators that had made her childhood such a delight. She longed to grasp the mademoiselle's shoulders and give her a good shake, to demand that she show Nonc P'tit her truly lovely smile and bell-like laugh.

Court, watching Coco, saw the frustration in her taut mouth and the flame in her eyes. A flame that warned she was ready for action. Any action, appropriate or not. She might be quick to make amends for a slight, but she expected her machinations to work. And she was not getting an iota of cooperation from the oblivious objects of her good deed.

He bit back a smile, unsure whether it had taken a massive dose of self-confidence or an equally large portion of naiveté to expect these fainthearted souls to change the timid habits of a lifetime in one short evening. But then Coco had never been shy. Right or wrong, she always knew exactly what she wanted, and she didn't hesitate to demand it.

Right now she wanted the miracle of a match between her uncle and the mademoiselle. Like them, Court could not break the habit of a lifetime. He leaned forward to rescue her: "Coco, did you know that Mademoiselle Dupree is none other than Tante Helene, the author of *Des Creoles*?"

All eyes turned to the mademoiselle, even Nonc P'tit's. *Des Creoles* was an anthology of the nursery rhymes and songs taught to the children of the French Quarter by the old aunts who rocked them to sleep. It had recently appeared in the bookstores of the city, creating a minor sensation among the family-oriented, French-speaking populace.

"Is this true?" Coco asked eagerly.

The mademoiselle nodded, a flush rising from her smooth, slender throat to her shining black hair.

"Maman bought copies for each of us. We had such fun singing the songs with Tante Tata, and remembering how she always sang 'Frère Jacques' when we had a fever."

Nonc P'tit cleared his throat, sounding like a steamboat grating against the dock. "I—I, too, um, bought a copy, M-mademoiselle D-dupree. I—I particularly, ah, particularly liked the section on Lenten customs. You . . . you are to be, ah, be, um, com-commended for . . ."

Coco waited with bated breath for him to finish his sentence, but he'd run out of either courage or inspiration. Still, she was heartened. It had been an oratorical triumph for a man who mumbled at any female older than twelve.

More astonishing yet, the mademoiselle dared to glance at him, her color flaming higher. "*Merci*, Monsieur Robichaux."

Coco saw the faint light of victory on the horizon, but imagination failed her. She could think of no way to nurture this tenuous beginning.

"The mademoiselle," Court said to the table at large, his gaze meaningfully probing Coco's, "is now collecting the stories that we were all told as children."

While her family bombarded Mademoiselle Dupree with eager questions, Coco stared at Court. He had ignored her throughout dinner, sharing his tales of Parisian fashions with Cécé, his descriptions of Italian museums with Mémé, and his anecdotes of strange English customs with Tante Tata. Now he was watching Coco intently, as if conveying a silent message. The message escaped her, but the fact that he knew what she was doing, that he approved and was trying to help her, did not.

He had always helped her when she needed it, and she had always taken that help for granted, as if, somehow, it were her due. She had never thanked him for the times he had snatched her away from danger or made her laugh, rather than cry. And it seemed to her now that a single pattern had marked their long friendship: he had given and she had taken.

Her gaze wandered over Court, as if she were seeing him for the first time. She didn't remember his shoulders being quite so broad or his jaw quite so square or his mouth being so . . .

"Coco," he said with an edge in his voice, "perhaps you would like to tell the mademoiselle about Cousin P'tit's stories."

. . . well-defined. And when had those golden flecks appeared in the velvety brown of his eyes? She'd always envied the long, lush sweep of his lashes, but they seemed to have thickened and grown longer still. And . . .

"Coco," he said sharply, "Cousin P'tit's stories."

She started violently, her gaze hastily shifting away from the entrancing frown that etched parenthetical lines between his slashing black brows. Stories? Nonc P'tit? What was Court saying?

Her mouth rounded into an astonished oval, and her gaze swept back to meet his. It was inspired! Truly inspired! Her smile blossomed, bright and sunny, and the corners of his mouth kicked up in a response she had seen thousands of times. Yet now it was as new to her as the strange lurch of her heart and the odd catch in her breath.

He nodded to the couple sitting opposite Tante Tata, and Coco, unusually compliant, turned her attention to them. "Mademoiselle, you must ask Nonc P'tit to tell you his stories of Beaucoup Gator and Crevi Crawfish. Per . . ." She cast a swift glance at Maman, hoping she was not presuming too much. "Perhaps you could visit us on Christmas day. Every year he tells the children how Beaucoup and Crevi helped Papa Noël find New Orleans on a foggy Christmas Eve."

The mademoiselle turned her head stiffly, obviously summoning every ounce of courage to look directly at Nonc P'tit. "I should . . . should very much like to, if . . . if you would not . . . not mind, monsieur."

His crimson complexion grew redder, until, it seemed to Coco, his ears must be sizzling. Clearing his throat, he bobbed his head, his glance grazing the mademoiselle and darting away. "If . . . If you wish t-to, mademoiselle, but . . . but they are only tr-trifling t-tales that I—I made up."

"But . . ." she began in a fainting voice. "But that is . . . is exactly what I . . . I am looking for, Monsieur Robichaux."

Coco, triumphant, thought her night's work well done, but Court had yet another morsel of aid to throw her way. As the guests were departing he deftly arranged that she, he, and Nonc P'tit would walk the mademoiselle home, accompanied by that vigilant guardian of Coco's virtue, Tante Tata.

As they reached the broad wooden planked banquette, he offered one arm to Coco, the other to her aunt, and they strolled into the fog, lit at regular intervals by the golden orbs of light fanning out from gas street lamps. Nonc P'tit and the mademoiselle trailed behind, as silent as the tombs in the City of the Dead.

On the return journey, her uncle having hurried home from the Duprees' door, Coco suffered so dizzying a round of elation and depression that she wondered whether she might be falling ill. She flushed like the shy mademoiselle when Court spoke to her; she paled when he looked away. She longed to kick Tante Tata in the shins for demanding so much of his attention; she longed for her to demand more. She wanted to tell him how much she appreciated his help, but her facile tongue was curiously tied.

At the massive wooden door leading into the Colomb carriageway, Court leaned over her hand, kissing the back and holding it in the warm cradle of his palms. "I'm proud of you, Coco. They don't know it yet, but you've made two people very happy."

His *à bientôt* lingering as a promise that she would, indeed, see him again, Coco held the hand he had kissed against her breast and watched him vanish in the fog.

3

COCO REACTED POORLY TO UNCERTAINTY. SHE WAS AC-customed to the absolutes of childhood and the convictions of her own healthy self-confidence. A self-confidence which had deserted her.

Court had told her he was proud of her. He'd kissed her hand. *Why should she care!* Yet she did care. Her heart soared with every memory of the tender light in his eyes.

She spent anxious hours before her mirror examining her smooth, white skin, fearing it was as blotchy as a magnolia petal bruised by a touch. She complained of her hair so incessantly Papa ordered Maman to summon the *coiffeureuse* who came to style her hair for evenings at the opera. Coco's luxuriant sable tresses were trimmed in the back and snipped about her face, freeing the springy, natural curl. She was horrified. She was ruined! She wouldn't show her face again until it grew out! While she wept before the mirror in utter despair, Papa threw up his hands and departed "this madhouse!"

Tante Tata, in a misguided effort to appease her, stroked Coco's cheek and ran a frail hand over the curls that corkscrewed around her temples. "Do not fret, *ma petite*. Your papa was just so when he was falling in love with your *maman*. Nothing could please him—"

"Falling in love!" Coco rounded on her aunt, her tears sucked back to their source by this astonishing deduction. Nothing could be farther from the truth. It was preposterous! She was no shy and shrinking violet like the mademoiselle, who took every blow life offered her without complaint. Court had rejected her once. She would not succumb to his charms again! She certainly would not chance another rejection by him!

"But of course," said Tante Tata expansively. "Do you think we can fail to see your growing affection for Court?"

"Affection for Court," she echoed, terrified that it was true. "I despise him! I loathe him! I wish he was dead!"

"You only think that now, but soon you will see—"

"If this is what love is like, I want no part of it!" Coco flung herself away and raced to her bed, throwing herself across it to sob in earnest.

Her tears spent, she curled up in a ball of misery atop the patchwork quilt, knuckling her burning eyes. Her life had been so simple, until Court returned.

She sat up abruptly. And it could be again! He was the source of her emotional turmoil. All she had to do was rip him out of her heart and life, then she would be happy. And she knew just how to do it! If it was games he hated, it was a game he would have.

* * *

By the night of the Fortiers' soirée, Coco had herself
firmly in control. Court despised nothing more than flirtatious belles with changeling moods. So, she would lose
no opportunity to flirt then grow cold, to advance and
retreat in a courtship dance—all within the bounds of
propriety. And when he had turned from her in disgust,
she would be free of him, free of her uncertainty and
misery. Never again would she pray to Saint Nicholas,
hoping for a black-haired man who would make her heart
beat faster. Her heart had been pounding since her first
sight of Court, and she'd never suffered so much grief
and aggravation. She would be well rid of him.

Yet the thought made her feel as cool as the silvery
moon, as distant from the ebullient dancers thumping
through a polka as were the stars shining through the
lace curtains.

The Fortiers' double parlors were filled to bursting
with familiar faces. Rugs had been taken up, and the oak
floors polished. The heavy mahogany upholstered furniture was pushed back to the walls, strategic seats
claimed by the old aunts who exchanged gossip while
keeping a meticulous watch over their charges. No tidbit
of scandal was so absorbing that Tante Tata would not
take immediate note should Coco commit a faux pas.
She would then be subjected to a hissing lecture behind
the shield of Tante Tata's fan. Though it had happened
often enough in the past, Coco was determined it would
not happen tonight. Tonight she would act the *grande
dame*—if it killed her!

Court strode toward her with a smile and a warm,
welcoming look. Coco's heart did a somersault, leaving
her breathless and excited and afraid.

The fear put steel to her back and sent her chin climbing arrogantly. He was only Court, after all. She'd seen
his face smeared with mayhaw jelly and his clothes

muddy from crawfishing in the bayou. She remembered the days when he hated to take a bath, when he was sent away before every meal to scrub his filthy hands. Of course those days had long passed. The Court who bowed before her now was immaculately garbed, spotlessly clean, and smelled of bay rum.

Bon Dieu! Bay rum. The most masculine of scents.

Coco unfurled her mother-of-pearl *brisé* fan and fluttered it languidly beneath her nose, zephyrs of air sweeping away the scent. Over the filigreed rim her black eyes danced coquettishly beneath the challenging arch of her brows.

"Court," she said warmly, lowering the fan a trifle to expose the blinding brilliance of her smile. At least, she hoped it was blinding and brilliant. Her cheeks were so stiff and cold she might have been strolling the French Quarter in the frigid wind of a winter's day, rather than wilting in the overheated Fortier parlor.

He paused, his eyes widening, his expression both surprised and pleased. So pleased that Coco experienced an unexpected dagger of guilt and doubt, which only confirmed the necessity for the course she planned. Doubt was intolerable. Uncertainty was unbearable. Soon, she would suffer neither.

"How handsome you look tonight," she said. "After your tour of France you must find us quite rustic here in New Orleans."

"Never could I find you rustic, Coco," he said, a smile quivering at the corners of his mouth. "Exasperating, infuriating, impossible, perhaps, but never rustic."

"You are mocking me," she said lightly, giving his arm a flirtatious tap with her fan.

"Am I?" he queried.

His growing smile affected Coco like her first sip of fragrant anisette liqueur. It went straight to her head, leaving her pleasantly dizzy. She dragged her gaze away from his swarthy face and sparkling eyes, casually surveying the room and briskly plying her fan. How hot she had become.

"You are looking exceptionally lovely tonight, Coco," he said softly, his deep gravelly voice caressing her like a hand.

"You know very well that white is not my color," she said archly.

"Do I?"

How very unforthcoming of him! Didn't he know that he was to play the gallant and assure her that she was perfection itself? "Would you please not respond to my every comment with a question!" she commanded acidly.

"Temper, temper," he chided, reaching for her hand and pulling her onto the dance floor, gracefully guiding her into the first steps of a waltz.

She wanted to jerk away, but that would not suit her plan. She must first seduce him, and then reject him. But . . . but truly he was a marvel on the dance floor, as light on his feet as the sylphlike Florian Breaux, as sure of every step as the athletic Gaspard Trouard. What had happened to the days when he clumped through the square pattern of the waltz, mumbling one-two-three under his breath and crunching her toes at every turn?

"You are smiling," he whispered beneath the lilting strains of Nonc P'tit's fiddle.

"I was remembering when you first learned to waltz."

He chuckled. "It's a wonder you were not permanently maimed."

"Perhaps you have not noticed my limp," she riposted, her gaze climbing to meet his. For a moment their gazes meshed, and she was taken captive by an exquisite sensation of homecoming. How she longed to yield herself willingly, to grasp and never release the peace that snared her in a grip as gentle as the hand at her waist.

"No," he said, his voice low and sweet, "I've only noticed that you dance, as you do everything else, divinely."

The graceful compliment pleased her to an absurd degree. She blushed and paled, then blushed again, her cheeks scalding hot and a host of butterflies whipping against her ribs. On the brink of a blazing smile, Coco wrenched herself back. What was she thinking? What was she doing?

Melting like the sugar Tante Tata boiled for her pralines! she thought scornfully. And worse! She was enjoying it! Did he only need to offer a verbal bouquet for her to forget everything?

The strains of the waltz closed with a flourish. Coco, clapping politely, cast him a stormy look.

Florian Breaux approached, requesting her hand for *le galop*, and she spun away with him, leaving Court staring after her with a narrow frown.

He had planned to abandon circumspection and launch into his wooing of Coco tonight, but she had succumbed so easily, it made him suspicious. Nothing about this new Coco was coming easily. She was like the Chinese puzzles that arrived by clipper ship from the Orient: no sooner was one door opened than another was found to bar the way. But then, he had always enjoyed puzzles, especially when they came in such lovely packages.

Coco romped across the dance floor with that upstart puppy, Breaux. Court, unaccustomed to the impatience—dare he admit it? the jealousy!—that chafed him, turned for the punch table.

But Coco was not thirsty. She wanted to dance, and only Gaspard Trouard would do for the Virginia reel—which Tante Tata deplored as an invention *américain*.

Impatience metamorphosing into irritability, Court

waited through the reel, noting the brittle quality to Co-co's gaiety and the cold core at the heart of her flirtatious glances. Had she changed so much? The Coco he remembered had never blown hot and cold. She had always been honest, brutally honest on occasion. If she was angry, she said so. There were no games with her.

Yet he suspected that she had learned much—much that he did not like—while he was away. He saw it in the triumphant smile she turned upon him when he requested a second waltz.

"Surely you would not want Papa to think your intentions more serious than they are." She batted her lashes in imitation of a vapid belle, while plucking a *dragée* from a tray. "Really, Court, I could almost think you have forgotten what a"—she pressed the candy into his palm, her smile as sugary as the almond coating— "*child* I am."

His hand closed around hers in a hard and hurting grip, his temper soaring. He had meant to let her have her revenge, but she had pushed him to his limits and beyond. While he might choose to dance attendance on a warm and willing woman, he'd have nothing to do with a spiteful child.

"You have given me no chance to forget it, *chèrie*," he said, his voice as hard as the look in his eyes. "And I have grown weary of waiting for you to grow up."

In the dark of night, Mémé's elbow sank into Coco's ribs. "Would you be still!" she hissed. "I'm trying to sleep!"

Coco curled up on her right side, gulping back tears, the taste of revenge lingering in her mouth like the taste of ashes. She should be happy. She'd gotten exactly what she wanted. Court would bother her no more. But what would she do without him to laugh with her and mourn with her and steady her flights of fancy?

She rolled to her left, seeing in the glimmer of light reflected in the mirrored armoire doors the hot, angry light in Court's eyes. She'd *wanted* him to turn from her in disgust, so why did she feel so lost, so alone, so much like the child he had suggested she still was?

She stretched out, lying flat on her back, pointing her toes toward the foot of the bed she had so recently leaped in one bound to pray that Saint Nicholas send the one she was to wed. Had he answered her prayer? Had she not recognized that answer when Court appeared before her?

I have grown weary of waiting for you to grow up. The implication was unmistakable.

How . . . how romantic to think that he had waited for her. Why . . . why, it was like Heathcliff and Catherine in *Wuthering Heights*—and if Papa ever learned that she had been reading the gallicized versions of those barbaric English novels, he would take a cane switch to her.

Dizzy from the seesaw of her own emotions, Coco stumbled into the kitchen at dawn. A fire crackled in the fireplace. Leggy pups gamboled underfoot, begging scraps of the bacon frying atop the iron stove. Jubilee, the cook, prepared feather-light *beignets*. Tante Tata ground roasted beans and set out the *cafetière*—the drip pot—for Papa's ritual of making the morning coffee when he came down for breakfast.

Coco flopped into a chair, earning a stern look from her aunt. "Sit up straight, *bébé*," Tante Tata said sharply. "Remember the string pulling up through the top of your head. It straightens the spine, and—"

"I'm not a baby any longer." Coco frowned.

"It is the curse of the youngest to be the baby, no matter how old she gets. Does not your grandpapa still call me *bébé*, and I only a year younger than he?"

"Well, *I* think people should see when a girl is grown up!" Coco responded testily.

"And who has not seen that you are all grown up, *pauvre petite*?" asked Tante Tata, her dark eyes shining with amusement.

"Court!" she burst out. "He said that I was a child! A child! I'm sixteen and a half!"

Tante Tata paused in grinding the beans to study her grandniece. "And why would Court say such a thing to you?"

"Oh, I should have known you would take *his* side!" said Coco, flaring up. "You've never thought Court Fortier could do any wrong! Just because he's Cousine Zaza's grandnephew—"

"Which hardly recommends him to me," said Tante Tata dryly. "Court is *un garçon gentil*, a *very* well-bred young man. Too well-bred to have called you a child, unless he was provoked. So, *bébé*, what have you done?"

"Me?" queried Coco, squirming in her chair. "Nothing! Nothing at all!"

"Coco," said her aunt, as only she could, a note of warning darkening the unspoken I-know-you-too-well.

"I . . . I flirted with him."

"And?"

And? She had insulted him, deliberately, maliciously, and she'd never been more miserable.

"And?" prodded Tante Tata.

"I . . . I . . ." Coco found herself bereft of an explanation that would shed the best light upon herself. Worse, she found herself yearning to erase all she had done, to begin anew with Court. "What must I do to make him see me as a woman?" she cried.

"*Pauvre petite*, you must become a woman."

"I've had my come-out! I'm of marriageable age! I can sew and cook and haggle at the French Market! I *am* a woman!" Coco protested.

"No, *bébé*, you *act* like a woman, which is not at all the same thing as *being* one."

"Riddles!"

"A woman, Coco, does not think only of herself."

She slumped in her chair, her lower lip trembling. Obviously growing up would be more difficult than she had foreseen. "You think I'm selfish," she said mournfully.

"I think you are young, with much to learn."

Which was not at all what Coco wanted to hear. "And what of a man?" she asked sharply.

"If he is a good man, he does not think only of himself either."

"What of Court? Do you think he is a good man?"

Tante Tata, pouring the ground coffee into *la grecque*—the upper part of the *cafetière*—stopped to settle a pensive gaze on Coco. "A woman would find that answer for herself, not ask for the opinions of others."

Left to find her own answer, Coco believed that Court was perfectly wretched—until she wandered into the courtyard to stand beneath the shade of the oak tree. How glorious it had been to climb into the topmost branches, to feel like a bird ready to take wing, to hear Court's hearty laugh below her. That laugh had always made her feel as safe and warm as the kitchen fire on a cold winter night with Papa smoking his pipe and keeping the demons of darkness and whistling wind at bay. Court had always been nearby when she needed him; he had never judged her harshly—until now.

Was Tante Tata right? Did she only act like a woman, while she was still a child inside?

As November marched into December with its promise of the fast-approaching holiday season, Coco tried to *become* a woman. Yet she delayed the first and most necessary step—an apology to Court, the honest and forthright apology that a mature woman would make. Sheer cowardice stilled her tongue, but Court didn't help.

At the soirées and dances and at homes where they met, he was courteous but distant. Like an old uncle of the curmudgeonly variety, he tolerated her presence without taking any pleasure in it. The safe and warm feeling he had once engendered in her was gone, and she had not realized, until now, how important it was to her.

Since she could not find the courage to confront him, Coco channeled her frenetic energy into ''thinking of others.''

She accompanied Tante Tata to the French Quarter, not to dawdle after the sights but to carry her aunt's packages. She fetched Papa's slippers and pipe in the evenings, unfolding *L'Abeille* and laying the newsprint carefully across the arm of his chair. She insisted on dusting the parlor and polishing the furniture so that Maman could rest. She scolded her sisters for their heedless demands on their parents, shaming Cécé into darning her own cotton stockings and Mémé into refurbishing an old party frock rather than beg Papa for another.

This sudden industry and concern over their well-being had Maman and Papa whispering in their bed at night, wondering what had happened to their fun-loving and thoughtless *bébé*. Overhearing themselves referred to as ''aging parents''—they were in the creaking dotages of forty-two and forty-five years—sent them careering off into gales of giggles in the privacy of their bedchamber.

Unaware that she had been the source of much hilarity, Coco spurred her industry on to new heights. She spent a day in the kitchen helping her aunt make fruitcake for the Christmas and New Year's *réveillions*. She accompanied Maman to Canal Street, for a day of holiday shopping. She offered to mend the torn lace of Cécé's gown and to help Mémé decorate her new hat, which sent her sisters flying to Tante Tata carrying the news that Coco was sickening with something that was sure to be fatal!

But no matter what she did, Coco didn't *feel* any more like a woman. And she wouldn't until her apology to Court was made and her mistake put behind her. She did not doubt that he would quickly forgive her, for he always had. But she could not—would not—have her humiliation exposed to a crowd at the opera or a soirée. It must be done in private, but they had no private moments.

She must contrive one. A secret meeting! A tryst! How appealing that sounded. No sooner had the thought come than she penned a cryptic note: *Monsieur Fortier, please meet me in Saint Anthony's Garden at the stroke of midnight tonight on a matter of the utmost urgency. A matter, Monsieur, of life and death,* she added with a dramatic flourish. That should pique his interest and bring him to her.

Court Fortier was at work on the trading floor of the Sugar Exchange when he was informed that a chimney sweep wished to speak to him. The Negro sweep, wearing the frock coat and tall silk hat that was the uniform of his trade, shifted the ropes hanging at his shoulder and set his bundle of palmetto fronds on the banquette. "M'sieu"—he proferred the note—"me, I am told to give this to M'sieu Harcourt Fortier."

Court rapidly scanned the unsigned missive, his eyes dilating, his color paling, and his mouth thinning into a grim line. Crumpling it in his hand, he tossed the sweep a silver dollar and a warning: "Don't ever carry messages for this . . . lady again!"

"*Oui*, m'sieu. *Non*, m'sieu," said the sweep, hefting the palmetto fronds and backing away.

Court stood on the banquette, his rage building—not that it had far to go. Since Coco had spitefully pressed the *dragée* into his palm, he'd teetered on the edge of an explosion. The last of his patience had been used up, and now—this!

The little fool! Didn't she know he would recognize her handwriting? *A matter of the utmost urgency. A matter of life and death. Meet her in Saint Anthony's Garden at midnight!* She had less sense than the hen scratching in the dirt of the street!

Though he was eager for a confrontation, he could not abandon his work during its busiest season. By the time he reached the Colomb town house hours later, his venom had been distilled to a deadly poison. He failed to knock at the gate, rushing through as he had when a boy. Abandoning every courtesy, he barged through the courtyard's multi-paned glass doors, bellowing "Coco!" in a voice that rattled the spider's-web fanlight overhead.

The family Colomb was gathered around the dining table, dipping spoons into a fragrant shrimp-and-oyster gumbo. Papa missed his mouth and poured a healthy dollop down the front of his best vest. Maman dropped her crust of bread and turned disbelieving eyes to the archway where Court had suddenly appeared. His rich brown hair tossed wildly about a face as red as the strings of cayenne peppers hanging in the kitchen. Coco choked and gulped down a succulent oyster, her stomach threatening to revolt. Wh-what was he doing here?

"You will pardon this intrusion," Court commanded in a tone that said I-don't-give-a-damn-whether-you-do-or-not, "but I must speak with Coco—alone!"

"Alone?" said Tante Tata sharply. "I am shocked at you, Court Fortier. You know that is impossible. Why, a young, innocent girl and a man—alone! It would be the talk of the Quarter, besmirching Coco's good reputation!"

Coco could have kissed her aunt. The last thing she wanted was to be alone with this stranger whose eyes burned and whose hands balled into angry fists at his sides.

Papa, absently dabbing at the gumbo on his vest, stared

at his unheralded guest. While his expression held a portion of outrage, Coco noted a stronger overlay of wry amusement that did not bode well for her. He, unlike Maman and Tante Tata, was never predictable. "Perhaps," he said mildly, "you could explain the need for this, ah, unusual request."

"It is, monsieur, a matter of"—Court's hot gaze swiveled toward Coco—"the utmost urgency."

Bon Dieu! He knew that she had sent the unsigned note!

Papa leaned back in his chair, locking his hands across his rotund belly. "And what, may I ask, is so urgent that you must see my, ah, innocent daughter without the protection of her guardian?"

The blood rushed from Coco's head, leaving her reeling in her chair. If Papa learned what she had done, he would confine her to room until she was thirty at the very least. *Mary, Mother of God, I pray to thee in this my hour of need . . .*

"I would prefer not to say, monsieur," said Court stiffly.

Coco wilted against the back of her chair, weakly oblivious to Papa's curious perusal of her white and stricken face.

"Which only means that my daughter has involved herself in something outrageous or dangerous, and you, Court, have come to her rescue once again." The curling tips of his luxuriant handlebar mustache began to twitch. "Very well, perhaps a stroll in the courtyard?"

Coco sat up, pricked by anxiety. "But . . . but Papa, I don't think—"

"Jean!" chorused Maman and Tante Tata, aghast.

"But Papa," Coco wailed, "I don't want to—"

"Which, I do not doubt, is all the more reason why you should!" he said, slamming a fist onto the table and autocratically ending all opposition. "Go!"

Coco hesitated, unable to believe that she had been so cruelly deserted by her loving papa. Court marched around the table, caught her beneath the arm, and jerked her out of her chair, hauling her unceremoniously into the misty night. Following them through the courtyard door was Tante Tata's needling, "Are you mad, Jean? An innocent young girl—"

"Innocent!" Court hissed in Coco's ear as he dragged her across the flagstones toward the shadowy corner where the winter-tattered banana leaves hung limp and dripping.

Never had she seen him so angry. Never had she feared him, until now. "Court, I—"

He yanked her around, his hands clamping around her shoulders. "Are you mad?" he echoed her aunt. "Asking me to meet you at midnight! Dare I hope you planned to bring your Tante Tata along to act as chaperone?"

"Well, no, I—"

"Of course not!" he raged in a whisper, giving her a shake that rattled her teeth. "You don't have that much sense!"

"But I—"

"Do you know what could happen to you alone on the streets at night? It would be assumed that you were a lady of the evening and fair game."

"But—"

"And if this little tryst should have been discovered, you would have been ruined and I with you! Frankly, Coco," he said coldly, "you are not worth that risk."

She gasped and wrenched away, her eyes glittering with tears. "Then . . . then why are you here?"

"To warn you that I am done with dancing to your tune," he said savagely.

"I—I'm sorry," she whispered, her throat thick and aching, her heart a hollow void slowly filling with remorse.

"So am I," he bit out, turning away, raking his hands
through his hair and staring up at the moon bathed in a
halo of mist. "*Sacré*, Coco, what has happened to you?
You were the most honest girl I ever knew, but now . . .
now . . ."

She was the most *dis*honest, even with herself. She
watched him stride away, his heels clicking on the paving
stones. If only she could find the courage to call him
back, to say that she had been blind and afraid.

Tante Tata had warned her that her inability to forgive
would someday come back to haunt her, but she had
thought the delicious satisfaction of retaliation was worth
any risk. Well, she had taken the risk and suffered its
consequences.

She had lost Court's respect, his friendship, his love.

Now it was too late for pleas and protestations. It was
too late to say, "I love you."

MAMAN AND TANTE TATA WERE HOVERING ANXIOUSLY
when Coco returned to the house after sobbing herself
dry of both tears and hope. "Papa has forbidden us to
question you, *chérie*," Maman said gently, "but if you
need to talk . . ."

What was there to talk about? Court was gone; he
wouldn't come back. She had succeeded in disgusting
him so thoroughly he never wanted to see her again.

Coco shook her head and stumbled away to bed. She expected Cécé and Mémé to fall upon her, agog with curiosity and demands to be told all. Instead, they quietly laid out her nightgown and helped her plait her hair and put her to bed as tenderly as if she were an invalid. Had she had any tears left, she would have wept with relief.

Still, she felt her world had turned topsy-turvy, for no one was acting as they always had. Her sisters were strangely compassionate. Maman and Tante Tata had, for the first time, respected her privacy. Papa had not just allowed but insisted that she be alone with a man. And Court . . .

It was too late.

But was it?

Surely there was something she could do. Something she could say. He could not turn off his feelings like the spout on the water cistern, and now . . .

Hope burgeoned within Coco's breast, bringing with it a new determination. Now that she knew exactly what she wanted, she would not give him up so easily.

What had he said? *Sacré, Coco, what has happened to you? You were the most honest girl I ever knew, but now . . . now . . .*

Honest. That was it! She would tell him everything: what she had planned, what she had done, and what she had felt from the moment she vaulted over the footboard of the bed with a prayer for Saint Nicholas to the moment in the garden when she realized that she loved him.

And if he rejected her offer of the truth he prized so highly?

She wouldn't think about that. He wouldn't. He couldn't.

But it seemed that he could. At the Breaux soirée the following night, his only greeting was an abrupt nod of his head.

Coco had dressed carefully in her come-out gown of Mechlin lace. She'd coaxed short curls to frame her face, and rolled the long length of her hair in a smooth chignon, tucking a cool, white camellia into the curls at her temple. But she could keep no color in her cheeks, nor could she hide the mauve circles of sleeplessness that ringed her eyes. It was easy to say that she would bare the secrets of her heart, but more difficult to contemplate actually doing so when Court was so cold to her.

She did not lack for partners to spin her through waltzes, to skip through polkas and clap through Virginia reels. But at every turn on the dance floor her gaze sought Court, who was ever at the center of a field of flirtatious belles. And why not? While he lacked the masculine beauty of a Gaspard Trouard, he had a ruggedly handsome face, a winning smile, and that least resistable of traits in a man—he liked women and let them know it.

While watching him smile at one, laugh with another, bow gracefully to yet another, Coco's temper slowly climbed out of the morass of guilt and despair, inching up the scale degree by degree. He obviously thought he could ignore her with impunity. Just as obviously, he considered himself free to pluck the fair flowers from this all-too-willing field.

Her newly discovered humility vanishing as quickly as it had come, Coco insinuated herself into his circle of admirers with a carefully placed elbow.

"*Bonjour*, Court." Her smile did not reach her eyes, nor did it soften the belligerent set of her jaw.

"Coco," he said neutrally, though his expression was as wary as a fox padding around an unleashed hound.

"Perhaps you have forgotten that you promised me this dance." Should he deny it, he would look the cad—and that he would never do. Coco, certain she had won the first skirmish, began to raise her hand.

"Forgive me, Coco"—one slashing brow arched over

his hardening gaze—"but I injured my ankle while walking through . . . Saint Anthony's Garden, and I am unable to dance tonight."

Her fingers curling into a fist, she drew her rejected hand to her waist. Despite the pain that lanced through her, Coco's chin climbed arrogantly. "A romantic spot, monsieur. Dare I ask if you were alone?"

"Of course you may ask, mademoiselle," he said coolly, offering no further explanation.

She snapped her fan shut, slapping it in the palm of her hand. "How . . . silly of me, monsieur. A gentleman would never tell."

"Never," he said shortly.

"I myself have been in the garden of late," she said with a casual air belied by the angry flashing of her eyes.

"Have you?" he asked, his tone implying that no subject could interest him less.

"*Oui*," she bit out. "I find its romantic reputation has been vastly overstated."

"Perhaps," he said, a frown gathering between his brows, "you were not in the proper frame of mind to appreciate it."

"*Au contraire*, monsieur. My frame of mind was quite precise."

"Might I suggest then," he said stiffly, "that the perceptions of your heart failed you."

"Of course you might suggest it, monsieur," she said, offering no further explanation. Her gaze dropped to his mirror-shined shoes, to the feet planted as firmly as the roots of a great oak. "You wear the injury to your ankle lightly, monsieur."

Her gaze met his briefly, scornfully, before she spun on her heel and walked away.

Tata Colomb and Zaza Fortier had a relationship as prickly as a cockleburr, but they agreed on three things.

The stunningly handsome Maintenon youth they had vied over as girls in their come-out year had proved himself unworthy of their attentions by marrying an *Américain*—which did nothing to allay the enmity that had flourished between them.

The pine Christmas tree holding court in a corner of the Breaux family's best parlor was another sign of the deplorable encroachment of *américain* customs on the Creole community, whose old ways could hardly be improved upon. However, like all doting aunts, they had yielded to the exhortations of their nieces and nephews for a tree that glittered with gilded ornaments and danced with candle flames. But they held firm against the *américain* pine, dragging into their parlors a tall, potted camellia. So much better. So much more French.

And the last thing they agreed upon? The thing that drew them together now? Coco Colomb and Court Fortier must marry. The cousins had shared this common goal since the first time they saw Court a boy, lift Coco, a toddler, onto his hip and carry her to the tiny pool in the Colomb courtyard to show her the frog croaking among the lily pads. They decided then and there that the two must marry, and for many years they sat back to watch, quite satisfied with the progression of events. But now it seemed their dream would be shattered.

Alarmed, they watched an angry Coco stride away from an equally angry Court. This would not do! Tante Tata's gaze shifted from the pair, catching the eye of her old enemy. Cousine Zaza nodded loftily, rising from her chair. In a corner of the Breaux parlor, they put their heads together to hatch a plan.

A week later Tante Tata pressed a scented handkerchief to her brow and moaned softly in an act that was worthy of the French Opera House's best tragedienne, whose performance that night the whole of the family Colomb was to see.

Instead of the usual last-minute flurry of finding the proper fans, of tucking ribbons into place, of checking hem lines and coiffures, they were gathered around their aunt's graceful four-poster like minions around a dying queen. Tante Tata was never ill. Papa always said she would outlive them all, but now even he was hovering anxiously. And Coco, desperately gripping her aunt's frail hand, was buffeted by painful memories of her every thoughtless act and rebellious word. If anything happened to Tante Tata . . .

"We can go to the opera another night," Papa began.

"I will not hear of it! You will be off, and you will enjoy your evening," Tante Tata commanded imperiously, and with a surprising vigor. "I have nothing more than the headache, and I need only one of you to remain and attend my few needs."

"Then I shall stay," said Maman.

"Absolutely not!" cried Tante Tata, sitting up. "You deserve an evening out, and you shall have it."

"Let me stay, Maman," Coco pleaded. "I don't mind, really. I want to help."

"Perfect!" said Tante Tata. "Our *bébé* will have many more evenings at the opera. It won't hurt her to miss this one."

Maman glanced worriedly at Coco. "But Tante, should you grow worse, do you think she would be—"

"Capable?" queried Tante Tata. "But of course! Our *bébé* is almost a woman now, and we have taught her well. She will know exactly what to do."

Maman and Papa appeared a trifle doubtful, but Tante Tata and Coco united in assuring them that she would send word by Jubilee should there be any need. A short time later, Coco, puffed up with her own self-importance, shooed her family out of the door and waved their carriage out of sight. The responsibility for her aunt's well-being might weigh heavily on her shoulders, but her parents' trust lightened that burden considerably.

She paused in the courtyard, clipping the greenest and least weathered banana leaf. Nothing was so cool and refreshing to a achy brow. Though her feet longed to skip, she climbed the stairs with a measured and womanly tread. Approaching Tante Tata's door, she heard an agonized groan that abruptly expunged every thought of self-importance, every feeling of adequacy.

Flying through the door, the banana leaf fluttering from her hand, she trembled to halt at the bedside.

"*Bébé*," moaned her aunt, "I feel so terrible. My head throbs. My stomach hurts. My legs ache. I think I have a fever."

"Sh-should I summon Maman?" asked Coco, her voice as high and breathless as a child's. And she felt like a child, helpless and unequipped for the task she faced.

"And ruin her pleasant evening? *Non!*" cried Tante Tata, one bright black eye peeping from the handkerchief draped across her face.

"Sh-should I send for *le docteur*?" asked Coco, frantically watching her aunt writhe upon the bed.

"That coconut head! *Non!*" said Tante Tata, so spiritedly that Coco blinked.

"But Tante, I . . . I . . ."

"*Oui*, I have it! Cousine Zaza! She will know what to do!"

"Cousine Zaza?" Coco stared at her aunt with growing terror. Was Tante Tata's fever so high she was delirious?

Another pitiful moan sent Coco racing for the door, stumbling down the stairs, and screaming for Jubilee.

Within minutes Cousine Zaza came panting into the kitchen where Coco was brewing a tisane from the leaves of the ham-and-egg bush, which Tante Tata claimed was good for any ailment. Where her aunt was tall and thin, Cousine Zaza was short and broad, with a deep and cushiony breast that tenderly cradled Coco's head while she stammered out her fears.

"Do not take on so, *ma petite bébé*." Cousine Zaza pressed Coco into a chair and patted her cheek with a chubby hand. "I'll take the tea above and see to your aunt. Surely it is nothing so serious."

"But . . . but she is suffering so!" cried Coco, starting up from the chair.

"Then I must hurry up to her," Cousine Zaza said, waving her away. "*Non*, wait here with Court."

Coco's gaze sped to the door, where he stood with his opera cape swirling about his ankles, his top hat in one hand and his ebony cane in the other. Seeing the look of compassion in his dark eyes, she promptly forgot the anger that had simmered since the debacle of the Breaux family's soirée. It had always been Court she had sought to soothe her fears, and now she longed to throw herself on his broad chest and beg him to make this fear go away as he had so many others. But she was supposed to be a woman, and a woman would not be so weak and help-less—would she?

Coco insisted on carrying the tray of cups and teapot up to Tante Tata, unsure whether she wanted most to escape Court or help her aunt.

"I do believe I feel a little better now that Cousine Zaza is here," said Tante Tata, confirming Coco's fear that her fever must be high indeed. "Leave us, *bébé*. Take out the *cafetière* and make Court some coffee."

"Are you sure?" asked Coco, trembling at the door, equally as afraid to leave as she was to stay and watch her aunt suffer.

*   *   *

In the kitchen below Court stoked the fire against the cool of the evening. The December weather was, as always, undecided: a warm day, a cool day, then a frost melted by a balmy Southern breeze. Much better weather than the deep snows and frigid winds of Alpine regions. He was glad to be back home, even if his road had been as rocky, as steep to ascend, as precipitous to descend as the Alps had been.

Scowling into the fire, he squatted on his heels, one knee braced on the brick hearth, his forearm resting on his muscular thigh. His plans had been so simple: to court Coco, to win her, to wed her. But the more he had tried, the further apart they had grown, until now . . .

He heard the whisper of her step, the rustle of her lace skirt, and slowly swiveled around. Her face was as white as her gown, her eyes as black and lightless as the night sky in the limitless regions between the stars. Once he would have gone to her, gathered her in his arms, and whispered assurances that all would be well. Now he waited, unsure of himself, unsure of her, still caught in the lingering web of his anger and her deceit.

"How is Cousine Tata?" he asked, Coco's wringing hands and wretched sigh tearing at his heart.

"She seems better, but . . . don't you think it strange that she asked for Cousine Zaza?"

"I've always thought that they care more for one another than either will admit." And was that also true of him and Coco? Did she care more than she would admit? *Bon Dieu*, how gladly he would confess his love, if only she would give him some hope.

"Coco," he began.

"Court," she said, so urgently he paused.

"*Oui*."

She stared at him for a moment, then looked away. "Nothing. It is nothing. Would . . . would you like some coffee?"

"If it would not be too much trouble."

"No, no trouble." Coco hurried to the cupboard, withdrawing the tin of roasted coffee beans and her papa's cherished *cafetière*. She wanted to weep with fear for her aunt, with frustration for herself. This was her opportunity to tell all to Court, but the secrets of her heart were not so easily unlocked. Her throat ached with the antagonistic pressures demanding that she speak and commanding that she be silent. After all, he had made it perfectly clear that she was not worth any risk to his reputation. She was not worthy of so much of his time that a single dance would take. How that had stung!

She poured the coffee beans into the funnel of the grinder and began turning the handle. Court rose and crossed to a nearby chair with a firm, steady step.

"I see that your ankle is much improved," she said, her gaze meeting his squarely.

A flush scaled his cheeks, sped up his brow, and vanished in the wayward curls that clustered at his hairline. "There was never anything wrong with my ankle."

"I know." She swallowed the lump in her throat and blinked back scalding tears. Was she in danger of losing everyone she loved? Even Tante Tata, that loving and lovable scold. Drawing a shuddering breath, Coco fought back a sob.

Suddenly, Court was there, gathering her in his arms, and whispering, "Courage, *ma petite chatte*, courage."

But there was no courage left in her, nor any fight either. She flung herself against him, clutching at his lapels, and sobbing against his spice-scented carnation boutonniere. Though it seemed she had cried buckets of tears since his return, she did not cry easily or daintily. As he settled in the chair, pulling her across his lap, she bawled like a baby, her heaving shoulders rocking them both.

"Oh, Court, Court," she wailed, tears flowing, her nose reddening.

"Shhh, shhh," he murmured against her brow. "Cousine Tata will be all right. By the morning, she will be as feisty and frisky as a colt, and she'll have as many opinions as one of those *américain* politicians."

"B-b-but you didn't see her suffering so."

No, he hadn't. But he suspected Cousine Tata's suffering was an act worthy of the stage. Why else would his Tante Zaza have delayed his departure for the opera? Why else would she have had her tin of pralines conveniently waiting on the table to be whisked up as they rushed out in Jubilee's frantic wake?

He had long known of the hopes they shared for him and Coco. His Tante Zaza had no thoughts that went unshared, and much as he had longed for the blessed peace of silence, she had shared a number of them during the last week. *What a lovely girl Coco is. So amenable, so agreeable.* He'd held his tongue firmly beneath his teeth on that one! *What a wonderful wife she would make some lucky man.* He'd ignored his aunt's arch expression and found an errand in need of immediate attention.

Whatever plot the cousins had hatched to bring it about, however much he longed for it, it did not appear that he was to be that "lucky man." Nor was he sure the man would be so lucky. Coco was running as mad as English hares in the first rays of spring sunshine. However disagreeable, however baffling her fits and starts had been, she was in pain now. And he could not fail to comfort her.

He pulled out his handkerchief and pressed it upon her, biting back a smile as she blew her nose and sniffled. But when she snuggled against his chest and sighed as if all had suddenly become right with her world, the smile fled before a rush of desire. The womanly curve of her hip fit the cradle of his loins as if designed for him alone. The swell of her breast pressed sweetly against his chest, summoning passionate thoughts of bare flesh and hot nights, of hungry mouths and seeking hands.

As if propelled by that thought, his hand rose and his knuckles coasted across the silken curve of her cheek. She raised her face to him, her eyes spangled with tears and her full lips quivering with her every breath. Slowly, his head lowered, his gaze fixed on her parted mouth. Whether it beckoned him to heaven or hell, he wasn't sure and didn't care. He only knew that he had waited for her, for this, as long as he could.

His lips touched hers, gently, so gently, savoring the unique flavor of her, glorying in the first tentative response. He held her heart to heart and mouth to mouth, her hand curling around his nape to hold him fast. Her wine-sweet breath sighed through his lips, as heady as the finest cognac. It left him with the same giddy relief, the same soaring excitement he had felt on first stepping onto the Louisiana shore on his return. He was returning to the home of body and soul then. He was finding the home of his heart now.

His kiss deepened, fierce and hungry, and he knew he would do whatever it took to make her his forever.

Coco had never been kissed by a man, and she was ready for more than her kinsmen's gallic kisses on the cheek. She'd practiced on the back of her hand, eyeing herself in the mirror. She'd dreamed of it, but never had she dreamed that it could be so all-consuming, that the touch of mouth to mouth could waken her from slumbering innocence to a new and exciting world.

The gentle friction of his mouth on hers; the pounding of his heart against hers; the sigh of his breath and hers: all breached the first virginal barrier of innocence, expanding the horizons of her existence, awakening in her new sensations. The kiss tingled in odd places: the palms of her hands and the burgeoning tips of her breasts. Every sense was heightened to a painful acuity: the rough rasp of his beard against her cheek and the prickling of his hair against her palm. She could feel the ebb and flow of her pulse, the pounding of her heart. And when his kiss deepened, she met it eagerly, alive and loving.

A new knowledge seeped into her awareness, an understanding of herself, of her hopes and dreams. She had thought love would come like a bolt of lightning and leave her thunderstruck. But it had come instead on tiptoe, slipping into her heart and waiting patiently for her to recognize it. It wasn't shock, but delight. It wasn't heat, but warmth. It wasn't taking, but giving.

She leaned back against Court's strong arm and gazed into his dark, glittering eyes and rested her hand tenderly against his cheek. "I love you," she whispered. "I think I've always loved you . . ." His gaze shied away from hers, and Coco found herself unable to go on.

"Don't mistake what you've just felt for—"

"It was no mistake." She paused, fear clutching at her throat. "Was . . . was it for you?"

"No, God help me."

"Then what?" she pleaded.

"You"—still he would not look at her—"have not been . . . receptive—"

"I've been a fool!" She slipped from his lap and knelt before him, gathering his hands in hers. "Please listen," she begged, and began, "Do you know how girls pray to Saint Nicholas?"

He nodded, his gaze cautiously returning to her face, his expression softening, a smile tugging at his mouth as she told of how Cécé and Mémé had bedeviled her.

"Can't you see?" Coco said urgently. "He answered my prayer when you came home, but I didn't see it. I didn't want to see it. I wanted love to come with the excitement and thrills of the unknown, and what I got was my comfortable old shoe Court."

''How . . . dreary for you,'' he said, chuckling, running a caressing finger down her cheek.

''Hardly dreary. I was furious with you, and all I could think of was my revenge. But when I got it . . .'' She laughed softly, her eyes shining up at him. ''It certainly didn't give me as much pleasure as chucking Gaspard's tin soldiers into the river. In fact, it made me more miserable than I've ever been. And that made me more angry. Can you forgive me?''

He studied her face so pensively, Coco feared he would withhold his forgiveness and his heart. ''*Oui*,'' he said at last, adding, ''but you are so very young, *chérie*.''

''A problem cured by the years,'' she said uncertainly. She didn't like this odd mood of his, this strange hesitancy in a man who was always so sure of himself.

''But Coco, some decisions made in the heat of youth must be repented in the chill of age and maturity. Even you have admitted that you have not known what you wanted. How can you know that this is not another false turn?''

''Why won't you believe me?''

''Because I love you too much to hurt you or to let you hurt yourself.''

''Then I will prove it to you.''

''Saying does not make it so,'' he said.

Coco's fertile brain began to fly through the possibilities. Her growing smile blended three parts mischief with one part triumph. ''We could begin with another kiss.''

''So you liked that, did you?'' Grinning, he leaned down and pressed a kiss to her brow. ''I've abused your father's hospitality enough for one night.''

''Then I suppose''—she walked her fingers slowly up his lapel, touched the pulse sprinting in his throat, and gently toyed with his mouth—''I shall have to court you.''

"Coco," he warned, "I'll not have you make a spectacle of yourself for—"

"Only for you," she promised, "though I will remind you that I do not have your patience. And if you ever again refuse to dance with me, I will make a . . . spectacle such as New Orleans has never seen."

"I shudder to think—"

"And well you should."

"Hmmm." He frowned lightly, humor gleaming in his eyes. "Would it be as bad as the reception after Cécé's come-out, when you put a frog in the punch?"

"And she only refused to let me watch from the door," Coco reminded him.

"Then I take it my . . . ah, spectacle would be decidedly worse."

"Decidedly."

"Then you have my solemn promise that I will never refuse you another dance."

"And the next question is, will you refuse my proposal?"

"Coco! You shameless girl! What would your papa say?"

"Oh, what he always says," she responded with a burble of laughter. "Getting old will give him gray hair, but raising Coco will kill him."

Court, his good intentions drifting away on a gust of laughter, pulled her into his arms and kissed her until she was breathless and he was in danger of forgetting that he was a gentleman. "I—I think it might be best if you made the coffee," he said huskily.

"Are you sure?" she murmured, her gaze dazzled and dazzling.

"Quite sure." He set her from him, regretfully watching as she swayed gracefully toward the table, casting him a pert glance and a happy smile.

He yearned to believe that she loved him with the

enduring love of which a happy marriage was made, but he would make no mistakes now. Coco must convince not only him but also herself.

He leaned back, contented for the moment, watching the firelight play across her face as she turned the coffee grinder. No sooner had he wondered when she would notice than . . .

"Court, we are alone!"

"*Oui*, quite alone, *chérie*."

Now that Coco thought on it, Tante Tata had had a suspiciously healthy bloom to her cheeks. And . . . and Tante Tata had sent her here to entertain Court—alone! And Cousine Zaza, who was notoriously strict with her charges, not only allowed it, but had hurried her along!

"They planned it!" she burst out.

"Assuredly."

"Oh! *Oh!*" She spun the handle around and around, setting the grinder to whirring. "Tante Tata scared me witless! I was terrified that she was dying! How could she do this to me?"

"Because she loves us both." Court joined her, placing his hand over hers. "I think the coffee beans have been sufficiently ground. Much more and they will be powder."

Coco whipped to and fro between relief that her aunt was not ill and resentment that she had been manipulated—and so successfully! But how could she continue to resent her aunt, when she had made this reconciliation with Court possible? She couldn't, not when he was trying so hard not to laugh.

"How long have you known?"

"I suspected from the beginning."

"You should have told me!"

"And missed . . . this." He leaned down and brushed his lips against hers. "Why don't we go up and end their suspense?"

* * *

"Really, Zaza, I think they've been alone long enough."

Coco paused outside the door and put a finger to her lips, unable to resist this opportunity to hear what the conspirators had to say.

"This might not be wise," Court whispered, before he was roundly shushed.

"Do you suggest that my Court—"

"Certainly not! He is *un gentil garçon*. You've done a fine job raising him, Zaza."

"As you've done with Coco. *Ma petite ange.* Such lovely manners she has," said Cousine Zaza, unaware that the angel with the lovely manners was eavesdropping. "Do have another of my pralines, *ma amie*."

"I do believe you've outdone yourself with these, Zaza," said Tante Tata grudgingly.

Outside the door Coco heard the faint metallic creak of a tin lid being removed from its box.

"Perhaps you would like to try one of my pralines, Zaza," coaxed Tante Tata.

Moments later: "Delicious. You must have waited until the weather was right to make these."

"I have no need to wait for the weather to be right," came Tante Tata's tart response. "*My* pralines have never failed me."

"Oh?" said Cousine Zaza triumphantly. "Is that why Coco tells me that *my* pralines are better than yours?"

Coco straightened as if pricked with her aunt's foot-long hatpin. She wanted to fly through the door and end this conversation posthaste, but was paralyzed by a sinking feeling of imminent doom. Praying fervently that her sins would not find her out, she waited with bated breath.

"Humph! That's how much *you* know! Coco only told you that because you're getting so old and feeble, and she didn't want to hurt your feelings! She really thinks *mine* are best!''

"But . . . but she told *me* the same thing about *you*!" said Cousine Zaza.

Sagging against the door frame, Coco whispered, "Oh, no!''

"You didn't!" hissed Court, horrified.

"I did." She nodded, sickened by waves of icy cold and fiery heat.

"*Bon Dieu*, Coco! They'll have your hide!"

He caught her hand, yanked her down the stairs and into the kitchen, flinging her into one chair and throwing himself in another.

"Just act natural," he ordered.

How she was supposed to do that when she couldn't draw a breath, she could not imagine. And she didn't have to worry over it long, for the furies descended— all pretense of Tante Tata's illness abandoned.

Cousine Zaza, puffed up like the bullfrog croaking in the courtyard, glared at Coco with her snapping black eyes, as if *ma petite ange* had metamorphosed into the very devil. "Shame, shame on you, Coco. I know you've been raised better than this. Come, Court," she commanded brusquely. "*This* is no place for you.''

"Now, Tante," he began soothingly, "perhaps you could tell us what the problem—"

"Cousine Tata will see to that! It seems we have been sadly mistaken in Coco's character. She obviously is not ready for the responsibilities of courtship and marriage.''

"But Tante," he protested to her retreating back as she sailed out, leaving him no choice but to follow. No decent woman could be left alone to walk the streets at night. He swept up his opera cape, his top hat and cane, pausing to cast Coco a lingering, loving look.

Stricken with dread and remorse, she was unable to take heart from it. Shrinking in her chair, Coco waited for the ax to fall—which it did in such a flood of hurt feelings, she truly felt the shame Cousine Zaza had wished upon her. All of her stammering explanations, all of her protestations of affection were ignored. Tante Tata stomped off to bed with a last dire threat of "I will speak to your papa in the morning."

5
▲▲▲

THE PARLOR WAS USED NOT ONLY FOR RECEIVING GUESTS but for relaying bad news, for discussions of consequence, and for meting out punishments—all conducted under the stern and accusing portraits of the ancestors gazing down from the walls.

Coco stood before her papa, her feet aligned, her hands linked at her waist, her face hollow-eyed and wan, the very picture of penitence. "But Papa, I truly meant no harm."

"*Naturellement*, Coco, but it remains that you did cause great hurt to your tante and Cousine Zaza. If it had been anything but those damnable pralines! You could have chosen nothing to offend either of them more. I tell you, Coco, they've been at it since before *I* was born! Why, here in my own house I am denied my favorite sweet, simply because I will not be drawn into this feud! It's time it was stopped, though how that should happen I cannot imagine." He sat heavily in the upholstered chair whose mahogany carving rose like a throne behind him. "I'm sorry, *bébé*, but your *tante* is convinced that you are too irresponsible for courtship and marriage."

Coco closed her eyes and swayed dizzily. Why had this happened now? Now, when she knew she loved Court, when she needed so desperately to prove that love to him. "And you, Papa?" she whispered. "Do you think I . . . I am too young to . . . to be courted?"

"Unfortunately, what I think is irrelevant. It is our *tante* whom you must convince, for she has the last word in all matters such as this. I had, of course, hoped—"

"It's so unfair!" cried Coco.

"Is it, *bébé*?" Papa questioned softly, patting his knee, waiting while she sank into his lap with her chin drooping and her lips trembling. "Consider your Tante Tata's position, Coco," he urged her, smoothing thick, sable curls away from her cheek. "She has no man, no home, no child to call her own. Like all of our old aunts, she lives on the charity of her family. She has nothing but her pride and her usefulness to recommend her. Now you have hurt her pride, and I cannot damage it further by ignoring her advice."

But her aunt was so integral a part of the family, Coco could not imagine it without her. It was inconceivable that Tante Tata might question her place in it.

Coco cast her papa a quick, anxious glance. "But she must know how much we need her, how much we love her."

"*Oui*, but when was the last time you told her?"

She couldn't remember. Oh, she'd flung her arms around Tante Tata when she was a child, fervently proclaiming her love for a specially cooked sweet or a gift on her Feast Day or New Year's. But she never remembered saying, "I love you," simply because she did.

"*Bébé*," Papa said gently, "you must be patient with your *tante* for a while. You've always been her favorite, but now you are growing up and away from her, and she's afraid of losing you.''

''Papa, I'll never grow away from Tante Tata. She's a part of me.'' And it was true. Her *tante* might rigidly enforce every unwritten law of society, but she was also the first to offer a helping hand and an understanding heart.

''But Coco, growing away from your *tante*, from your *maman*, and from me is a part of growing up. Someday you will be a wife and mother, and your first thoughts should rightly be of your husband and children.''

''But Papa, I will always love you, all of you!''

''Of course you will,'' he said heartily, a smile twitching into place. ''And if you have a daughter like yourself, you will love us even more because you will understand us better. Perhaps you will even understand why I must say no if your Court comes to me.''

No, Coco thought, that would be impossible. She had only told the tiniest of white lies and in the very best of causes. She really hadn't wanted to hurt Tante Tata or Cousine Zaza, but they would persist in insisting that she choose between their pralines. Surely this punishment did not fit so trifling a crime.

The sliding doors rolled back, and Court stepped through like a dark angel come to save her. Coco leapt up with a cry of relief, but he did no more than cast her a quick compassionate glance, as if to assess the damage, before bowing gracefully to her papa. ''Monsieur, I apologize for this intrusion, but I must speak with you.''

Treading on his heels came Tante Tata. ''Jean, I assured him that you were unavailable, but he insisted—''

''You are dismissed, Tante,'' Papa said, a tinge of curtness in his tone, which would ensure his life being made miserable for some time to come. It was, Coco knew, a full measure of his state. He despised family squabbles and would do almost anything to avoid them—which did not bode well for Court's mission or for her.

Tante Tata marched out with an offended sniff, closing the doors behind her with a forceful slam.

Papa grimaced and sighed, while Court offered Coco an encouraging smile. "*Chérie*," he said gently, "I would like to speak to your papa alone."

"But I—"

"Alone," he said firmly, taking her hand. The last thing he needed was an impetuous and hot-tempered Coco setting all awry, when her father needed the delicate handling of a diplomat.

"Courage, *ma petite chatte*, courage," Court whispered in her ear before he closed the doors behind her and turned to face her father.

"If you've come seeking permission to court my Coco," said Papa Colomb, gesturing to a nearby chair, "I fear I must refuse it. Her *tante* has decided she is too young to be courted."

Court had been prepared for that. He tossed his hat into the chair, declining a seat. "How fortunate," he said with the ghost of a smile, "that I have not come with such a request."

"*Non?*" queried Papa, his thick black brows drawing together in a puzzled frown. "Then what?"

Court braced himself for the squall ahead. "I have come seeking your permission for Coco to court me."

Papa blinked, nonplussed, his mouth dropping open, his luxuriant mustache aquiver. "*Sacré tonnerre!* Thunderation!" He sat forward, glaring his displeasure. "What is this?"

"I suspect, monsieur, that you have long known of the . . . affection I feel for your daughter."

"But of course!" said Papa, scowling. "I am neither blind nor indifferent to the happiness of my Coco."

"Then perhaps you have also noticed that all has not

gone well between us since my return to New Orleans?''

"*Mon ami*," said Papa, his scowl swept away by a grudging gleam of humor, "I have seen that my Coco has led you a merry chase."

"Exactly." Court swept up his hat and sank into the chair, eagerly leaning toward the man who could grease the path of his courtship or obstruct it. "You know that Coco cherishes nothing she wins too easily."

"*Oui*," said Papa warily.

"She believes now that she is in love with me, but I am not so sure. You see, I fear that Cousine Tata may be right. Coco might yet be too young to know her own mind."

"Ah," said Papa sagely, nodding. "But what has this to do with—"

"In order to prove her feelings to me, Coco has proposed that she court me."

"*Bon Dieu!*" shouted Papa, shaking a hand at the heavens. "How could You send me this wretched, unnatural girl? She will be the death of me yet!"

"Monsieur, Coco has given me her solemn pledge that she will not make a . . . spectacle of herself."

"And you believe her?" boomed Papa, as if he suddenly doubted Court's wisdom.

"Should she . . . forget, I would not allow it. I love her, monsieur, as you do, too much to allow her to hurt herself."

"This is most irregular, *mon ami*. Most irregular. Her *maman*, her *tante*, should they learn that I have sanctioned such . . . such—"

"But think, monsieur, if Coco were wed . . ." Court paused, his smile growing. ". . . she would become her husband's problem. For you, she would simply be a loving daughter to be enjoyed."

Papa dragged out his handkerchief and mopped his sweating brow, leaning laboriously into the back of his chair. "*Mon ami*, if you could bring this blessed event about, you would have my everlasting gratitude. Unfortunately, we must be bound by Tante Tata's decision—"

"There must be something—"

"Impossible! Though I must confess that it has long been my dearest wish that you and Coco . . ." Papa spread his hands and shrugged. "Ah, well, if we let these tempers die down, perhaps . . ." He shrugged once more, wilting back into his chair. "Those damnable pralines!"

Court, leaning forward, braced his forearms on his knees and frowned thoughtfully. Perhaps, just perhaps there was a way to change Papa Colomb's mind. "Monsieur, if I could ensure that we are never again asked whose pralines are the best—"

Papa looked up, his eyes bright with hope. "Could you do it?"

"Yes," said Court with supreme assurance.

While Papa clapped his hands to his head, suffering the acute agony of temptation, Coco sat quietly in the rocker by the kitchen fire watching Tante Tata pound crisp sassafras leaves into powder—the pungent *filé* that seasoned gumbo.

Coco never remembered seeing her aunt take her leisure. Always she was busy: shopping, sewing, cooking, cleaning, thinking of everyone but herself. Even on the at-home days, she did not relax. Instead, she saw that every guest was comfortable, that every guest was served, that Maman was free to enjoy the gossip and chatter of her friends.

Was Papa right? Could Tante Tata possibly question her place here? Could she wonder if someday she would displease and be cast out? Surely, she could not. It was a point of pride that every Creole take care of his own.

No orphaned child lacked an uncle, an aunt, a cousin to take him in. No maiden aunt, no bachelor uncle went without a home where she or he was welcomed and honored.

Honored, as the Colombs honored Tante Tata. Loved, as they loved her. Needed, as they needed her.

Coco's gaze drifted away to the blue and yellow flames leaping from the log fire. Shame marked her cheeks with a mottled flush. She had always taken Tante Tata for granted. Like Court, her aunt had always given, while she always took. Wasn't it time for her to . . . to think of others? To become the woman she wanted to be?

If only she could go to Tante Tata, to hug her and tell her how much she was appreciated, how much she was loved. Coco had often charmed and wheedled her way back into her doting aunt's graces, but she couldn't do that now. Her "trifling crime" had been nothing less than a betrayal. There was only one way to show Tante Tata that she was sorry—and that way was to give up the man she loved.

Papa Colomb, in the parlor, squirmed on the needle-sharp horns of temptation. There was nothing he would not do to end the feuding between Tante Tata and Cousine Zaza. Almost nothing, he modified grudgingly. As much as he longed to see peace reign at family gatherings, he could not hurt Tante Tata by ignoring her advice. Good advice, for he was no more convinced than she and Court that Coco knew her own mind. His *bébé* was still too much the child, still too thoughtless of others.

"I'm sorry, *mon ami*, but I cannot . . ."

The sliding doors opened. Coco appeared.

"Pardon, Papa." She moved slowly into the room, her eyes downcast, the feathering fan of her lashes shielding their expression. Her hands entwined at her waist with a grip so tight her knuckles were white, and she faltered to a stop before him.

Papa sighed heavily, his dread growing. A woman's tears left him defenseless; his daughters' tears reduced him to abject helplessness—as his Coco well knew. Should she cast herself on his mercy, pleading and weeping . . .

"Coco," he said darkly, warning her, bolstering himself.

"Please, Papa," she said softly, her hot, dry gaze meeting his, gliding away to meet Court's. "I'm sorry, but I've come to ask Papa to refuse his permission—"

"So!" Papa thundered, furious that his fickle daughter had created so much turmoil to no purpose, equally furious that the faint hope of ending the feud of the pralines had been snatched away. "You've now decided you do not want Court—"

"*Non! Non!*" cried Coco, wheeling around, her face revealing her inner torment. "I do! I do! But . . . but . . ."

"But what?" he bit out. "Come, we haven't all day!"

"Court, please try to understand." Coco turned to him, stretching out her hands, and he came to her, folding her hands in his.

"Tell me, *chérie*," he said tenderly. "What must I understand?"

"It's Tante Tata. I can't . . . I just can't hurt her anymore. Perhaps, later, when she's over it, when I've shown her that I really—"

"*Bébé*," said Papa, rising from his chair, "am I to understand that you are doing this for Tante Tata?"

"*Oui*, Papa. It's the only way I can show her—"

"But you still want your Court?"

"More than anything—"

"Do you love him, *bébé*?"

"*Oui*, Papa."

Her shining gaze rose to Court's face, and Papa Colomb knew that he had lost his youngest and dearest to another man. He suffered a pang of jealousy, a sharper pang of loss, then a heart-swelling pride. His wayward Coco had become a woman at last. One who would be generous and kind and thoughtful and loving. Could any father ask for more?

"Excuse us now, *bébé*," he said gently. "I must discuss this with Court."

"But Papa, there's nothing to discuss. I must do this."

"Of course you must, but I am still your papa," he said, leading her to the door. "Until your Court steals you away from me, I decide what is best for you."

With that he closed the doors behind her and strode to the *secrétaire*, withdrawing a carafe of brandy and two glasses. Pouring, he slanted a glance at Court. "So, our little girl has grown up. Did you ever think to see the day?"

"I had begun to wonder."

Papa handed Court a glass, raising his own. "To Coco and her . . ." He paused, smiling, ". . . courtship, if you will pardon a very bad pun."

"In this case, easily, monsieur." Court raised his cut-crystal tumbler in toast. "To the end of the feud of the pralines."

"Ah," said Papa, approvingly, "I see we understand one another."

Papa informed neither his *tante* nor his daughter that he had agreed to promote the courtship, leaving each to believe that she had won. Though Coco could hardly consider refusing to see Court as "winning." Nor could she take any pleasure from knowing that she had chosen the right path, one that would cause the least hurt to Tante Tata.

The incense of Christmas might perfume the nippy air and carolers might stroll the length of Canal Street to mingle with bustling shoppers, but in the town house on

Orleans Street a siege was in progress. Tante Tata was the only Colomb who could hold a grudge as long as Coco, and she wasn't speaking to her niece.

On Christmas Eve mistletoe dangled from doorways and pine boughs draped mantelpieces and candles flickered on the branches of the camellia. The house was scented of candies and cookies and patty shells filled with oysters and shrimp. The table was laden with a piping-hot feast, a melange of everyone's favorite dishes. Papa dug into his eagerly awaited autumn delight— pumpkin baked in syrup, butter, and cinnamon. Coco shifted her own jambalaya around on her plate, listless and unable to take a bite.

"Ermina," said Tante Tata to Maman, "would you ask your daughter to pass the salt?"

Coco dutifully reached for the salt shaker, uncomfortably aware of the commiserating glances of her sisters and brother, all of whom had suffered their *tante*'s thundering silences.

"*Chérie*," she said to Cécé, "would you tell your sister that her *maman* spent the morning making her jambalaya. The least she could do is eat it."

Papa heaved a doleful sigh and set his fork aside, as if wondering whether he'd ever have peace enough to enjoy a meal again. "It's growing late. If you children don't leave soon, you'll miss the lighting of the bonfires."

The "children," Pierre and his Marie, Cécé and Mémé, leapt up hastily. Tante Tata set her napkin aside, preparing to rise.

"There will be no need for you to accompany them this year," Papa said firmly.

"What?" said Tante Tata in disbelief. "You cannot think Pierre to be a sufficiently alert chaperone!"

"I do," replied Papa, his temper rising, "and I'll hear

no more about it. Coco,'' he said, frowning, ''why are you dawdling?''

''I—I don't want to go, Papa,'' she said, biting back tears. Having never felt less like celebrating, she didn't have the heart to mingle with the revelers.

''Get up,'' he said sharply. ''You need the fresh air, and I'm tired of watching you mope around here.''

''But Papa, I—''

''Enough!''

Pierre had hastened after Coco's pelerine, rushing back to fling it around her shoulders and hustle her from the house with her sisters and his Marie racing after them. On the banquette he swung her around, tying the ribbon at her throat, perching on her sable curls a dainty black bowler with feathers and flowers.

''Pierre,'' she protested, ''this is Maman's hat, and it doesn't match my—''

''Foolish girl,'' he chided, chucking her under the chin, ''do you think your Court will care?''

''Court!'' she asked, her eyes wide with shock.

''*Oui*,'' he said, grinning. ''By Papa's order we are to pick up Court on our way to the docks.''

''By Papa's . . .'' Coco's voice failed her, smothered by the thick gladness crowding her throat. ''I . . . I shouldn't—''

''But you will.''

Court, having arranged all with Papa Colomb, cautiously approached his Tante Zaza, smoothing the way for Coco's arrival.

Zaza Fortier was a small, comfortable woman, broadfaced, broad-hipped, and forgiving—of everyone except Tata Colomb. She'd much rather love than hate, and Court appealed to her romantic nature, slyly suggesting that Cousine Tata was keeping the lovers apart—which gave his *tante* a more than adequate reason to foster their courtship.

As a boy, he'd awaited the New Year's Day arrival of Papa Noël with the same anticipation with which he now awaited Coco's. But his robustly healthy and happy beloved arrived hollow-eyed and pale, and as shy and subdued as the retiring Mademoiselle Dupree. The joy he had expected to feel quickly changed to alarm.

She stood before his Tante Zaza looking ethereally lovely in her cream-colored gown and pink pelerine, the black bowler an oddly emphatic keynote to her mood.

"I'm so sorry," she said, chastened. "I've hurt you, Cousine, and I—"

"You've been a naughty girl, *ma petite bébé*," said Tante Zaza, opening her chubby arms and folding Coco to her ample breast. "But then"—she laughed softly— "you've always been a naughty girl. I well remember the time you put Court up to stealing a batch of *my* pralines, when you had a choice of mine or Tata's."

"And they were delicious," Coco murmured, so softly Court wondered if she remembered that they had been trying to get *both* batches. They had shared so much in the past, he thought. Surely they would share more in the future.

"*Merci, bébé*," said Tante Zaza, patting Coco's cheek. "Now hurry off and have a good time. I'm not so old I've forgotten how romantic the Christmas Ève bonfires can be. And Pierre," she said sternly, "do not forget your duties as chaperone to your sisters."

"*Non*, Cousine." He pressed a kiss to her cheek. "I shall watch them as carefully as you would."

Which he, fortunately, did not do. Pierre was so besotted with his Marie that he was blind to the stars sparkling like dewdrops overhead, to the wanderings of Cécé and Mémé, to the lagging of Coco and Court.

The lighting of the bonfires on the Algiers levee, across the Mississippi from New Orleans, was a tradition so old its beginnings had been forgotten—though many thought it arrived with the Acadians, who used the bonfires to guide Papa Noël to their new home. At dusk each Christmas Eve the streets filled with merry crowds heading for the docks to watch the fires being lit as far up and down the river as the eye could see.

Those crowds pressed forward, jostling the lovers who strolled together, so close but not touching.

"You are heavyhearted, *chérie*," said Court, longing to take her in his arms and kiss away the sad droop of her mouth.

"It's Tante Tata," Coco said, guilt battling and defeating her pleasure in his presence.

"She's still angry?"

"She's not speaking to me. She won't listen when I try to apologize, though I've tried again and again. And if she knew about . . . about . . ."

"About tonight," he said, aching to take her sorrow away, "about me."

Coco nodded miserably. "Why did Papa arrange this?"

"He wanted to make you happy."

"And he has, only . . . only . . ."

Court thrust his hands in his pockets, to prevent them from reaching out for her. He could not add another feather's weight to the guilt she so obviously harbored. "That *only* is the reason he did it, Coco. You put your concern for your *tante*'s happiness above your own, proving to your papa . . ." He paused, his voice strumming low as he continued. ". . . and to me that you have become a woman who knows her own mind. I am proud of you, Coco."

"Are you?" she asked.

"More than I can show you now."

The promise in the dark intimacy of his voice brought a touch of color to Coco's cheeks. Invalorously, she skirted that treacherous ground. "I'm surprised that Papa would risk Tante Tata's ire by—"

"Oh, he had another, a more selfish reason, too." Court touched Coco's arm, guiding her around a puddle, then found himself unable to release her. He caught her hand, pulling it into the crook his elbow and covering it gently with his palm. "You see, I have promised to end the feud of the pralines."

"The . . . the feud!" Coco stopped in the street, staring up at him in astonishment. "But . . . but how? And when?"

"How? You will have to see. When? On New Year's Day, when we traditionally end all family squabbles. What better day could there be?"

Yes, what better day. To end the feud between Tante Tata and Cousine Zaza—if it was possible! But also, to end the feud between her and Tante Tata? Coco wondered. To show her *tante* how much the family loved her, how much they needed her?

"Court!" she said, breathless, excited. "You've given me the most wonderful idea! I know how to make my peace with Tante Tata!"

A new animation brightened her face, and the old sprightly bounce had returned to her voice. "Is that all?" he said, feigning disappointment in the midst of relief. "I thought surely that I must be at the center of any *wonderful idea* you might have."

"Cabbage head," murmured Coco, smiling as she used her oldest endearment for him. Nuzzling her cheek against his arm, she suddenly felt lighthearted and light-headed. The numbing worry that she would never be reconciled with her aunt had lifted, freeing her of despondency and gloom, freeing her to enjoy her papa's gift of an evening with Court.

"How handsome you look tonight," she said, smoothing his lapel with a proprietory touch. "I shall be the envy of every girl."

"And is that what you want, Coco?" he asked softly. "To be the envy of every girl?"

She paused a moment, thinking how recently that would have been true. "Once," she said dreamily, leaning her cheek against his arm, "but no more."

"And what do you want now?"

"I think . . ." She looked up at his face, lit by the dim light of the gas street lamp. In his every feature she saw the substance of his character: pride, faith, and honesty. Could she be less honest than he? Less revealing of her heart? "I think I want to be like Pierre's Marie. I want to be Court's Coco."

"Am I to believe that you will fetch my slippers and pipe, hang on my every word, and fulfill my every wish?" he asked, the dimple winking in his cheek.

"Surely you know better than that," she said, slanting him a provocative glance.

"I must have lost my head for a moment."

"Only for a moment?" she teased.

"Vixen," he said, laughing. "If I must admit it, I think I lost my head when I lost my heart long ago."

Court studied Coco's smiling face by the light of the street lamp. He remembered it in all of its guises: playful and fearful, full of mirth and mischief. He had always been able to read every nuance of her mood in the curve of her mouth and the shine of her eyes. He searched for any hesitation, any doubt. They were not to be found. Instead, he saw a new assurance, the poise and grace of a woman coming into her own. He was assailed by a fleeting sense of loss for the girl she had been. That poignant memory ebbed slowly into the recesses of his heart, to be put away as all childish things must be, never forgotten and always treasured. With the memory ebbed the regret, for the woman gave promise of much joy to come.

His smile blazed, wide and white and happy, and he took her hand as he had when a boy eager to embark on an escapade. Coco, conforming to an old habit, took fire from his enthusiasm, following where he led.

They raced down Orleans Street into narrow Orleans Alley, exiting behind St. Louis Cathedral into tiny Saint Anthony's Garden, the sight of many duels in the early days of the city. The duel to be fought now was equally dangerous even if more tender, for two hearts beat as one and two bodies yearned to be together.

In the darkest shadow of a rose arbor, Coco flowed into Court's arms, raising her lips to his. He held her fiercely, his strong arms a prison from which she had no desire to escape. Not while his mouth mated with hers, adding precious new colors to the spectrum of her knowledge. Her patient and cautious Court could be as impatient, as impetuous, as careless of convention as she.

She yielded herself up, a zealous student to his tutor. His tongue touched the corner of her mouth, and she trembled. It glided slowly along the seam of her lips, and they parted tentatively. It probed gently, and her knees weakened. In a swirl of disconnected thoughts and surging emotions, she matched him touch for touch, sigh for sigh.

His lips glided along her cheek, seeking her throat, finding the frantic pulse beating in the tender hollow at its base. Her fingers threaded through his hair, cupping his head, urging him closer still. And from the docks there rose a roar that seemed to be in celebration of her newfound love.

Coco nuzzled her cheek against his, her breath labored and uneven. "Are you not afraid that your good name will be blackened should we be discovered?" she asked, teasing.

He leaned back, his hands cupping her cheeks, his thumbs grazing her lips. "Your opinion is the only one I cherish," he murmured, leaning down to suckle gently at her lower lip. "But your good name must be considered, along with your brother's. I fear Pierre would never get over the shame—and your Tante Tata's ire—should it be learned he was so lax a chaperone."

"Good old Pierre," murmured Coco, allowing Court to guide her to the shell path.

"Tell me, *ma chérie*," he whispered, his voice deep and low, "do you still find the romantic reputation of Saint Anthony's Garden to be vastly overstated?"

Coco gazed up into his dark eyes, her face alight. "How wretched of you to toss that back in my teeth!"

"Ah, then I am to believe that the perceptions of your heart are much sharper now?"

"Much sharper."

She snuggled against his chest, and he held her tightly, his lips caressing her brow as he whispered, "We must join your brother and quickly, *chérie*."

"I could stay here forever," she mourned softly.

"As could I."

The bonfires blazed along the levee, lighting the sky. On the docks, a carnival atmosphere reigned. Vendors strolled through the crowds selling hot chocolate and café au lait and parched peanuts. Praline mammies strolled about with baskets heavy-laden with brown pecan and white coconut pralines. Cala women carried their wares of rice fritters in wooden bowls on their heads, singing, "*Bels calas, bels calas, tout chauds*. Fine fritters, fine fritters, very hot."

But it was the small woolly-headed boy with a big, toothy grin who caught Coco's eye. "*Cornets de dragée*," he shouted, hopping like a cricket and bouncing the white willow basket strapped around his neck.

While Court, lying quite masterfully, assured Pierre that they had simply become lost in the crowd, Coco slipped away to press a coin into the boy's hand. She returned with the paper cone filled with *dragées*.

"A peace offering," she whispered.

Court eyed it doubtfully, plucking one candy-covered almond from the top and raising it to her lips. She took it from his fingers, nipping it gently.

"Peace," he said, laughing aloud, "is the last thing I expect to find with you, *ma petite chatte*."

6

ON CHRISTMAS MORNING COURT RECEIVED A LOVING note in Coco's flowery script, one accompanied by a loaf of *pain-anis*, a sweet anise-flavored cake she had baked to show him, the note said, that his notorious sweet tooth would not suffer should he consider her suit favorably.

On Christmas night he received a nosegay of acorns and autumn leaves from the courtyard oak, accompanied by a longer and exultant missive. Excepting his absence, her day had been wonderful. Tante Tata had deigned to speak to her. Even better, Mademoiselle Dupree had been enthralled with Nonc P'tit's stories of Papa Noël, Beaucoup Gator, and Crevi Crawfish. Nonc P'tit, red to the tips of his ears, had puffed out his chest and answered her every question—without stuttering once! And the *coup de foudre*? He had asked the mademoiselle to attend

the Colomb family's New Year's Day celebration! Coco
was now impatiently awaiting her uncle's next bolt from
the blue: the announcement of his engagement to the shy
mademoiselle. Did Court think she hoped for too much?

The following day Coco received a delicate etching of
the sun breaking through storm clouds, for *ma petite
bijou*—his little gem, Coco smiled—who spreads sunshine wherever she goes. He had no doubt that, should
Nonc P'tit falter, she would nudge him gently back onto
the proper path. Further, Court wrote, he was impatiently
looking forward to the day when she would guide him
where she would.

Of course, Coco sighed, that day could not come until
he had ended the feud of the pralines and she had fully
reconciled with Tante Tata. Unfortunately, her aunt had
only called a short-lived truce for the day of peace and
goodwill.

Where Christmas day was a solemn occasion devoted
to the immediate family and marked by the exchange of
token gifts, New Year's Day was one of festivity. Papa
Noël arrived early in the morning, much like the *américain* Santa Claus—except for his gallic twinkle for the
ladies. Family members exchanged gifts, ate a hasty
breakfast, then prepared for the influx of guests—the day,
above all, was devoted to visiting and being visited.

Since no good housewife would allow the old aunts
to carry whispers of dust in corners, the week between
Christmas and New Year's was spent in a whirl of polishing silver, dusting, beating carpets, and scrubbing
floors.

No festivity was complete without a feast, and every
corner of the house was drenched in the yeasty, spicy,
heady aromas of cooking, baking, and candy-making.
Where Tante Tata was a queen in the kitchen throughout
the year, during this week she became a haughty em-

press—directing every pair of hands, even Papa's. He shelled walnuts and pecans, his grumbling reaching a crescendo until he was appeased with one of Maman's wine cakes or Tante Tata's pralines or Coco's *pain-anis*.

As if there were not hustle and bustle enough, Coco involved Maman and Papa, Cécé and Mémé, Pierre and his Marie, in a plot to show Tante Tata how much they all loved her.

Though she was sure it never would, *le Jour de l'An*— New Year's Day—arrived at last. Coco tossed off the covers, trembling with anticipation and hope. Even *le bon Dieu* smiled upon her, for the day promised warm and fair.

"Cécé! Wake up!" Coco got a weak cuff on the arm for her trouble. Where Mémé leapt from the bed, bright-eyed and cheerful, Cécé was as sluggish and cross as Monsieur Bear after his long winter nap.

"Shall we tickle her feet?" said Mémé, giggling.

Cécé rolled from the bed, heavy-eyed and growling. "I don't know why we can't do this at a decent hour!"

"You know very well that Tante Tata rises with the dawn. If we don't get an early start, she'll be up and about. And we want it to be a surprise."

"The real surprise will be if Pierre arrives in time," groused Cécé. "You know how horrible he is to get out of bed in the morning."

"Almost as horrible as you." Coco ducked the pillow that flew her way. "Shhh! We don't want to wake Tante Tata!"

But there was a tap-tap-tap at the door, and Tante Tata peeked in, her thin gray plait dangling to her waist. "What is all of this noise?" she scolded. "Do you want to wake your *maman*, your papa?"

Coco stood frozen with dread and disappointment, but quick-witted Mémé skimmed across the room, whispering, "Tante Tata, please go back to bed. We are planning a surprise for Papa."

"Well, it won't be much of a surprise if you arouse the whole house!"

"I know," said Mémé, guiding her out. "We'll promise to be as quiet as mice."

Coco released her pent-up breath in a gust, falling into Cécé's arms with hysterical relief. "Do you think she guessed—"

"*Non*, how could she?"

A short time later, they tiptoed down the stairs. Maman fried the last of the *beignets*. Papa carefully spooned the hot—not boiling; never, he always assured them, should it be boiling—water into the *cafetiére*. And most amazing of all, Pierre was there, reared back in the rocker, his Marie hanging anxiously over him, and his mouth crusted with sugar. He even looked wide awake, which was a miracle for that early hour.

"Coco, get the platter and plates," ordered Maman. "Cécé, the cups and saucers. Mémé, two trays should do it."

"And what," Papa said, "do you think our *tante* will say to us serving *petit déjeuner* in her chamber?"

"Oh, Papa, do you not have a trace of feeling?" Coco cried with an excess of rattling nerves. "Always Tante Tata serves us. It is time we served her."

"And you are right, *bébé*," said Papa, smiling. "So, my infants, do you all have your *compliments*?"

"Oh, dear!" shrilled Cécé. "I forgot to bring mine down."

"Cécé! How could you?" Coco nearly wept with frustration. It was so important that all go smoothly, that Tante Tata be made to see how much she meant to them all.

"I brought it with me," said Mémé, withdrawing the single sheet with its decoration of cherubs and cabbage roses surrounding a hand-lettered verse.

"What is this?" came Tante Tata's pointed question.

Cécé squealed like a guinea hen sighting an intruder. Mémé gasped and dropped the *compliment*. Coco spun around, the platter nearly flying from her hand. After all of the sneaking around, the whispering in corners, and the cautious planning, her wonderful surprise had come to this. There stood Tante, her arms folded across her narrow chest, her foot tap-tap-tapping like her earlier knock at the door.

"Tante Tata!" Coco cried with more vigor than sense. "You are supposed to be in bed!"

"Oh?" She looked at Maman. "Am I no longer a part of this family?"

"Don't be ridiculous!" gusted Papa, which earned him a reproachful look. "You are and always will be a part of this family. In fact," he said, lowering his voice, "we are up at this outrageous hour because Coco thought we should show you how very much a part of it you are."

"*Oui*," said Maman, "this is all Coco's idea. We were going to serve your *petit déjeuner* in bed—"

"In bed! Now that is *truly* ridiculous!" Tante Tata slanted an angry glance at Papa. "I am not ill—"

"*Non*," said Pierre, rising from the rocker to place an arm around her shoulders, "but you are being very ungrateful. This week while you have been refusing to speak to Coco, she has been planning this surprise for you."

"Coco, is this true?" asked Tante Tata stiffly.

She nodded, unable to speak.

"Well, I suppose I must appreciate it," said her *tante*, loftily.

"I suppose you should," gusted Papa, his thick brows beetling over his eyes. "Coco, give her your *compliment*."

Tante Tata had often encouraged Coco as she labored

over the *compliment du jour de l'an* that was presented to her parents on New Year's Day when she was a child. Though those days were behind her, she had thought this the best way to say *I love you* to her aunt. Now, she was not so sure.

Silently, she proferred the decorated sheet with its awkward verse: *My dear Tante Tata*, Bonne année; *A very good New Year; Thank you for all you have done for me; Thank you for all you have taught me; I love you with all my heart.*

Tante Tata read it slowly, sniffing all the while. With-drawing a handkerchief from the sleeve of her gown, she blew her nose. "You've been a naughty girl, *ma petite bébé*," she said, unconsciously echoing Cousine Zaza.

"I didn't mean to hurt you."

"Of course you didn't," said Tante Tata, thawing.

"Can you forgive me?"

"I suppose I must. It is said that how we act on New Year's Day is how we will act all year, and"—a touch of her old sparkle lit her eyes—"being angry with you is too difficult to sustain through the rest of the year."

Coco flew into her waiting arms, and Tante Tata smoothed the curls from her brow with a gentle hand. "Now, *bébé*, you must tell me what you have learned from this."

A smile curved Coco's lips, matching the deviltry in her eyes. "Not to be so greedy for pralines."

"What? What is this?" Tante Tata held her away, her expression poised midway between a smile and a frown.

"Well," Coco said, laughing softly, assured now of her *tante*'s forgiveness, "when I told you that yours were the best pralines, you gave me a big tin. And when I told Cousine Zaza that hers were the best, she gave me a big tin. So, I had pralines to eat well into spring."

Tante Tata struggled to look sternly disapproving, but a smile began to twitch at the corners of her mouth. "I

am shocked at you, Coco. It would have served you right
to grow as fat as Cousine Zaza!''

Tante Tata was inordinately pleased with her surprise,
even if she was uncomfortable with being the center of
attention in the bosom of the family. A discomfort that
bothered her not at all outside it.

When the Colombs hurried out for their morning round
of visits, she tucked her *compliments* under her arm and
sallied forth to show them to her small world. Godparents, aunts, uncles, and, of course, Grand-mère and
Grand-père Colomb: all had to read the verses and admire
the artwork of her nieces and nephew; all had to hear
every detail of the *petit déjeuner* that had been fixed
especially for her.

The *compliments* remained in her grasp, to be whipped
out for the perusal of every guest who arrived at the
Colombs in the afternoon.

Tante Tata's inordinate pleasure was Coco's best present of the day, one she was as eager to share with Court
as she was to learn how he would end the feud of the
pralines.

A balmy Southern breeze had taken the nip from the
air. In tribute to the glorious day the guests were received
in the courtyard. Papa dispensed libations from the sideboard, set up by the raised bed filled with lushly bloom-
ing chrysanthemums. Maman wandered from the shade
of the oak to the sun-drenched rectangle bordering the
brick wall and its swags of fresh, green ferns. Tante Tata
sat like a queen in the chairs reserved for the old aunts,
the *compliments* fluttering in her hands.

Hour upon hour passed. Still Court did not arrive.
Coco grew increasingly worried. Gradually an odd notion
intruded on that worry. More and more people were
arriving, but none were leaving. Was it imagination, or
did she detect a strange atmosphere of suspense? As if

all here were waiting as she was.

Grand-mére and Grand-père came toddling in, to be ensconced in the best chairs in a sunny spot where the weather-bedazzled periwinkles raised delicate blossoms to the sky. While the new babies and toddlers were brought for their inspection, Coco wandered the garden, finding Nonc P'tit proudly presenting the shy mademoiselle with a plate. The delicate flower pattern of Maman's best china was buried beneath a mound of fragrant French cuisine that would have daunted even that hearty trencherman, Coco's papa.

Mademoiselle Dupree studied it, her eyes widening and meeting Coco's with a gentle shine of mirth before turning to Nonc P'tit. "*Merci*, Monsieur Robichaux," she said sweetly. "You have chosen just as I would have chosen myself."

The red of his nose spread to his ears, and he swelled up on a suspender-popping breath, looking like a man who had just been handed the keys to the Pearly Gates. Surely a better response than the one Coco would have gotten from Court with an astringent, "*Bêtasse!* Blockhead! Do you think I am an ox?"

"*Bonne année*," she said, smiling. "How nice that you could join us, mademoiselle."

"Merci, but I must"—her tender gaze turned up to Nonc P'tit, whose ruddy complexion grew a brighter red—"thank Monsieur Robichaux for inviting me."

"Of course," said Coco, wishing that Court was here to see them. Where was he? Why the delay? Her gaze skimmed the courtyard and the guests, all standing shoulder to shoulder and more arriving. "From the looks of it we are the only ones entertaining today."

"*Non*," said Nonc P'tit, "as always we have many stops to make."

Coco stared at him, more interested in his lack of hesitations, of stutterings and stumblings, than in what he was saying. Surely Mademoiselle Dupree had worked a miracle here.

"You apparently are unaware," he continued, his wide mouth slipping into a smile, "that the news of your quarrel with Tante Tata and Cousine Zaza has spread through the French Quarter. And with it, Court's promise to solve the problem of the pralines."

She blinked rapidly. "What? But how?"

"Your papa spread the word, and everyone—which, as you know, is all of us—who has been forced to make a choice between them, then suffer the consequences, is here. They won't leave until they have seen either the fireworks or the solution."

"Let us hope," she said fervently, "it is the solution."

"Coco! Coco! Hurry!" Cécé and Mémé urgently beckoned to her from the broad double doors.

"What is it?" she asked, running up to them.

"Oh, you've always asked too many questions!" groused Cécé, taking her arm.

"And we've decided we'll never forgive you for this!" said Mémé, taking her other arm.

Between them, they hustled her through the dining room and into the kitchen.

"Forgive me for what?" she managed to ask, as they jerked her to a stop before the storage room door.

"For marrying before us!" they chorused, opening the door and thrusting her in.

She stumbled over the broom and fell into Court's waiting arms.

"So eager, *ma chérie*," he chuckled at her ear. "Hasn't your *maman* taught you that a lady should be decorous and aloof?"

"But then," she whispered, raising her lips to his, "you would be denied this."

His mouth covered hers, gliding to the corner. "*Bon Dieu*, I have missed you."

"And I you." How good it felt to linger in his embrace, to feel his heart beating against hers, to feel the heat of his breath washing across her temple. How safe it felt, and contrarily, how deliciously dangerous.

"Your sisters tell me that Tante Tata has forgiven you."

"Now," she murmured, leaning back to gaze up at him, to trail loving fingers over the curve of his cheek, "we must hope that she will forgive you after your work is done here."

"Ah, my work."

"Tell me, what will you do? I've thought and thought, and—"

A light tap sounded at the door, and Court gently shoved her away. "Your papa's coming," he said, turning to the two platters of pralines sitting on the shelf.

A moment later, the door opened and Papa stepped through, pausing. "Most irregular, *mon petit*," he said, casting a frown at Coco. "You should have waited . . ." He stopped and shrugged, reaching out to playfully pinch the tip of his daughter's chin. "Well, I might be an . . . aging parent, but I am not so long in the tooth that I've forgotten what it is like to be young and in love."

"Papa!" Coco blushed. Really! He could be so . . . so unpredictable.

"So, *mon petit*," he said to Court, "am I to learn at last how you will bring about a truce in the war?"

Coco was astonished at how simple it was. Tante Tata's pralines were transferred to Cousine Zaza's distinctive platter, while Cousine Zaza's were transferred to Tante Tata's cherished Niderviller *faïence* tray.

"But Court," she asked, "how will you—"

"Ah, *ma petite chatte*," he said, grinning, "you obviously have not yet realized what a wise man you have chosen."

"*I* have chosen!" She sank an elbow ungently into

his ribs, earning a chiding, "Behave yourself, *bébé*," from her papa.

"But Papa," she protested, "he knows very well that he pursued me until I—"

"And here"—Papa waggled his moustache—"I had thought it the other way around."

She considered denying it, but he knew her too well. Instead she raised a laughing gaze to Court. "So, most wise of men, how will you achieve this incomparable feat."

"I will do nothing. Your Grand-père Colomb has agreed to do the honors."

That Nonc P'tit was right, that all had lingered in the hope of seeing the end of the feud, was evidenced by the expectant hush that spread when Court exited the house, a tray balanced on each hand.

Every gaze followed him across the courtyard. A collective breath was indrawn and suspended as Grand-père stood slowly, leaning on his cane. "*Bébé*, Cousine Zaza, if you would be so kind as to join me," he said, his voice ringing with the prestige and pride of the eldest, the most respected and cherished member of the family.

Truly, Coco thought, her heart racing, Court had been wise. As a comparative youth, he would only offend should he attempt what was nothing more than the basest of tricks. But what he could not do, Grand-père could, for he wore the mantle of age and authority.

"For years," he said, "you two have forced us all to choose between your pralines. Now, we have decided it is time for *you* to choose. *Bébé*," he said to Tante Tata, "taste one of Cousine Zaza's pralines."

"Ti-Jean," she said to her brother, one of the very few who dared to question him, "this is monstrous! Why—"

"No more monstrous than you demanding this of us!" he thundered. "Taste one!"

Court offered the tray. Tante Tata dithered, selecting the smallest praline she could find, nibbling at the corner, rolling it around on her tongue, like Papa with his first sip of decanted wine. "*Bien*," she said stiffly. "Good, but . . . a trifle . . . only a trifle too sugary. I am sure, Cousine Zaza, had you beat it just a moment—only a moment!—longer, it would have been creamier."

Cousine Zaza, her lips pursed as if she'd bitten into a lemon, selected the smallest praline from Tante Tata's tray. She nibbled and sucked and nodded her head sagely. "*Bein*," she said stiffly. "Good, but . . . a trifle . . . only a trifle too fresh. I am sure, Cousine Tata, had you added only a few more grains of salt—only a few!—it would have been better."

Exchanging haughty glances, they turned to Grand-père. He stood as straight as a lance, as proud and haughty as they were, giving Coco a glimpse of the young man he must have been.

"My dear *bébé*, my dear *cousine*, you have just judged your own pralines."

"What? What is this?" They rounded on him, shrill with indignation.

He raised a hand, his expression so forbidding that they both fell silent. "The pralines were switched, and this was done in the very best of causes. We've all grown weary of this endless feud. Dear ones," he said, softening, "none of us have your discerning taste. How can you ask us to choose between perfection and perfection?"

"Well, of course, Zaza is very good," said Tante Tata.

Not to be outdone, Cousine Zaza graciously admitted, "As you are, Tata."

"Then it is my wish"—and his wish carried the weight of a command—"that you will in future combine your extraordinary talents, working together to give us the best pralines the French Quarter has to offer.''

Tante Tata closed her eyes and shuddered. ''I—I suppose we could.''

Cousine Zaza, more yielding, leaned over to tap her arm. ''Tata, don't be such a martyr. Don't you remember how we learned to make pralines together as girls? We had such fun.''

''Well, I suppose—''

''*Bien*,'' said Grand-père. ''Then I am assured that none of us will ever again be required to choose between you.''

''*Non*,'' clipped out Tante Tata.

''Never,'' said Cousine Zaza.

A ragged cheer went up, racing around the courtyard to become a full-throated roar. But Grand-père was not done yet. He thumped his cane on the bricks, waiting for silence to fall.

''Coco, come to me,'' he said, his dark eyes losing their stern frown. He took her hand, gallantly raising it to his lips. ''How quickly you have grown up, *ma petite*. Grand-mère and I are very proud of you,'' he murmured for her ears alone.

''Court, come.'' He joined their hands together, covering them with his, and raised his voice to be heard. ''My son Jean has given me the privilege of announcing the engagement of our Coco to Court Fortier. You must all join me in wishing them a long and prosperous life together.''

While the well-wishers thronged around them, Court murmured in Coco's ear, ''Your grand-*pére* would have done better to wish us a peaceful life.''

''Cabbage head! How dull that would be for you,'' said Coco, laughing, slipping her hand into his.

How much better love was when it came on tiptoe, nestling in her heart, patiently waiting for her to recognize it, to accept it, to grow with it.

MANY GOOD TIDINGS
from . . .

DIANE WICKER DAVIS

Christmas to me is remembrance of times past. Each year my husband and I sit in the glow of the Christmas tree lights, remembering the many holidays we've shared. In the midst of the day's festivities at my parents', I remember my young-at-heart great-aunts Tenna and Sara, who entertained us one year with a song and dance from their youth. Never will I forget the English Racer bicycle that Santa brought me, and more important, the miles Daddy trotted at my side trying to teach me to ride it. Remembering reminds me to give thanks for the many blessings of family and friends.

May each of you have a holiday to treasure in the years to come.

Avon Romances—
the best in exceptional authors and unforgettable novels!

HIGHLAND MOON Judith E. French
76104-1/$4.50 US/$5.50 Can

SCOUNDREL'S CAPTIVE JoAnn DeLazzari
76420-2/$4.50 US/$5.50 Can

FIRE LILY Deborah Camp
76394-X/$4.50 US/$5.50 Can

SURRENDER IN SCARLET Patricia Camden
76262-5/$4.50 US/$5.50 Can

TIGER DANCE Jillian Hunter
76095-9/$4.50 US/$5.50 Can

LOVE ME WITH FURY Cara Miles
76450-4/$4.50 US/$5.50 Can

DIAMONDS AND DREAMS Rebecca Paisley
76564-0/$4.50 US/$5.50 Can

WILD CARD BRIDE Joy Tucker
76445-8/$4.50 US/$5.50 Can

ROGUE'S MISTRESS Eugenia Riley
76474-1/$4.50 US/$5.50 Can

CONQUEROR'S KISS Hannah Howell
76503-9/$4.50 US/$5.50 Can